MW01692000

One-Year Interactive Daily Devotional

FOR **TEENS**

QUIET TIME

Word of Life
Local Church Ministries

QUIET TIME **INTERACTIVE**

One-Year Daily Devotional

Word of Life Local Church Ministries

A division of Word of Life Fellowship, Inc.
Don Lough – Executive Director
Jack Wyrtzen & Harry Bollback - Founders
John Collins – Director, Local Church Ministries

USA
P.O. Box 600
Schroon Lake, NY 12870
lcm@wol.org
518-494-6000

Canada
617796 Grey Road 18, RR #8
Owen Sound, ON N4K 5W4
lcm@wol.ca
1-800-461-3503

Web Address: www.wol.org

Publisher's Acknowledgements:

Writers and Contributors:
Barry Beebe, Brandon Collins, Jeff Harkins, Angelina Hartzler, Beth Horst, Chelsea Huizing, David and Amanda Kirabira, Andrew Krop, Whitney Miller, Andrew Nippert, Cindy Skeffington, Jason Skeffington, Matt Vanderwiele

Editor: Cindy Skeffington
Curriculum Manager: Don Reichard
Cover and Page Design: Ottoman Creative Group

© 2018 All rights reserved. Published by Word of Life Local Church Ministries. A division of Word of Life Fellowship, Inc. Word of Life creates faith-defining experiences that give students and families the opportunity to encounter God and grow in their spiritual walks. No portion of this publication may be reproduced in any form without prior written permission of the publisher.

ISBN - 978-1-935475-78-1

Printed in the United States of America

Interacting with God
changes your life.

The Bible Changes You

The Word of God, the Bible, is the most powerful weapon that every Christian has. It changes us as we read it, think about it, and do what it says. The Holy Spirit who lives inside every believer also uses the Bible to speak to us. He takes the words written in the Bible and tells us what God wants us to know for our lives. When something is interactive, it works in a way to have an effect on another. Quiet Time Interactive does just that: it is a tool that helps you to interact with the powerful weapon of the Word of God and with God Himself, which will have an incredible effect on your life.

Getting Started

Quiet Time Interactive is all about spending time with God. In order to be friends with someone, you have to do two things: talk to them and listen as they talk to you. Quiet Time Interactive teaches you how to develop a relationship with God: learning how to listen to Him (by reading the Bible) and learning how to talk to Him (by praying to Him).

That's what Quiet Time is all about: **spending time with God**.

Prioritize

Think through your day and decide what time you will do your Quiet Time. Make it a consistent time, when things are quiet and you can really think. Put it on your schedule. Put a reminder on your phone. Ask a friend, leader, or parent to check in on you daily to see how your time with God was.

Pray

Before you open God's Word, ask God what He wants to speak to you about from it, and ask Him to help you obey it after you read it.

REMEMBER TO PRAY FOR YOUR UNREACHED FRIENDS

"You have 100 times more influence on your friends than a stranger does!"
– Dare 2 Share

The **CAUSE CIRCLE** is a simple tool that will help you be more intentional about sharing Jesus' message with your friends. It's built around three simple priorities that Jesus lived out during His earthly ministry. These same priorities will help you effectively share your faith: Prayer. Care. Share.

PRAYER – Asking God to prepare my friend's heart to hear the good news of Jesus.

CARE – Asking God to help me love my friend by listening to them and caring for them.

SHARE – Asking God to help me lovingly share the gospel message clearly and confidently with my friend.

Peruse: to examine with attention

Look at your Quiet Time and look at the Bible verses chosen for that day at the top of the page. If you aren't sure where the book is in the Bible, you can look at the index in the front of your Bible. From your computer or smartphone, you can use a Bible search engine or Bible app and type in the passage of the day.

Read the verses, answer the questions, check the boxes, and fill in the blanks that are on the page of your Quiet Time. Quiet Time Interactive is made to help you go through each verse and think about it more deeply.

Practice

Now that you prayed and heard from God as you have read through the Bible passage, the last step is to apply it to your life. Applying God's Word is where you take what you read and do something about it.

- Post a verse from the reading or the quote at the bottom of the page from the Share It! section on your favorite social media platform.
- Tell some friends, small group leader, parents, or pastor about what you learned.
- Write down what you learned somewhere and read it a couple of times a day.
- Create a reminder on your phone that will pop up and remind you what you learned at a specific time during the day.
- Text a friend what you learned and ask them what they learned.

As you keep reading, praying, and applying, you will be amazed at how interacting with God changes your life.

QUIET TIME INTERACTIVE

My Personal Prayer Journal

PRAYER LIST

DATE / REQUEST **DATE / ANSWER**

DARE 2 SHARE CAUSE CIRCLE STRATEGY

PRAYER: Asking God to prepare my friend's heart to hear the good news of Jesus.

CARE: Asking God to help me love my friend by listening to them and caring for them.

SHARE: Asking God to help me lovingly share the gospel message clearly and confidently with my friend.

PRAYER LIST

DATE / REQUEST **DATE / ANSWER**

PRAYER LIST

DATE / REQUEST **DATE / ANSWER**

DARE 2 SHARE CAUSE CIRCLE STRATEGY

PRAYER: Asking God to prepare my friend's heart to hear the good news of Jesus.

CARE: Asking God to help me love my friend by listening to them and caring for them.

SHARE: Asking God to help me lovingly share the gospel message clearly and confidently with my friend.

PRAYER LIST

DATE / REQUEST	DATE / ANSWER

PRAYER LIST

DATE / REQUEST **DATE / ANSWER**

DARE 2 SHARE CAUSE CIRCLE STRATEGY

PRAYER: Asking God to prepare my friend's heart to hear the good news of Jesus.

CARE: Asking God to help me love my friend by listening to them and caring for them.

SHARE: Asking God to help me lovingly share the gospel message clearly and confidently with my friend.

PRAYER LIST

DATE / REQUEST **DATE / ANSWER**

PRAYER LIST

DATE / REQUEST **DATE / ANSWER**

DARE 2 SHARE CAUSE CIRCLE STRATEGY

PRAYER: Asking God to prepare my friend's heart to hear the good news of Jesus.

CARE: Asking God to help me love my friend by listening to them and caring for them.

SHARE: Asking God to help me lovingly share the gospel message clearly and confidently with my friend.

PRAYER LIST

DATE / REQUEST **DATE / ANSWER**

PRAYER LIST

DATE / REQUEST	DATE / ANSWER

DARE 2 SHARE CAUSE CIRCLE STRATEGY

PRAYER: Asking God to prepare my friend's heart to hear the good news of Jesus.

CARE: Asking God to help me love my friend by listening to them and caring for them.

SHARE: Asking God to help me lovingly share the gospel message clearly and confidently with my friend.

AILY PRAISE LIST

TE / I'M PRAISING GOD FOR...

DAILY PRAISE LIST

DATE / I'M PRAISING GOD FOR...

SATURDAY WEEK 1

TRUTH: PHILIPPIANS 2:17-23

Paul the Apostle led Timothy to Christ when he was a young man. I was led to Christ by ______________________________.

☐ I will send them a quick message to thank them.

Paul took Timothy with him on his second missionary journey and discipled him to be a follower of Jesus. (**Acts 16:1-5**)

I was or am being discipled by: ______________________________.

☐ I would like to be discipled; I will talk with my youth leader about this.

Paul and Timothy became co-workers in Christian service, and together with Silas helped to plant the church in Philippi.

I am serving in my local church alongside of ____________________in this ministry: ______________________________.

PHILIPPIANS 2:19-21

Why did Paul send Timothy back to the Philippian Church? ______________________________

____

What special quality did Timothy have? ______________________________

Whom have I taken the time to sincerely care for lately? ______________________________

Today I must focus on ______________________________
and not on my own things or interests.

PHILIPPIANS 2:22-23

Timothy was Paul's son in the faith. Who is your son or daughter in the faith? (Who have you led to Christ?) ______________________________

Timothy was tested and proven faithful and therefore Paul could trust him in the Gospel ministry.

Have you proven yourself a faithful Christian? Are you someone who could be sent forth to serve Jesus? ☐ **YES** ☐ **NO** ☐ **HOPE SO!**

Paul wrote two letters of encouragement and instruction to Timothy. They are called ____________________ and ____________________.
(Hint: What two books of the Bible are named after Timothy?)

SHARE IT

A disciple is one who cares for others more than themselves.

WEEK 2 SUNDAY

TRUTH: PHILIPPIANS 2:24-30

Epaphroditus was a Christian man sent by the Philippian church to help Paul during his imprisonment in Rome. Paul now writes that he is sending Epaphroditus back to the congregation in Philippi with his letter.

PHILIPPIANS 2:26

Write five descriptions of Epaphroditus.

1. ______________________ 4. ______________________

2. ______________________ 5. ______________________

3. ______________________

We are also to exhibit these roles, attitudes, and activities to our fellow Christians in God's family. List two people you have recently helped in one of these five ways.

1. ______________________ 2. ______________________

PHILIPPIANS 2:26-27

How serious was Epaphroditus' sickness? ______________________

Have you ever been severely sick? ☐ **YES** ☐ **NO**

Has anyone you know been so sick that they died? ☐ **YES** ☐ **NO**

Do you know someone who is currently ill whom you could help or encourage?
Who? ____________ How? ______________________

PHILIPPIANS 2:28-30

Paul instructs the congregation to welcome Epaphroditus home, not as one who in weakness failed on his mission, but as one who succeeded and should be honored and respected.

Some pastors, missionaries, and Christian workers have become physically, emotionally, mentally, and spiritually ill in their service. We should not criticize or look down on them, but speak well of them in our conversation with others and our prayers to God.

☐ I will speak well of pastors, missionaries, and Christian workers.

SHARE IT

No sacrifice is too great for Jesus and others.

MONDAY WEEK 2

TRUTH: PHILIPPIANS 3:1-6

PHILIPPIANS 3:1

Paul wrote this letter of truth to the Philippians so that they would rejoice in Christ and what He was doing in Paul's life.

The word ***rejoice*** is found in every chapter of this book, a total of twelve times.
I will rejoice today in Christ for these three reasons: 1. ____________________
2.____________________ 3. ____________________

PHILIPPIANS 3:2

Paul also wrote this letter of truth to protect them and keep them safe from false teachers who attack Christians and the truth like vicious dogs. There were false teachers who demanded circumcision and other legalistic laws instead of grace, faith, and truth.
Name one false teaching that is going on today. ____________________

PHILIPPIANS 3:3-4

True salvation is to: Worship God in the __________, Rejoice (glory) in __________ __________, Have no confidence or dependence in the works of the ____________________.

It's not what I have done, can do, or will do that makes me right with God; it's what Jesus has done for me.

PHILIPPIANS 3:5-6

Paul gives a list of several things that he trusted in or was proud of before his conversion:
His circumcision under the law on the ____________day.
His nation's Jewish heritage of being from the tribe of ____________________ .
His position and education as a ____________________.
His zeal for ____________________the Church.

I know people like this who are very religious and dedicated to their beliefs yet are not trusting in the work of Jesus alone. **YES** **NO**

Am I this way? **YES** **NO**

SHARE IT

True salvation is in Christ alone, faith alone, and grace alone.

WEEK 2 TUESDAY

TRUTH: PHILIPPIANS 3:7-14

All of the things that Paul was proud of (**vv. 5-6**), all the things that he had accomplished in life, and all of the religious observances that he was devoted to, he had to give up in order to know Christ and to experience His righteousness.

PHILIPPIANS 3:8

In Christ we win and gain by losing and giving up. Please write out **Matthew 16:25**. ____

____

I am willing to give up whatever is necessary in order to know Jesus and follow Him.

YES **NO** **MAYBE**

PHILIPPIANS 3:10

Our desire to know Christ in a deeper way should also include:
Experiencing the power and victory of life because of His resurrection.
Experiencing the sufferings of life as a Christian as He suffered for us.

Lately I have experienced this victory: ____________________________________

____

Lately I have suffered in this way as a Christian: ____________________________

____

PHILIPPIANS 3:11-14

The Christian life is one of continually growing in holiness, purity, and Christlikeness. We are never fully perfected here and now, but we will one day be like Jesus there and then.

Am I becoming more Christ-like? **YES** **NO** **HOPE SO**

Do I know a person who continually reminds me of Christ? **YES** **NO**
If yes, who? ______________________________

I will write them a quick note to thank them for their example.

SHARE IT

I am willing to give up whatever is necessary in order to know Jesus and follow Him.

WEDNESDAY WEEK 2

TRUTH: PHILIPPIANS 3:15-21

As we move forward in our Christian lives, we are to grow spiritually mature by following the example and teaching of Scripture and godly leaders.

PHILIPPIANS 3:15-16

I am confident that ____________________ will show me if I am thinking properly about truth and Christian living. I know that through the Holy ________, the ___________ of God and godly _____________, I can be directed to believe and live properly.

PHILIPPIANS 3:17-19

What caused the Apostle Paul to weep? ____________________________________

____

Some professing believers are in reality enemies of the _____________ of Christ.
What are the four descriptions of false believers in **verse 19**?

1.___________________________ 3.___________________________

2.___________________________ 4.___________________________

Have I ever met false believers? ☐ **YES** ☐ **NO** ☐ **NOT SURE**

PHILIPPIANS 3:20-21

We are citizens of Heaven who still live as strangers and pilgrims on the earth. We are constantly __________________ for the coming of our Lord Jesus Christ. Our spirits and souls are fully saved/redeemed but our bodies are not. Jesus returns to change our ____________ bodies. We will experience a miraculous makeover so that our body is made ______________ like His heavenly body.

When Jesus returns, the bodies of believers will be resurrected from the graves and changed. Those who are living will be instantly changed to be like Jesus is now in Heaven.

I want my body to be:

☐ Just like it is now forever.
☐ Just like Jesus' body is forever.
☐ Just like someone else's body forever.

SHARE IT

Waiting patiently for my Heavenly makeover!

WEEK 2 THURSDAY

TRUTH: PHILIPPIANS 4:1-7

PHILIPPIANS 4:1

The Philippians are urged to stand fast (stand firm, stand faithful, stand strong) in following Christ. I sometimes feel like giving up, giving in, and falling down in my commitment to follow Jesus. ☐ **YES** ☐ **NO**

Jesus stood firm for me as He went to the cross bearing my sin. Jesus stands firm for me each day interceding in prayer for me, and I need to trust Him to strengthen me even when I am weak.

Read **2 Corinthians 12:9-10** ☐ Done

PHILIPPIANS 4:2-3

Two of Paul's former co-workers in Philippi were apparently not getting along. Their names were ______________________ and ______________________.

Paul urges another former co-worker who he calls a yoke fellow, a true companion, in service to get involved and help these women to be reconciled.

Is there another Christian I am not getting along with? ☐ **YES** ☐ **NO**
What am I going to do about it? ______________________________________

____

How will I help others who are not getting along?
☐ Pray ☐ Ignore it ☐ Don't take sides ☐ Talk about them ☐ Speak to them in love ☐ Walk away from them ☐ Be a peacemaker ☐ Be an example

PHILIPPIANS 4:5

I am to rejoice in the Lord ______________________ . Am I to rejoice in all the events of my life or am I to rejoice in Jesus who is with me in all the events of my life?

____

PHILIPPIANS 4:6-7

I am not to be full of needless care, worry, or anxiety about anything in life. I am to bring all of my concerns to God in ______________with ______________________________. (**v. 6**)

My biggest concern today is ______________________________________.

God promises to give me His ______________ to comfort my heart and mind when I pray even if I cannot understand all that is happening. (**v. 7**)

SHARE IT

Why worry when you can pray?

FRIDAY WEEK 2

TRUTH: PHILIPPIANS 4:8-13

PHILIPPIANS 4:8-10

Paul tells the Philippian believers how to think and what they are to focus on daily in their thoughts.

God wants us to think right not wrong. How you think affects how you feel and how you will act.

Paul lists eight good ways of thinking. List the eight bad ways of thinking.

1.____________________ 5. ____________________
2.____________________ 6. ____________________
3.____________________ 7. ____________________
4. ____________________ 8. ____________________

How is your thought life? ■ Good ■ Not so good ■ Quite bad

PHILIPPIANS 4:11-12

What lesson did Paul learn? To be ____________________ regardless of his condition or circumstances.

I need to learn to be satisfied with whatever God allows for me, whether I am to have more than I want or whether I am to be without what I want.

■ **YES** ■ **NO** ■ **NOT SURE**

What am I going without right now that I greatly want? ____________________

PHILIPPIANS 4:13

All things – whatever God calls me to do or to go through – can be done through Christ's strength. Jesus said that "without Me you can do nothing." **John 15:5**

I remember two special times when Christ's strength helped me:

1. ____
2. ____

SHARE IT

Whatever God calls me to do or to go through can be done through Christ's strength.

WEEK 2 SATURDAY

TRUTH: PHILIPPIANS 4:14-23

PHILIPPIANS 4:14-16

The Philippians were the first church in Macedonia (Eastern Europe) to support Paul financially in his ministry to the Gentiles.

Does your church help Christian workers to preach the Gospel in other lands?

YES **NO** **NOT SURE**

I am giving some of my finances to help others preach the Gospel.

YES **NO** **I WILL.**

PHILIPPIANS 4:17

Even greater than Paul's desire for financial help was his desire for them to be fruitful before God and for God to bless and reward them for giving.

How has God blessed me when I have given to others? ______________________________

____

PHILIPPIANS 4:18

Epaphroditus had brought the gift from Philippi. Paul knew their gift was a generous, sweet act of sacrifice and that God was well pleased with their offering.

Someone in ministry that I will help/have helped financially is:

____.

PHILIPPIANS 4:19

Their gift to Paul was so generous that they were now facing needs of their own. Paul promised that God would take care of them through His ____________________ in glory in Christ.

PHILIPPIANS 4:20-23

Paul's conclusion in his letter to the Philippians was to give ________________ to God the Father, give a ______________ to every saint from those with him in Rome, and give a request for the ______________ of Jesus to be upon them all in the Philippian church.

Who will you send a special greeting to today? ______________________________

SHARE IT

You can't out-give God!

SUNDAY WEEK 3

TRUTH: JOB 1:1-12

JOB 1:1-5

Job had quite the reputation! How is he described? (**v. 1**)

____

Blameless ***means to make no offenses to God or to others.*** When I do offend, I need to confess my sin, ask for forgiveness, and do my best to make it right. Is there any offense I need to deal with now? **YES** **NO**
If so, whom do I need to talk to today? ______________________

Do I truly fear God? **YES** **NO** **SOMETIMES**

The fear of God reigned in Job's heart and governed all he did. Job dreaded the thought of doing wrong so he stayed far from evil.

The fear of God controls my heart and behavior:

Never 1 2 3 4 5 Always

What does *shun* mean? ______________________

Job didn't even give evil a chance! I face evil temptations every day; what in particular do I need to stay clear of? ______________________

JOB 1:4-5

Most scholars believe Job lived prior to the Mosaic Law and Temple, so Job acted as a mediator or priest between his family and God, leading his family in repentance. His family was his priority!

If I haven't already, I will add my family members to the prayer journal in the front of this Quiet Time. Done

JOB 1:6-12

The angels appeared before God, and Satan followed. God pointed out Job's upright character and instantly Satan attacked it.

Has my character been attacked before? **YES** **NO**

As a Christian, people will attack my character, but as I will see in this study of Job this can be an opportunity to grow and glorify God.

JOB 1:9-11

Satan said Job only loved God because ______________________.
Is this true of me? **YES** **NO**

JOB 1:12

TRUE OR FALSE.
T F God allows bad things to happen in my life.
I may never know why on earth, but God uses all things for __________ (see **Romans 8:28**).

SHARE IT

"Satan can only touch God's people with God's permission, and God uses it for their good and His glory."
~ Warren Weirsbe

WEEK 3 MONDAY

TRUTH: JOB 1:13-22

JOB 1:14-19

When our lives are falling apart, it's hard to think that God is in control. But Job defied the devil and any personal doubts!

Job faced a series of major tragedies. List them here:

vv. 14-15: ____________________

v. 16: ____________________

vv. 17: ____________________

vv. 18-19: ____________________

JOB 1:20-21

Job, who was the richest man in the land, had now become the poorest.

We often wonder why God allows horrible things to happen to people who have been obedient to Him. Job lost everything—all his children and his way of living. But what was Job's response? ____________________

If I'm honest, I would have responded like: ____________________.

Job WORSHIPED! He held to the unshakeable truth that God is always GOOD. He understood that everything he had came from __________.

Job said God __________and God __________ away.
He was committed to praising God in the good times as well as the bad times because he loved GOD for HIS character not for His gifts!

How often do I believe God is good?

Never 1 2 3 4 5 All the Time

Just like Job couldn't see what was going on between God and Satan, neither can I. That is why, like Job, I need to be committed to truth—so that when hard times come, I don't doubt God. Google/search for a verse that talks about God's goodness or faithfulness and write it here: ____________________

____

I won't always know why bad things happen to me or to others. I must learn to trust God's goodness regardless. The Lord is in control: He gave to Job, He took away from Job, and He also let Satan try Job. But GOD never left Job.

God is at work to make me more like His ____________________ . (**Romans 8:29**)
God will also use my story to help others, just as Job's story is still teaching us.

SHARE IT

"The purpose of life is the building of character through truth."
~ Phillips Brooks

TUESDAY WEEK 3

TRUTH: JOB 2:1-13

Job passed his test. He lost all his possessions and all of his children, but he still praised God. But that doesn't mean the enemy would relent after Job's victory.

JOB 2:1-3

Again, we see the Lord praised Job, this time for being faithful under suffering. Was there a time when I was obedient to God even though it was really hard?

☐ **NO** ☐ **YES, WHEN I** ____ .

Know that God sees that and will reward for obedience! (**Romans 2:6**)

JOB 2:4-8

Who gave Satan permission to further torment Job? ________

Can we understand everything God does? ☐ **YES** ☐ **NO**

Look up **Isaiah 55:8-9**. God's ways are ______________________ than my ways. Though I may not understand everything God does, I can trust His goodness.

JOB 2:9

Next, Job's wife encouraged him to sin! Why do I think she encouraged Job to curse God?

____

When I go through a trial, I must look for what there is to learn instead of only focusing on a way out. How do I respond to my friends' bad advice?

☐ I don't even recognize it as bad. ☐ I reject it and seek spiritual advice.

JOB 2:10

Job proved not to be a "fair weather fan" of God and rejected bad counsel.
Am I willing to praise God in the hard times as well as the good? ☐ **YES** ☐ **NO**

JOB 2:11-13

What did Job's friends do? ______________________________________
Sometimes when a friend is hurting, we just need to be there for them and show them we care. Explanations don't erase the pain.

Who do I know right now that is going through a hard time? ____________________
I will decide on a way to show them I care:

☐ Message/write them a note saying I am praying for them.
☐ Get them their favorite snack.
☐ Other: ____

SHARE IT

Dear God, if today I lose my hope, please remind me that Your plans are better than mine.

WEEK 3 WEDNESDAY

TRUTH: JOB 7:1-16

Was there a time when I felt like no one cared or understood how I felt? ▢ **YES** ▢ **NO**
Have I had someone quote a Bible verse to me in a hard time, but it didn't seem to help?
▢ **YES** ▢ **NO**

Our tendency is to look for a quick fix—like Job's friends were offering in chapters 3-14. As mentioned earlier, sometimes the best thing I can do for a hurting friend is to simply be there for them.
Am I willing to take the time to simply listen when others are hurting?
▢ **YES** ▢ **NO** ▢ **SOMETIMES**

Job's friends sat with him, but it does not seem they understood his hardships, though they thought they had all the answers.
Define the word *empathy*: ____

____

Yesterday I was challenged to show a friend I cared.
Did I do it? ▢ **YES** ▢ **NO** ▢ I will pray God shows me an opportunity.

For starters I will try to listen to others more instead of being focused on what I have to say!
▢ **AGREE** ▢ **DISAGREE**

JOB 7:1-7

Job had no relief. His life was brief. His time was running out.
When I can't control my circumstances, I feel ______________________.

Job couldn't change anything! He felt hopeless.
When I feel this way, I need to cry out to the Lord.

Is it sinful to question God? ▢ **YES** ▢ **NO**
What did Jesus do? See **Matthew 27:46**. ______________________
But Jesus trusted and obeyed as He asked.

I am confused why God has allowed ______________________________

____.

But I am committing today to trust the All-Knowing God.
▢ I prayed about this. I will share my commitment with this friend or mentor to keep me accountable: ______________________.

Can God be anything but loving toward His children? ▢ **YES** ▢ **NO**

PRAY: *God, please help me to remember that the God Who willingly gave Himself for Job—and me—would never allow anything to happen that was not designed to grow me. Help me to stay thankful and trust You!*

SHARE IT

The true grace of God sometimes comes in strange packages.
~ Whitney Miller

THURSDAY WEEK 3

TRUTH: JOB 9:1-20

How often is God just? **Never 1 2 3 4 5 Always**

In **chapter 8**, Bildad, another friend of Job, told him that since God is always just, Job must have sinned! Is punishment the purpose of all the trials that God allows in our lives?
☐ **YES** ☐ **NO**

When trials or hard times happen in my life, I feel like:

- ☐ Questioning God's goodness.
- ☐ Doubting that God's way is best.
- ☐ Getting bitter at God for letting this happen.
- ☐ Confused, but I pray for strength to obey Him.

Look up **James 1:2-4**. What do these verses say about what trials can do for me?

____

JOB 9:1-13

These verses speak of God's great wisdom and power over all the earth.
Could I win a debate with God? ☐ **YES** ☐ **NO** (**v. 3**)

In **chapters 38-41** God asked Job 77 questions, and Job was not able to answer one of them!
Could I win a fight against God? ☐ **YES** ☐ **NO** (**v. 4**)

Will I be able to understand everything God does? ☐ **YES** ☐ **NO** (**v. 10**)

JOB 9:14-20

Job was able to defend himself to his friends, but could he defend himself before God?
☐ **YES** ☐ **NO**

What would Job ask for? (**v. 15**) ______________________________

Job knew there was no sense in debating with the All-Knowing One. He knew there was no sense in struggling against the All-Powerful One.

When I am confused by why God is allowing difficulties in my life, I must trust God's purpose in it all.

Write a short prayer below expressing to God something you are hurting about or are confused about. Then ask Him to help you trust His goodness and power. ______________

____

____

____

____

SHARE IT

"God never uses anyone greatly until He tests them greatly."
~ A.W. Tozer

WEEK 3 FRIDAY

TRUTH: JOB 9:21-35

Have I ever felt hopeless? Or maybe do I now? ☐ **YES** ☐ **NO**
This passage shows that Job was full of hopelessness. He had not found any answers as to why he was suffering, and he still had all the emotional and physical pain plaguing him.

JOB 9:21

Job said he was ________________________. He did not sin to bring this suffering upon himself. According to Job 1:8 and 2:3, God would agree with him. But Job had not heard that heavenly conversation.
What was Job's attitude toward his life? ________________________________

JOB 9:22

Job said God destroys:

- ☐ Only the wicked.
- ☐ BOTH the wicked and blameless.
- ☐ Only the blameless.
- ☐ No one.

JOB 9:21-24

Like Job, when I am hurting, it's easy to focus on what I feel like is true rather than what is really true. **Jeremiah 17:9** says, "The heart is ____________above all things, and ____________________; who can know it?" I cannot trust my heart! It will deceive me! But I can trust God's Word. I must choose one or the other:

- ☐ I will believe what God tells me about the circumstances of life.
- ☐ I believe what my heart tells me about my trials.

JOB 9:27-31

If Job changed his attitude, would that change anything? ☐ **YES** ☐ **NO**
Do I need to change my attitude today? ☐ **YES** ☐ **NO**

JOB 9:32-35

What is a mediator? (Google it if you don't know.) __________________________

____

Job wished he had someone to go between him and God.
Who does that for me as a believer? ____________________ (see **1 Timothy 2:5**)
Jesus is ready to listen to me! Will I listen to Him? Talk to Him!
Write a prayer to God where you are choosing to trust that He is always good – despite how you feel! ____

____

SHARE IT

My feelings do not determine truth.

SATURDAY WEEK 3

TRUTH: JOB 13:1-18

Do I trust in the Lord when things go wrong?

No, never 1 2 3 4 5 Yes, always

Job was responding to Zophar's speech from **Chapter 11**. Zophar had been pretty harsh with Job.

Have I ever been given advice that was really harsh? ☐ **YES** ☐ **NO**
Have I ever given really harsh advice? ☐ **YES** ☐ **NO**

JOB 13:1-12

Had Job's friends revealed anything new to him? ☐ **YES** ☐ **NO**
When I talk to others, do I make them feel inferior? (**v. 2**)

No, never 1 2 3 4 5 Yes, all the time

I need to be pointing others to Christ and encouraging them rather than dragging them down. The problem is that Job's friends thought they had all the answers but didn't really listen to Job. (**vv. 5-6**)

Ask a close friend today: How well do I listen? Then record their answer here: ________

____

If their response shows room for growth, first bring this matter to God in prayer. Add it as a prayer request in the prayer journal of this Quiet Time. Then ask your friend to help you practice listening! ☐ Done

Job said they were ________________ physicians. (**v. 4**)

Do I care deeply with others when they are struggling? ☐ **YES** ☐ **NO** ☐ **SOMETIMES**
Or do I get impatient with them? ☐ **YES** ☐ **NO** ☐ **SOMETIMES**

When I criticize others but don't care for them, I act selfishly.
Am I quick to judge others?

No, Never 1 2 3 4 5 Yes, all the time

JOB 13:13-18

Job desired to defend himself before God! He knew God is just and would hear him out. He said in **v. 15**, "Though He slay me, yet will I __________ Him."

Job was confident that God would, in the end, clear his name.
Take a moment to pray over these principles from today's passage.

☐ Give me patience to listen to others.
☐ Help me to love others selflessly.
☐ Help me to trust Your goodness each day no matter my circumstances!

SHARE IT

My advice is worth more if I truly care for the person.

WEEK 4 SUNDAY

TRUTH: JOB 14:1-15

Job continued expressing his hopelessness. Charles L. Allen wrote, "When you say a situation or a person is hopeless, you are slamming the door in the face of God."

Have I ever given up on someone? ☐ **YES** ☐ **NO**

Have I ever given up on a situation? ☐ **YES** ☐ **NO**

I will ask God to renew my hope about: ______________________________.
Add this to your prayer journal. ☐ Done

I need to continue to trust God and watch Him work!

JOB 14:1-6

As part of the human race, my days are: **many / few**. (Circle)

Who gives man life and numbers his days? (**v. 5**) ____________

So I need to use my time wisely! I have only one life to live for Christ!

On a scale of 1 to 5, how do I spend my time?

Not very wisely 1 2 3 4 5 Very wisely

JOB 14:7-10

Job said there was more hope for a ____________(**v. 7**) than for ____________ (**v. 10**). A tree's roots can bud again, but man's life on earth is never restored once he breathes his last.

JOB 14:13-15

Job was so miserable he asked to be ____________.(**v. 13**)
As a believer, who is my hope? ____________
Look up **1 Peter 1:3**. The resurrection of ____________ has brought me hope! Death is not the end of my story!

Whether it's myself, someone else, or a situation in my life, I will hold on to hope in Christ! I refuse to give up on God. Hold on to hope. Because God is faithful and all-powerful, I can trust Him for every situation!

Write a prayer to God thanking Him for the hope that only He can and will give.

____

____

SHARE IT

"God is the only one who can make the valley of trouble a door of hope." ~ Catherine Marshall

MONDAY WEEK 4

TRUTH: JOB 17:1-16

JOB 17:1

Job suffered so much his spirit (breath) was ______________! He feared death was near!
☐ I can relate. ☐ I can't relate.

JOB 17:2-6

How were people treating him? ____________________ He was consumed with their hostility to him. ☐ I can relate. ☐ I can't relate.

JOB 17:7

What was Job's physical condition? ____
Physical suffering wears on our souls! ☐ I can relate. ☐ I can't relate.

JOB 17:9

"Those with clean hands will grow __________________ and __________________ ."
I have been encouraged to focus on God's goodness throughout this study of Job. The more I do that, the stronger I will become. Making godly decisions is not always easy, but the more I obey God, the stronger my "new man" becomes!

Read **Ephesians 4:22-24**. These verses tell me to put off what?

____

And put on what? ____

If I focus on how I feel and what I see, instead of the truth, which will become stronger?
☐ Old Man ☐ New Man

As I make decisions this week, I will ask myself:
"Am I feeding **my new man in Christ** or am I feeding **my sinful nature** ?"

What did I do yesterday that would strengthen my new man? ______________________

____

JOB 17:10-16

Job was crushed, and his friends had no wisdom or comfort to offer him.
It has been said that there is wisdom in a multitude of counselors. But I need counsel grounded on the promises of God, not someone who gives me false hope (**v. 12**).
Who is someone who would give me false hope therefore I should avoid his or her counsel? ____________________________________
Who is someone I can go to that would give me Biblical counsel? __________________

This week I will ask that person to pray for me about this specific issue: ____________

____ .

SHARE IT

"Hardships often prepare ordinary people for an extraordinary destiny." ~ *C.S. Lewis*

WEEK 4 TUESDAY

TRUTH: JOB 19:19-29

In **chapter 18**, Bildad insisted that since God is just, Job must have done something to earn this trial and was being disciplined for it. But stop and think for a moment:
Is discipline always bad? ☐ **YES** ☐ **NO**

What about the parent who puts boundaries on their young child so he doesn't play in the street and get hit by a car?

TRUE OR FALSE.
T F Discipline can be used for my growth and protection.
The Lord disciplines those whom He ____________ (**Hebrews 12:6**).

JOB 19:19-22

Job's situation was truly desperate! How were his friends and loved ones treating him according to these verses? ______________________________

It seemed everyone in the world was against him, even God.
I felt like this when: ______________________________.

Do I know someone who could be feeling like this right now? ☐ **YES** ☐ **NO**
If so, I will find a way to encourage him or her this week. ☐

JOB 19:23-29

Amidst all his suffering, Job made some amazing statements of faith in these verses! In my own trials, I must shift my thoughts to truth!
Did Job's desire in **verses 23** and **24** get fulfilled eventually? ☐ **YES** ☐ **NO**

In **verse 2**, Job said, "I know my _______________ lives!"
Define *redeem*. ______________________________

In his suffering and rejection by his own loved ones, Job held on to his hope that God would redeem him. Always hold on to this—God will never quit on me! (**Philippians 1:6**)

In faith, Job said that even after his death he would _______ _________.

Job was talking about the resurrection! He didn't have the New Testament to tell him this! But he focused on God's goodness and righteousness. I won't have all the answers in life; but like Job, especially in the hard times, I need to focus on God's faithful character.

JOB 19:28-29

Job warned his friends—there is judgment for all—including them!
Napoleon Bonaparte said, "A leader is a dealer in hope." Job shared his hope with his friends. How can I share hope this week with someone?
☐ Write an encouraging note to someone who is struggling
☐ Invite a friend to church
☐ Pray with someone who needs some encouragement

SHARE IT

"…indeed hope is nothing else but the constancy of faith."
~ John Calvin

WEDNESDAY WEEK 4

TRUTH: JOB 23:1-12

JOB 23:1-3

Job wanted to find __________!
Have I ever felt like God was far off? ☐ **YES** ☐ **NO**
When? ____

Job wanted to go to God, but little did he know that one day God would come to man! Christ would come to be man's mediator and Savior!

JOB 23:4-7

What did Job want to do? ______________________________________
Would I want to defend myself before God? ☐ **YES** ☐ **NO**
Thankfully I don't have to because Christ is my defender! (**1 John 2:1**)

Job believed God would decide that he was: **guilty / not guilty**
Job trusted that God would let him—a man who had walked in obedience to God—present his case and then be delivered. Job wanted his reputation cleared before God and man.

JOB 23:10

Though Job could not find God, could God find Job? ☐ **YES** ☐ **NO**

No matter what happens to me, God knows what is happening to me!

What is the purpose of testing? ______________________________
Fire is used to purify gold. It burns away the non-valuable parts. Often God allows trials in my life so that I will grow and mature.

Think about the last hard time in my life, did I grow? ☐ **YES** ☐ **NO**

God is using the hard times in my life to bring me closer to Him. My choice is to get better or become bitter. What areas do I feel God is trying to grow me in? ____________
____

Am I allowing Him to work? **Not at all 1 2 3 4 5 Yes**

If I resist God's will in these trials, the testing will hurt and not help me.

JOB 23:11-12

Was Job committed to the Lord's commands? ☐ **YES** ☐ **NO**
He valued God's Word more than his ____________________.
How important is God's Word to me? ____________________________

How faithful am to studying His Word? **Daily Weekly Randomly**

How faithful am I to obey His commands?
- ☐ When it's convenient, I obey.
- ☐ Even when I don't want to, I obey
- ☐ When I see the benefit for me, I obey.
- ☐ I am choosing to obey daily.

SHARE IT

God is not saying the pain is good. But because of this pain HE will be made known, and I will be blessed.

WEEK 4 THURSDAY

TRUTH: JOB 38:1-18

In **chapters 33-37**, Job's final friend Elihu spoke up. Elihu was closest to the truth when he told Job that God refines the righteous through trials. But God would answer Job. It is important to remember that God cares about the process and not just the product. I need to look for God's will in the midst of the trial and not just focus on the end results.

JOB 38:1

From where did God answer Job? ______________________

God spoke to Job not in a timid manner, but through the power of a mighty whirlwind! God speaks in many ways!

Which is true about me? (Check the ones that apply most often.)

- ☐ I humbly yield to God's still small voice.
- ☐ I'm constantly defending myself to the Lord.
- ☐ It will take a display of His power to get my attention.
- ☐ As I go throughout my day, I will stop and listen for the Lord's voice.

JOB 38:2-3

Have I ever felt wronged by God? ☐ **YES** ☐ **NO**

Do I really think I could prove God wrong? ☐ **YES** ☐ **NO**

God rebuked Job for his ignorance. Job wanted to defend his innocence to God, but Job would not be able to answer even one of the 77 questions God asked him!

JOB 38:4-18

Who created this world? ___________

God used building terms to illustrate His creative process.

Who created the sea? ______Who made the clouds? _______

Oceans cover more than 70% of the earth's surface!

Who commands the sun? ________

Who knows every inch of earth? _________

Job was not at Creation, nor did he know the vastness of creation, nor did he have power over creation. However, my God does all of that!

I can tend to think my way makes more sense than God's. But I must remember He is all-powerful and all-knowing. Today I am committing to trust His power and knowledge about: ____

____.

SHARE IT

A humble faith and sincere obedience shall see further into the secret of the Lord than all philosophies and science.
~ Matthew Henry

FRIDAY WEEK 4

TRUTH: JOB 40:1-14

JOB 40:1-5

Job had been waiting for this moment! Finally, he could defend himself to God! But...did he?

☐ **YES** ☐ **NO**

Instead what was Job's response? ______________________________

Why? Job had been humbled by God's revelation of Himself, of His power, and of His knowledge. I may be discouraged and see hardship all around, but in these times, what must I choose to hold on to?

☐ The goodness of God's character ☐ How I feel ☐ My logic

Job realized that he went too far in his complaints. He crossed a line when he assumed that he was capable of judging an act of God.

Have I complained too much about something lately? ☐ **YES** ☐ **NO**

Have I acted as if God wronged me? ☐ **YES** ☐ **NO**

If so, take some time now to ask God for forgiveness and ask Him to help you trust His plan. ☐

I will not get the help I need if I keep making excuses and defending myself.

JOB 40:6-8

Job insisted that he had been treated unfairly. While the world will be unfair to me, is that God's character? ☐ **YES** ☐ **NO**

Would God ever act unjustly? ☐ **YES** ☐ **NO**

If I complain to God that He has not treated me right, I am accusing God of being unjust. Examine your heart: Is there anything I am holding against God? ☐ **YES** ☐ **NO**.

If so confess to Him here: ______________________________

Is there anything that I am upset about because He is withholding something from me?

____

JOB 40:9-14

God challenged Job to try to do better than Him! God asked Job these questions. Could I answer them any differently?

Can I humble all the proud in this world? ☐ **YES** ☐ **NO**

Do I have power to defeat all the wicked of this world? ☐ **YES** ☐ **NO**

Could I really save myself? ☐ **YES** ☐ **NO**

If I could have saved myself...the crucifixion of Jesus Christ would not have been needed! Who knows what is best for me? **God / Me**

SHARE IT

Will I believe the pain I feel or the God I serve?

WEEK 4 SATURDAY

TRUTH: JOB 42:1-17

Today we read the end of the story!

JOB 42:1-6

Job admitted that God can ________ ______________.(**v. 1**)
What are God's plans for me? See **Jeremiah 29:11** or **Romans 8:28-29**. Just like this verse says to Israel, God's plans are *always* for my____________. So, nothing can stop God's goodness for me!

JOB 42:3-5

Job admitted his wrong: ______________________________

Have I spoken to God arrogantly? Like I knew more than He did? ☐ **YES** ☐ **NO**
Take time now to confess like Job did!

Did Job get an explanation for why he suffered? ☐ **YES** ☐ **NO**
Instead Job got a personal experience with God. That showed him God's sovereignty—that He is all-powerful and in control of all that happens to His children.

Would I be okay if God doesn't give me an answer for my suffering?
No 1 2 3 4 5 Yes

Would I trust His purposes still? **No 1 2 3 4 5 Yes**

JOB 42:6

Job despised the way he had questioned and accused God.
With no explanation of his suffering, Job decided to submit to the omnipotent and loving God.

JOB 42:7-17

Spurgeon said, "The door of repentance opens into the hall of joy." Though I may not have my perfect, happy ending here on earth, repentance leads to a relationship with God that will bring joy and peace.

Who was rebuked here? (**v. 7**) ______________________________

What happened to Job after he prayed for his friends? ____________________

____

Job had been so focused on himself throughout this book. Amidst my own hardships, I need to look to the needs of others instead of being wrapped up in myself. As I think about this last week: Have I been focused more on myself and my problems or have I tried to help others?

Focused on myself 1 2 3 4 5 Focused on others

☐ Take time now to talk with God about the truths you have learned from Job's experience and share that truth with a friend.

SHARE IT

No matter what comes your way, trust that God's goodness cannot be stopped.

SUNDAY WEEK 5

TRUTH: PSALM 104:1-13

PSALM 104:1-13

David is very descriptive as he blesses the Lord in these verses.
What elements of creation does David use in telling us of God's greatness? List 5.

____

____

Write out **Psalm 34:1**. ______________________________

____

Describe how I have seen God's greatness in my life. ______________________________

____

How do I bless the Lord to others? ______________________________

____

Can I say with confidence, "O Lord my God, You are very great"? ☐ **YES** ☐ **NO**
Or, if I am honest, am I struggling with believing God is great? ☐ **YES** ☐ **NO**

This week I will commit to: (Circle one)

Share God's greatness in my life with someone.

Or, if I am struggling,

Pray daily for God to show me His greatness in my life.

PSALM 104:9

What did God set so that something may not pass? ______________________________

I believe that boundaries are important. ☐ **YES** ☐ **NO**
How can boundaries help me to bless the Lord at all times? ______________________________

____

What are some boundaries I have in place in my life? ______________________________

____

What are the boundaries that I have crossed that have kept me from seeing God's greatness? ______________________________

Today I will write an acrostic using the word, "GREAT," and hang it up to remind myself of God's greatness. ☐ **YES** ☐ **NO**

SHARE IT

God IS Great!

WEEK 5 **MONDAY**

TRUTH: PSALM 104:14-23

Write out **Genesis 1:1**. ____

____

What did God provide for each of these in His creation?

Livestock ______________________________ **v. 14**

Man ______________________________ **v. 14**

Trees ______________________________ **v. 16**

Birds ______________________________ **v. 17**

Storks ______________________________ **v. 17**

Goats ______________________________ **v. 18**

Lions ______________________________ **vv. 21-22**

God created each of these, and He provides shelter and food for them as well. How have I seen Him provide for me? ____

____

Now read **Matthew 6:25-30**.

Does God think I am valuable? ☐ **YES** ☐ **NO**
Does God know what I need? ☐ **YES** ☐ **NO**
Can I trust God to take care of me? ☐ **YES** ☐ **NO**

What is my biggest worry right now? ______________________________________

____

Philippians 4:6 says not to worry about anything but to pray about everything with thanksgiving.

I will consistently pray with thanksgiving about ______________________________ ______________________ until I am no longer worried about it because I know God is great, and I know God cares for me even more than the animals He created.

Sometimes writing down our worries in a prayer to God can help. Use the Prayer List section in this Quiet Time or use a journal or notebook. Don't forget to look back and write how God answered those prayers!

SHARE IT

Worrying doesn't change anything, but trusting God changes everything.

TUESDAY WEEK 5

TRUTH: PSALM 104:24-35

PSALM 104:27

"These all look to (wait for) You, God." Who are "these" referring to? ____________________

____

All of creation looks to God for its food, its sustenance, and its very breath.

When I am in need, who or what do I turn to? ______________________________
Do I look to God first for all that I need? ☐ **YES** ☐ **NO**

Philippians 4:19 says that God will provide for ALL of my needs.
Do I really believe this? ☐ **YES** ☐ **NO**

Ephesians 3:20 says God wants to give me far more abundantly than all I can ask or think. How does this make me feel?

Write out **Psalm 37:4**. (This is a great verse to memorize.)____________________

____

Look to God. Ask Him for your deepest need. He wants to give it to you.

PSALM 104:34

To meditate is *to think deeply or carefully about something or someone.*
On a scale of 1-5 how would I rate my prayer time?

Not Great 1 2 3 4 5 Meaningful

What about my time in the Word of God?

Not Great 1 2 3 4 5 Meaningful

Is my meditation pleasing to God? ☐ **YES** ☐ **NO**

PSALM 104:33-35

A heart that looks to God will SING, PRAISE, REJOICE, and BLESS the Lord. Is this the attitude of my heart today? ☐ **YES** ☐ **NO**

Write some thoughts about this here. ______________________________

____

____

____

____

SHARE IT

When my meditation is pleasing to God I can bless Him at all times, tell of His greatness, and trust Him to supply my every need.

WEEK 5 WEDNESDAY

TRUTH: PSALM 105:1:1-12

PSALM 105:1

TAKE ACTION: Give thanks. What are five things I am thankful for today? ________

____

TAKE ACTION: Call on His name. Today I am praying for: ______________________.

TAKE ACTION: Make known His deeds. Who is on my heart I know needs to hear about God's greatness? ______________________________

I commit to call, text, write, or talk to this person today. ☐ **YES** ☐ **NO**

PSALM 105:2

TAKE ACTION: Sing praises to Him. What kind of music do I listen to? Does it praise God?
☐ **YES** ☐ **NO**

TAKE ACTION: Tell of His works. Do I talk about God in my regular conversations?
☐ **YES** ☐ **NO**

When I spend time with God in prayer, in the Word, and in my thoughts, I will want to talk about Him. Who will I share my quiet time with today? ______________________________

PSALM 105:3

TAKE ACTION: Rejoice. Write out **1 Thessalonians 5:16**.
How often do I rejoice? ____

PSALM 105:4

TAKE ACTION: Seek the Lord. How often should I seek Him? ________________
I commit to be in the Word of God at least 5 minutes every day for a week. ☐ **YES** ☐ **NO**

Dates: 1._______ 2._______ 3._______ 4._______ 5. _______ 6. _______ 7. _______

PSALM 105:5

TAKE ACTION: Remember. I will spend some time journaling how God is speaking to me today and what God has done in my life.

PSALM 105:8

How long does God remember His covenants/promises to His people? ________________

SHARE IT

God is faithful to me. I will take action and live out my faith.

THURSDAY WEEK 5

TRUTH: PSALM 105:13-25

PSALM 105:13

God's people wandered for a long time. They were following the path God set them on. Some days it felt like they were going nowhere.

Do I ever feel like I am on a path to nowhere in this world? ☐ **YES** ☐ **NO**
Am I (circle):
on the path of God's goodness or **wandering from one worldly thing to another** ?

What is stopping me from following God's path today? ____________________

____

God's plan for my life is eternal life. If something were to happen to me today, do I know for sure I would spend eternity in Heaven? ☐ **YES** ☐ **NO**
Read **John 3:16**.
If I am unsure of where I am headed, whom will I talk to today about this?

____

If I am sure I will spend eternity in Heaven, I will pray God will give me an opportunity to share with someone how they can know for sure where they will spend eternity.
☐ **YES** ☐ **NO**

PSALM 105:14

Do I believe that God will protect and guide me? ☐ **YES** ☐ **NO**
Read **Psalm 119:105**. What can I use for direction in my life? ____________________

PSALM 105:16-25

What man is remembered in these verses? ____________________
Did Joseph have it easy in life? ☐ **YES** ☐ **NO**
What are some things I know about Joseph? (You can read all about him in **Genesis 37-50**.)

Match how God is always at work in the lives of His people.

God's Protection (**v. 14**)	God provided during the famine.
God's Provision (**v. 16**)	Israel became stronger than their foes.
God's Plan (**vv. 17-22**)	No harm was done to God's people.
God's Providence (**v. 24**)	God's people increased in number.
God's Power (**v. 24**)	Joseph went from prison to a prominent position.

SHARE IT

When things do not seem to be going my way, I can trust and know that God is looking out for me.

WEEK 5 FRIDAY

TRUTH: PSALM 105:26-36

PSALM 105:26

Who are the two men that God chose for this mission?

______________________ ______________________

God has chosen me for a special purpose as well. According to **1 Peter 2:9** what is that purpose? To proclaim (shew forth): ______________________

One practical way that I will do that today is:

- ☐ Post today's Share It on social media.
- ☐ Tell a friend what today's Quiet Time was about.
- ☐ Give a gospel tract to someone.
- ☐ Help someone willingly with a task.
- ☐ Have a good attitude with my family.

What are some ways to stay on mission for God? ______________________

____

I will circle one way I will stay on mission for God this week and will set a daily reminder for myself.

PSALM 105:28-36

This Psalm reminds me of the plagues that God sent to Egypt.

What are the 10 plagues?

1) **Exodus 7:17** ______________________
2) **Exodus 8:2** ______________________
3) **Exodus 8:16** ______________________
4) **Exodus 8:21** ______________________
5) **Exodus 9:3-4** ______________________
6) **Exodus 9:9** ______________________
7) **Exodus 9:18** ______________________
8) **Exodus 10:4** ______________________
9) **Exodus 10:21** ______________________
10) **Exodus 11:5** ______________________

A way God has shown His power in my life is: ______________________

______________________.

SHARE IT

God's power is greater than anything in this world.

SATURDAY WEEK 5

TRUTH: PSALM 105:37-45

PSALM 105:37

God's people had been in slavery for many years.
Who brought them out? __________
What is enslaving me today? ______________________________

Is there a friendship I need to let go of? ☐ **YES** ☐ **NO**
Is there an activity that I need to stop? ☐ **YES** ☐ **NO**
Are there things I am listening to or watching that are keeping me from seeing God's greatness in my life? ☐ **YES** ☐ **NO**

God wants to bring me out. Will I let Him today? ☐ **YES** ☐ **NO**
Spend time surrendering this to God now.

PSALM 105:37-43

Once I am set free from the things that bind me, God will abundantly bless me with His goodness.
What did God send with the Israelites when they left Egypt? (**v. 37**)

____

God will give me more than I can ask or imagine.

How did God guide the Israelites? (**v. 39**) ______________________________
God will guide my daily steps.

What did God provide for the Israelites to eat and drink? (**vv. 40-41**)

____

God will provide what I need.

When the people ____________________, God brought food and satisfied them. (**v. 40**)
God will answer me, when I ask.

How did God bring the Israelites out? (**v. 43**) ______________________________
God will give me gladness and joy.

PSALM 105:45

What two things does God ask of me? ______________________________

How am I doing with these? ______________________________

SHARE IT

God guides, provides, and answers.

WEEK 6 SUNDAY

TRUTH: JOHN 1:1-8

JOHN 1:1-2

These verses refer to "The Word" as a person; Who is the "He" that John is referring to?

____

What does it mean that "the Word was in the beginning"? ______________________

JOHN 1:5

"The light shines in darkness, and the darkness did not comprehend it."

- ☐ I actively try to make my light shine in the darkness.
- ☐ I desire to make my light shine in the darkness, but I often struggle with that.
- ☐ It is too hard to make my light shine in the darkness so I don't even try.
- ☐ I am always surrounded by Christians, and I have trouble finding places to let my light shine in the darkness.

What are the top 3 things that prevent me from shining my light in the darkness?

____________________ ____________________ ____________________

JOHN 1:6

"There was a man sent from God, whose name was John."

On April 17,1997, John Von Casper "Jack" Wyrtzen (co-founder of Word of Life) died. When Joe Jordan spoke to the Word of Life Bible Institute students, he started out with this verse saying, "There was a man sent from God, whose name was John" and went on to talk about the things that John "Jack" Wyrtzen accomplished for God in his lifetime.

Imagine at the end of your life if someone were to stand up and say, "There was one sent from God whose name was __________________."

Write about what they would say after that line: ______________________________

____

JOHN 1:8

People often asked John if he was the Messiah.

- ☐ No one would ever have any reason to confuse me with Jesus.
- ☐ My friends know that I follow Jesus, but my life isn't that much different than theirs.
- ☐ People often wonder why I am so much like Jesus.

SHARE IT

"There was a man sent from God..." ~ **John 1:6**

MONDAY WEEK 6

TRUTH: JOHN 1:9-13

JOHN 1:9

Who is a friend of yours that has heard about "the light" but still just doesn't see Him?

____

Write out a prayer to God about this friend that they will be able to see "the light" of Jesus in some way this week. ____

____

I will go out of my way this week to be "the light" in my friend's life, to love that person in a way that Jesus would. ☐ **YES** ☐ **NO**

JOHN 1:11

How likely would I have been to receive Jesus if I were one of "His own people" when He came into the world?

Not Very Likely 1 2 3 4 5 Very Likely

How likely would my church (today) have been to receive Him if we were there when He came into the world?

Not Very Likely 1 2 3 4 5 Very Likely

Someone I know now that I am certain would have received Jesus despite what anyone else in that time was saying is ____ .

JOHN 1:12

Becoming a child of God is the most important decision you will ever make. Briefly write out your story of when and how you decided to "become a child of God". (If you are not a child of God, skip to the next section.) ____

____

____

- ☐ I am very interested in becoming a child of God, and I will talk to a youth leader or a Christian friend about this today.
- ☐ I am somewhat interested in becoming a child of God, and I would like God to make Himself real in my life today.
- ☐ I am certain that I am a child of God, but it doesn't mean that much to me.
- ☐ I am a child of God, and I know it's the best decision I've ever made!
- ☐ I am not a Christian yet, but I'm looking into it.

SHARE IT

"Being born again happens in an instant; learning to live like a child of God takes a lifetime." ~ Derwin L Gray

WEEK 6 TUESDAY

TRUTH: JOHN 1:14-18

JOHN 1:14

"Became flesh and dwelt among us." Just picture it: Jesus chose to come in the form of a baby when He left Heaven to enter earth.

Circle the words that best describe a baby.

Helpless **Confident** **Vulnerable** **Needy** **Dependent**

Defenseless **Humble** **Self-Sufficient** **Independent**

What do these words tell me about the position that Jesus chose to put Himself into when He "became flesh to dwell among us"? ______________________________

____

JOHN 1:15

John was so excited to point out Jesus because he had been telling everyone about Jesus for a long time.
In what ways have I been telling people about Jesus in my life? ______________

____

Two people that I have been talking to about Jesus are:

__________________________ __________________________

- [ ] Throughout the day today I will pray for these specific people.
- [ ] Today I will look for the opportunity to start talking to someone about Jesus.

John had been getting a lot of attention and popularity, but now he was pointing to Jesus to be sure everyone knew Jesus outranked him.

Where do I struggle the most with taking the credit?
☐ Sports ☐ Academics ☐ Relationships ☐ Talents ☐ Other

JOHN 1:16

In my own words the definition for *grace* is: ______________________________

____.

Bono Vox once said, "Grace is what happens when love interrupts the consequences of my actions." Respond to that definition here: ______________________________

____

SHARE IT

"Grace is what happens when love interrupts the consequences of my actions." ~ Bono Vox

WEDNESDAY WEEK 6

TRUTH: JOHN 1:19-28

JOHN 1:19

Doing the right thing for God often confuses other people. A time that I was doing what God wanted me to do, but others didn't understand was: ______________________

____

JOHN 1:24

Who sent these priests and Levites to John to ask him these questions?

☐ Roman government ☐ Pharisees ☐ People from the town

Define what a *Pharisee* is: ______________________

Throughout John's and Jesus' lives, the Pharisees were usually:

- ☐ Helpful and interested in what they had to say.
- ☐ Uninterested and ignored that they even existed.
- ☐ Untrusting and scared of what would happen next.

Is there someone in my life that I would see as a Pharisee? ☐ **YES** ☐ **NO**

Both Jesus and John were often sarcastic and somewhat aggressive when addressing the Pharisees, but in **John 3** when Jesus talked with a Pharisee who seemed genuinely interested, Jesus treated him differently. Why did Jesus speak this way in this situation in **John 3**? ______________________

____

When I interact with Pharisees in my own life:

- ☐ I am always aggressive or dismissive of them.
- ☐ I am looking for a way to "win" and look better than them.
- ☐ I am trying to have compassion and figure out how to best love them in my interactions with them.

JOHN 1:25

John was prepared to give them an answer for what he was doing. If someone were to ask me what I am doing, what my purpose in life is, I would say: ______________________

____

SHARE IT

"…always be ready to give a defense to everyone who asks you a reason for the hope that is in you…" ~ **1 Peter 3:15**

WEEK 6 THURSDAY

TRUTH: JOHN 1:29-34

JOHN 1:29

How did John react when Jesus approached? ______________________________

____

In the Jewish culture, lambs were sacrificed daily for the sins of the people as a picture of Jesus coming to be sacrificed for the sins of the whole world.

JOHN 1:30

John pointed out to everyone that this was the Man he had been speaking about. A time that I told people about God and then God actually showed up in that person's life was:

____

JOHN 1:32

What did John see descend from Heaven? ______________________________

If I were John and I had been preaching about the Messiah coming and now He was finally here before me, I would:

- jump for joy since He had finally arrived.
- be a little hesitant to decide if it was really Him or not.
- be a little surprised because in the back of my mind I sometimes wondered if I would ever really see this day come.

There are things that we talk to God about for a long time and sometimes we start to wonder if God will ever really do anything about it.

- Sometimes I am praying for things so long that I would actually be shocked if God did decide to do something about it.
- I never lose faith and find it easy to be patient and wait for God's timing.

This is one way I have been asking God to show up in my life.

____

____

JOHN 1:33

What are some ways that God communicates with you? ______________________________

____

____

SHARE IT

"When you read the Bible, you must think that here and now, God is speaking with me." ~ Dietrich Bonhoeffer

FRIDAY WEEK 6

TRUTH: JOHN 1:35-42

JOHN 1:35

"John stood with two of his disciples." The definition of a disciple is ***the follower of a teacher, leader, or philosopher***. It is possible to be a disciple of anyone that leads. These were two of John's disciples, meaning that they followed his teaching and leading and actively learned from him.

By this definition I would say that I am a disciple of (don't use Jesus for this answer, that will come later; think of a person whose teaching and lifestyle you follow and try to emulate): ______________________.

What draws me to this person or makes me want to be like them is:

____.

JOHN 1:40-41

One of the two who heard John speak and then followed Jesus was:

JEDIDIAH KYLE ANDREW RYAN LIAM MICHAEL JUDAS

John is an example of the ultimate goal of everyone who has "disciples" or people who follow them; the ultimate goal is to point your followers to: ______________________.

When Andrew decided to follow Jesus, who did he choose to go to first?

____

Who are the first people that I go to with important information?

______________________ ______________________

- The above people know all about my relationship with Jesus.
- I have never talked to those people about Jesus.

JOHN 1:42

Andrew brought his brother to Jesus. The person who brought me to Jesus is:

____.

Today I will talk with, send a note, or send a text to the person who brought me to Jesus and tell them what that meant in my life.

- Yes, I sent that note today. - No, I just don't feel comfortable doing that.
- I have no contact with that person today.
- I've heard about Jesus, but I can't really say that anyone has brought me to Him, or that I have a personal relationship with Him.

SHARE IT

Bring someone to Jesus today!

WEEK 6 SATURDAY

TRUTH: JOHN 1:43-51

JOHN 1:43

"Jesus found Philip." It appears that Jesus simply found Philip and told Philip to follow Him. My story with Jesus is a bit different than that. Here is the story of how I started following Jesus, starting with who I was, what happened, and concluding with who I am now: ______________________________

____

____

____

JOHN 1:46

Nathanael's first reaction when Philip told him that the Messiah came from Nazareth:

______________________________.

Apparently, Nazareth was not the place that people expected greatness from. The area in my life that people would be surprised to find greatness would be my:

Hometown Family School Church Group of Friends

JOHN 1:47-50

When Nathanael came, Jesus started telling him things about his life. This obviously impressed Nathanael, and he called Jesus the:

Greatest Magician Ever Original Sherlock Holmes Son of God

Where did Jesus tell Nathanael that he had been sitting? ______________________________

Why did Nathanael initially believe in Jesus?

- Because of what his brother told him
- Because Jesus' words were inspiring to him
- Because Jesus did something that seemed impossible

JOHN 1:50

What did Jesus say to Nathanael about the fact that Nathanael only believed after Jesus told him he was sitting under a fig tree?

- Oh, you of little faith.
- You will see greater things than these.
- Oh, that you would have the faith the size of a mustard seed.
- Get thee behind Me, Satan!

SHARE IT

"Jesus is not looking for fans. He is looking for followers."
~ Dr. Tony Evans

SUNDAY WEEK 7

TRUTH: JOHN 2:1-11

JOHN 2:1

Jesus and His disciples were at the wedding feast.
Do I ever alienate myself from others? ▢ **YES** ▢ **NO**

JOHN 2:5

Jesus's mother told the servants to do "whatever He says to you."

- ▢ I find it easy to know what is right and do it most of the time.
- ▢ I struggle figuring out what Jesus wants me to do, but when I know what He wants me to do, I will do it.
- ▢ Knowing what Jesus wants me to do is easy, but doing it is a different story.
- ▢ I am actively trying to do the best I can to know what to do and then to do what I know is right.

JOHN 2:10

The master of the feast was given the wine to taste; what was his reaction? ____________

____

Even though the master of the ceremony didn't know that he was drinking miracle wine, the servants with him knew it. A time that I saw Jesus work and the people affected didn't recognize it was Jesus working: ________________________________

____

What is a situation in my life where I decided to hand it over to Jesus and the outcome was so much better than if I had simply relied on myself? ____________________

____

JOHN 2:11

This was the ________ of Jesus' signs.

Second **Last** **Tenth** **First** **One Hundredth**

"And His disciples believed in Him." Jesus had been gathering these disciples. They started to believe in Him after they saw Him perform a miracle.

Does this make them **weak** or **normal** ? (Circle)

SHARE IT

"Those who leave everything in God's hands will eventually see God's hands in everything." ~ Unknown

WEEK 7 MONDAY

TRUTH: JOHN 2:12-25

JOHN 2:14-16

What did Jesus do when He found people selling things in the temple? ______________

____

"Jesus's anger was pure and completely justified because at its root was concern for God's holiness and worship. Jesus was never out of control. He controlled His emotions; His emotions did not control Him." (gotquestions.org)

When I see things that make me upset:

- ☐ I react without thinking and yell at people and come across judgmental.
- ☐ I get really upset but don't say anything at the time; I complain to other Christians later because they understand.
- ☐ I'm very level-headed and approach the person with respect.
- ☐ Other: ______________________________

JOHN 2:17

What did the disciples remember reading in the past that they connected with this?

____

People often take things that are meant to help us focus on God and instead use it for their own personal gain. One thing that specifically bugs me is: ______________

____

JOHN 2:18-19

When the Jews asked for a sign, Jesus told them to destroy the temple, and He would raise it again in three days. What did Jesus mean by that? ______________

____

It had to be hard for the disciples to follow Him when they didn't understand what He was saying until years later.

An area where I find it hard to simply follow Jesus in is: ______________

____.

SHARE IT

Follow Jesus even when it doesn't make sense.

TUESDAY WEEK 7

TRUTH: JOHN 3:1-12

JOHN 3:1

Who did Nicodemus work with? ____________________

If the Pharisees didn't like Jesus, what was this guy doing coming to Jesus to talk to Him?

- ☐ Nicodemus was trying to trap Jesus into saying the wrong thing.
- ☐ Nicodemus had genuine questions for Jesus.

Why did Nicodemus go to Jesus in the night? ____________________

____

When someone who represents those who don't like me comes and talks to me, how do I respond? ____________________

JOHN 3:2

Nicodemus pointed out that he believed Jesus came from God because of the miracles that Jesus performed. Is believing that Jesus comes from God enough?

- ☐ Yes, if a person believes that Jesus comes from God that is enough.
- ☐ No, belief is the first step, but I need to have a real relationship with Jesus.

James 2:19 points out that even the demons believe Jesus is who He says He is, but that doesn't make them Christian. Why is my belief not enough? Why do I need a personal relationship with Jesus? ____________________

____

Someone I know who believes in Jesus but does not yet have a personal relationship with Him: ____________________

This is my story, when I went from simply believing that Jesus is from God to accepting His sacrifice on the cross and asking Him to have a personal relationship with me:

____

____

If I don't yet have this personal relationship with Jesus, I will call a youth leader, pastor, or Christian friend today and ask them about it.

☐ **YES** ☐ **NO, THANKS**

SHARE IT

"Knowing God is more than believing in His existence. Even Satan and his demons believe in God!" ~ Crystal McDowell

WEEK 7 WEDNESDAY

TRUTH: JOHN 3:13-21

JOHN 3:16

This is the most famous verse in the entire Bible, and rightfully so, because it captures the whole theme of the Scriptures. Most people memorize this verse first, before any other verse. Have I memorized it?

☐ **YES** ☐ **NO, BUT I PLAN TO** ☐ **NO THANKS, NOT INTERESTED**

This is what **John 3:16** means to me: ______________________________

____.

JOHN 3:17

For God did not send His Son into the world to ______________ the world but that the world through Him might be ______________.

- ☐ I know some people who believe that Jesus came simply to condemn and point out what people do that's wrong.
- ☐ Most people I know already have a healthy understanding of why Jesus came into the world.

Someone I know who believes that being a Christian is just about following the rules:

____

JOHN 3:20

Why does this passage say that people like to live in the darkness? ______________

____

The area of my life that I keep most in the darkness because I'm afraid to expose it in the light is ______________________________.

I know that the first step of getting rid of evil practices in my life is to "expose them to the light." The biggest reason I'm struggling with exposing this thing to the light right now is:

- ☐ I'm not really done with it yet; I don't want to stop and get rid of it.
- ☐ I'm afraid it will hurt me or someone else if I share the truth.
- ☐ I'm ashamed and don't want people to think badly of me.
- ☐ It will affirm my belief that I am not good enough so that God won't even accept me.

One person I could talk to about this area of my life is:

____.

☐ I will contact them today. ☐ I'm not ready yet.

SHARE IT

Cover your sin, God will expose it. Expose your sin, God will cover it!

THURSDAY WEEK 7

TRUTH: JOHN 3:22-30

JOHN 3:22-23

What was John's job that he was put on earth to do?

- ☐ Pastor the largest church of Jesus' day
- ☐ Prepare the way and tell the world that God was sending the Messiah
- ☐ Build a big following of people who would listen and fight for him
- ☐ Fight against the Pharisees in everything that they did

There are a lot of things that I do because I love God and want to do what He says. Some of these things I do for God, but I also get a lot of credit for doing them. A few of these things are: ______________________________

Is it wrong for people to acknowledge the good things that I do?

☐ **YES** ☐ **NO** ☐ **I DON'T KNOW**

Is it wrong for me to accept all the credit for everything I do?

☐ **YES** ☐ **NO** ☐ **I DON'T KNOW**

JOHN 3:28

When people give me credit for the good things that I do:

- ☐ I am super quick to point to God as the One who deserves the credit.
- ☐ I thank God for making me into the person that I am today.
- ☐ I instantly note what I did so I can keep doing it to continue to receive their praise.
- ☐ I note their praise and then I work it into the conversation with everyone that I know.

A person I know who is always getting praise but remains incredibly humble and points people to God is ______________________.

JOHN 3:30

The phrase, "He must increase, but I must decrease" is one of the most powerful statements. What does it mean to me? ______________________________

____

SHARE IT

"Doesn't matter who gets the credit as long as God gets the glory." ~ Dr. K. Keith Megilligan

WEEK 7 FRIDAY

TRUTH: JOHN 3:31-36

JOHN 3:31

Who was John talking about in this verse?

______________________ and ______________________

Would it be difficult for me to be like John and develop such a big following but then see everyone go follow Jesus? ■ **YES** ■ **NO**

Is it enough to follow Jesus because of the miracles He did but not accept what He says about God? ■ **YES** ■ **NO**

What has God done in my life that helps me to know that He really is who He says that He is?

____

JOHN 3:36

He who believes in the Son has ______________________; and he who does not believe the Son shall not see ______________________ but the wrath of God abides on him.

What does **John 3:36** mean to me? ______________________

____

Three people I care about who I do not think have a personal relationship with Jesus are:

______________ ______________ ______________

Today I will pray for each of them by name. ■ **YES** ■ **NO**

Today I will pray that God gives me the opportunity to talk to each person within the next 24 hours. ■ **YES** ■ **YES, BUT I'M REALLY SCARED.** ■ **NO**

Today I will go out of my way to connect with each of these people in some way.
■ Yes ■ I will try, but I will need God's help. ■ I'm not ready for that.

SHARE IT

My own relationship with Jesus is more than just a way to get out of going to Hell when I die.

SATURDAY WEEK 7

TRUTH: PSALM 119:1-8

PSALM 119:1

What does it mean to be undefiled/blameless?____

____

Who makes me blameless? ____

PSALM 119:1-8

There are 6 names used for God's Word in this passage. List them here.

1.________________________________ 4. ____________________________________
2.________________________________ 5. ____________________________________
3.________________________________ 6. ____________________________________

Do I love God's Word? ☐ **YES** ☐ **NO**

How do I show that God's Word is important in my life:

Do I read it daily? ☐ **YES** ☐ **NO**

Do I memorize Scripture? ☐ **YES** ☐ **NO**

Do I have a daily quiet time and share it with others? ☐ **YES** ☐ **NO**

There is a high standard of behaviors to follow listed in this passage. Check all that I am following well. Put an X next to the ones I need to work on.

n Walk in the Law of the Lord

n Keep His testimonies

n Seek Him with my whole heart

n Do no wrong

n Walk in His ways

n Diligently keep His precepts

n Be steadfast in keeping His statutes

n Keep my eyes fixed on His commandments

n Praise with an upright heart

n Learn His righteous judgments

The only way to seek a life that is undefiled/blameless is to love God and His Word above all else. How much time do I devote to God and His Word daily? ________________________

SHARE IT

The only way to seek a life that is blameless is to love God and His Word above all else.

WEEK 8 SUNDAY

TRUTH: PSALM 119:9-16

PSALM 119:9

Am I living a life of purity? ☐ **YES** ☐ **NO** ☐ **SOMETIMES**
Am I committed to staying pure before and during marriage? ☐ **YES** ☐ **NO**

Think about this. **Give each a rating**	**1: not pure at all**				**5: pure**
Are the things I watch pleasing to God?	1	2	3	4	5
Does the music I listen to point me to HIM?	1	2	3	4	5
On social media am I looking at things honoring to the Lord?	1	2	3	4	5
Are my friendships bringing me closer to Jesus?	1	2	3	4	5

According to **verse 9**, how can I keep my way pure? ______________________________

____

PSALM 119:10

How should I seek God? ______________________________
Do I search for Him with my whole heart? ☐ **YES** ☐ **NO**

PSALM 119:11

How can I hide/treasure/store up God's Word in my heart? ____________________
Am I currently doing any of these things? ☐ **YES** ☐ **NO**

PSALM 119:12

Am I teachable? ☐ **YES** ☐ **NO** ☐ **DEPENDS ON WHO IS TEACHING ME**
Who am I currently learning from? ______________________________

PSALM 119:13

What kind of words come out of my mouth? ______________________________

Who will I talk with today about what I am learning in God's Word? ________________

PSALM 119:14

What is more important to me right now than God's Word? ____________________

SHARE IT

Do you value financial success and worldly gain above the Word of God?

MONDAY WEEK 8

TRUTH: PSALM 119:17-24

PSALM 119:17

I need to live and keep/obey ______________________________.
An area of my life where I know I am not keeping/obeying God's Word is:
______________________________.

I will talk with this trusted person to help me stay on track with this:
______________________________.

PSALM 119:18

According to this verse, what should I pray every time before I read God's Word?
____

PSALM 119:20

Does my soul long for more of God's Word? **YES** **NO** **SOMETIMES**
What foods do I have cravings for? ______________________________
God wants me to crave His Word more than anything!

PSALM 119:21

What does God do to those who stray from His commands? ______________________________
When has God rebuked me for straying from His commands? ______________________________

PSALM 119:23

If someone plots against or gossips about me, what should I think about instead?
____

Today, instead of dwelling on what people have done to hurt me, I will think about this verse instead: ______________________________.

PSALM 119:24

Write out **verse 24**. ______________________________
____

God wants me to run to Him first in prayer and to His Word.
From now on, will I choose to let the Word of God be my counselor? **YES** **NO**

SHARE IT

"You can't do the will of God
if you do not know the Word of God."
~ Jack Wyrtzen, co-founder of Word of Life Fellowship

WEEK 8 TUESDAY

TRUTH: PSALM 119:25-32

PSALM 119:25, 28, 31

Have I ever been in such despair that it feels like everything is falling apart?
■ **YES** ■ **NO**

What are some things that are out of my control? ____________________
What causes me to worry? ____________________
To fear? ____________________
To get angry or frustrated? ____________________
To doubt God's goodness? ____________________

As I cling to/hold fast to/stick to ____________________, life will not feel like I am clinging to dust. (**vv. 28-31**)

Someone that I can talk to that points me back to God's Word when I am feeling like life is falling apart is: ____________________.

PSALM 119:26

What does God do with my prayers? ____________________
How often do I talk with God? ____________________

PSALM 119:27

According to this verse, as God helps me understand His Word, then it helps me do what with His wonderful works? ____________________
Someone that is great at helping me understand God's Word is: ____________________.
I will take a minute and write them a quick note to thank them. ■ **YES** ■ **NO**

PSALM 119:29-30

Do I struggle with lying or falling for people's lies? ■ **YES** ■ **NO**
What should I choose instead? ____________________
How often do I put God's Word in front of me? ____________________

When I am afraid, He will give me courage.
When I worry, He will give me peace.
When I am sad, He will give unexplainable joy.
When I am angry, He will calm me.

What do I need Him to give me right now? ____________________

SHARE IT

I pray that I will run to God when life feels like dust.
He will redirect my thoughts, my actions,
my desires, and my dreams to Himself.

WEDNESDAY WEEK 8

TRUTH: PSALM 119:33-40

PSALM 119:33

The Psalmist promises that if the Lord will teach him the way of His statutes, the Psalmist will keep it how long? ______________

Being a surrendered Christian is not a one-time decision. It is a daily, moment by moment commitment. Am I willing to use everything I have and everything I am to the very end of my life to follow Jesus? ☐ **YES** ☐ **NO**

Am I willing to use everything I have and everything I am to the very end of this day to follow Jesus? ☐ **YES** ☐ **NO**

Am I willing to use everything I have and everything I am to the very end of this minute to follow Jesus? ☐ **YES** ☐ **NO**

PSALM 119:35

Delight. Do I delight in the Word of God? ☐ **YES** ☐ **NO** ☐ **SOMETIMES**
What are the things I delight in doing? ______________________________________

____

Do I like to spend time with my friends? ☐ **YES** ☐ **NO**
Do I like amusement parks? ☐ **YES** ☐ **NO**
Do I like reading? ☐ **YES** ☐ **NO** Sports? ☐ **YES** ☐ **NO** Music? ☐ **YES** ☐ **NO**

Does delighting in these things bring me closer to Jesus? ☐ **YES** ☐ **NO**

Which of these do I delight more in than God's Word? ______________________
How can I use these things to point others to Christ? ______________________

____

PSALM 119:36-39

Duty. As I dedicate my entire life to following Christ, I have a duty to live in obedience to Him and His Word.

Are there any areas of disobedience in my life that need to be addressed? ☐ **YES** ☐ **NO**
What are they? ____

PRAY: *God, please help me to obey You by choosing Your way over the ways of this world. Turn my eyes from worthless things, and turn my heart to You, God, and not to my selfish pursuits. In Jesus' Name, Amen.*

SHARE IT

"Ignorance of God's Word will always strangle the allegiance of those who say they want to follow Jesus." ~ Kevin J. Moore

WEEK 8 THURSDAY

TRUTH: PSALM 119:41-48

PSALM 119:41-43

When there is trouble, I can trust in God's ______________.
Who is my biggest enemy? ____

In **Matthew 5:44**, Jesus says I should love my enemies, bless those who curse me, do good to those who hate me, and pray for those who spitefully use me and persecute me. How do I do this? In His Word, I will… Match the corresponding verses.

Trust	**v. 48**
Hope/Wait	**v. 45**
Keep/Obey	**v. 42**
Walk	**v. 43**
Seek	**v. 47**
Delight	**v. 44**
Meditate	**v. 45**
Speak	**v. 46**

PSALM 119:45

Satan wants to bind me in shame, guilt, doubt, hate, bitterness, etc., but God will help me to walk in ____________________ from all this and will give me joy, peace, love, courage, and delight in the midst of tribulation and taunting.

A time that God gave me joy during a trial was: ______________________________.

I'm in the middle of a trial right now and am having a hard time finding joy. I will pray, reread these verses, and talk with this trusted person, __________________________, who will point me to God and His Word to help me during this time.

PSALM 119:46

I can love and trust God's Word so much that when I speak of Him to others, I do not have to be ____________________________________.

Read **Romans 1:16**: I am not ___________________ of the ___________ of Christ, for it is the power of God to ________________________ for everyone who believes.

SHARE IT

"I'm not ashamed of the One Who saved my soul!"
~ Passion (Lyrics from "Not Ashamed")

FRIDAY WEEK 8

TRUTH: PSALM 119:49-56

PSALM 119:49

GOD'S WORD IS MY HOPE.

To hope is *a feeling of trust or a feeling of expectation for a certain thing to happen.*

What do I hope or dream about? ________________________________

I "hope" to see you again.
I "hope" I pass this test.
I "hope" I get that promotion.
I "hope" this relationship lasts.

Do I really hope in the eternal? ☐ **YES** ☐ **NO**
Do I hope in my inheritance in Christ? ☐ **YES** ☐ **NO**
God's Word gives hope. If I am not reading it, I cannot find true hope.

PSALM 119:50-52

GOD'S WORD IS MY COMFORT.

How have I felt God's comfort? ________________________________

Have I been wounded by pain, brokenness, divorce, death, or persecution? ☐ **YES** ☐ **NO**
What have I turned to for comfort?

☐ Work? ☐ Shopping? ☐ Social Media? ☐ Food? ☐ Sports?
☐ Relationships? ☐ ________________________

I can instead turn to God's Word and find true comfort and true hope.

PSALM 119:51

Even when people make fun of me, like the Psalmist, I will not turn from __________ .

PSALM 119:54-56

GOD'S WORD IS MY SONG.

What comes out of my heart when I face trials? ________________________

Am I quick to complain, grumble, or criticize? ☐ **YES** ☐ **NO**

Spending time in God's Word will fill up my heart to be able to rejoice and praise God even in the difficult times.

SHARE IT

Comfort is not the absence of trials, but it is God's grace to help me live life in the midst of them.

WEEK 8 SATURDAY

TRUTH: PSALM 119:65-72

PSALM 119:66

PRAY: *Dear God, please teach me good* ______________________ *and* ______________________ *for I believe Your* ______________________.

Have I ever made a bad decision? ■ **YES** ■ **NO**

If yes, was it because I wasn't following God's Word? ■ **YES** ■ **NO**

PSALM 119:67-68

TRUE OR FALSE.

T F In difficult times, I am frustrated with God.

T F In difficult times, it is easy for me to draw near to God.

T F I believe that God is always good even in trying times.

T F Disobedience results in difficulties.

Am I experiencing any trial or difficulty right now? ■ **YES** ■ **NO**

Do I believe God is good in the midst of it? ■ **YES** ■ **NO**

What positive things can I learn from this trial? ______________________

Turn to God, not things of this world, during trials.

I want to turn to God, but ______________________ is what gets me.

How can I stay on God's path and keep a right attitude in trials? ______________________

____

PSALM 119:71

According to this verse, why is it good for me to go through trials? ______________________

____

How much time do I spend in God's Word daily? ______________________

I would like to spend **more** / **less** time in God's Word. (Circle)

What is one thing I will do this week to spend more time in the Word of God? ______________________

____

Who do I know that I can learn God's Word from? ______________________

PSALM 119:72

TRUE OR FALSE.

T F God's Word is more valuable to me than anything this world has to offer.

SHARE IT

Nothing can extinguish the goodness of God;
He is always good.

SUNDAY WEEK 9

TRUTH: JOHN 4:1-15

JOHN 4:4

This verse says that Jesus had to pass through this area… list some of the things that you have to do today:

______________________ ______________________

______________________ ______________________

JOHN 4:6

Forget for a moment that Jesus knows all things including what was about to happen; why did Jesus have a seat by this well? ______________________

JOHN 4:7

Jesus spoke to the Samaritan woman, and that surprised her because:

- She was popular and she didn't know who Jesus was.
- She could tell He was a Jew, but Jews hated the Samaritans.
- He didn't say "please."

When Jesus talks to me through His Word, the Bible:

- I also am surprised because I feel unqualified.
- I am always quick to listen because I am expecting Him to talk to me.
- I can't hear it.

JOHN 4:10

When she questioned Him about the water, Jesus responded by offering her ________ water.

FRESH **PURE** **LIVING** **HOLY** **FILTERED**

JOHN 4:12

She asked Jesus if He was greater than ______________________ .

JOHN 4:15

Her response showed that she was:

- Tired of talking to this guy.
- Very interested.
- Polite but only answering what was necessary.

A time that Jesus offered me something that I was excited to take: ______________________

____

SHARE IT

"Let us not drink from broken cisterns because we have access to living water." ~ Charles Simeon

WEEK 9 MONDAY

TRUTH: JOHN 4:16-30

JOHN 4:16

Jesus started the conversation about the woman's husband, knowing that she had had five husbands and currently lived with a man she was not married to. She tried at first to play it off by saying she had no husband.

Was her "creative answer" a lie? ☐ **YES** ☐ **NO**
The last time I answered "creatively" instead of admitting my faults:

____

JOHN 4:19-20

After Jesus told her what He could not have naturally known, she recognized Him as being a ____________________.

If I had one chance to talk to a prophet (or God Himself), the first thing I would ask would be:

____.

JOHN 4:25-26

The woman stated that she knew the Messiah was coming soon and Jesus answered by saying:

- ☐ "Seek and you shall find."
- ☐ "I who speak to you am He."
- ☐ "I do not know what you are talking about."

He clearly stated that He is the Messiah. People have said that Jesus was merely a "good man" or a "good teacher," but "Lewis' Trilemma" is an apologetic argument that C.S. Lewis posed stating that because Jesus claimed Himself to be God then He must fall into one of the categories: Lord, Liar, Lunatic. Explain why He has to fall into only one category (answer one category at a time).

Lord: ____

Liar: ____

Lunatic: ____

SHARE IT

"Jesus was either a Liar, a Lunatic, or Lord." ~ C.S. Lewis

TUESDAY WEEK 9

TRUTH: JOHN 4:31-42

JOHN 4:31

When the disciples returned with food, Jesus did not eat, but answered: ____________

____

Sometimes when Jesus talked, the disciples were so confused.

- I am disappointed in them because they should understand Him.
- I would be confused right with them and ask a lot of questions.
- If I am confused, it must mean that I am not good enough for God.
- If I am confused, it must mean that Jesus is not who He claims.

Is it ok for me to question God when I don't understand things?

YES **NO** **I THINK SO.** **I HOPE SO.**

Something that I don't understand is why God would ____________________

____.

JOHN 4:35

In this passage what does Jesus mean when He is talking about a "harvest"?

Wheat Fruit People

JOHN 4:37

"One sows and another reaps."

- It is hard for me to trust that; I always feel like I have failed in witnessing if a person doesn't follow Jesus every time I talk to them.
- I have to remind myself that I am one step in the process that this person will take in meeting Christ.
- God will save them anyway so I don't invest any time talking to people about Jesus.

When I became a Christian, it wasn't a 1-minute process. These are some of the people who God used along the way and some of the ways that He brought me to Himself:

____

____

____

SHARE IT

"Don't judge each day by the harvest you reap, but by the seeds you plant." ~ *Robert Louis Stevenson*

WEEK 9 WEDNESDAY

TRUTH: JOHN 4:43-54

JOHN 4:44

"A prophet is without honor in his own hometown" means that those who know us well, like family and people we grew up with, are often the last to recognize us as being able to do special things. A time that I have seen this at work in my own life was:

____.

JOHN 4:46

Those in Canaan remembered Jesus for doing what?

- Turning water into wine
- Walking on water
- Healing a blind man
- Making the Statue of Liberty disappear

JOHN 4:48

Jesus pointed out that unless people see signs, they will not believe. I'd like to think that this is not true about me, but I often find myself asking God to prove Himself by:

____.

Some of the areas that I find it hardest to simply believe are with:

Money **Family** **Friends** **School** **My Health** **Work**
Health of Loved Ones **Purpose** **Talent** **Relationships** **Parents**

JOHN 4:52-53

When the man's son was healed and he asked for the time of the healing, the Bible says that the man himself believed and who else? ______________________________

Who in your own family believes and who doesn't believe? ____________________

____

Who is one person in your family that you are praying will believe in God? __________

Today I promise to pray for ________________________ at least 3 times and look for opportunities to show Christ to them.

YES **NO, I WILL NOT DO THAT.**

I am a Christian today because this person in my family prayed for me: ______________

Today I will go out of my way to thank that person and remind them of how amazing it is that they did that for me!

YES **NO, I WILL NOT DO THAT.**

SHARE IT

"Believe God's love and power more than you believe your own feelings and experiences." ~ Samuel Rutherford

THURSDAY WEEK 9

TRUTH: JOHN 5:1-9

JOHN 5:5

38 years ago was the year ______________________________ .

38 years ago the president of United States was ______________________ .

38 years ago my parents were ______________________________ .

38 years ago computers were ______________________________ .

In 38 years, I will be ______________________________ years old.

In 38 years, I see myself ______________________________ .

How would I feel if I had the same disease for 38 years? ______________________

JOHN 5:6

How would I respond to the guy who said, "Do you want to be healed?"

- ☐ Annoyed since I obviously would want to be healed
- ☐ Excited because this man might offer to help
- ☐ Unimpressed because no one has helped me before
- ☐ Unbelieving since it has been 38 years with no change

JOHN 5:8

When Jesus said, "Get up and walk," would I have actually tried to walk?

- ☐ Yes, I would trust Him right away.
- ☐ No, I would hesitate. I've been disappointed and hurt too many times before.

When have I seen Jesus' healing power in effect in my life? ______________________

____

I have seen Jesus' healing power in this person's life: ______________________ .

Someone I am praying for that they will be healed is: ______________________ .

Today I will write them a note and let them know that I am thinking about them.

☐ **YES, I WILL DO THAT.** ☐ **NO, I DON'T PLAN TO DO THAT.**

SHARE IT

"Heal me, O LORD, and I shall be healed; save me, and I shall be saved, for You are my praise." ~ **Jeremiah 17:14**

WEEK 9 FRIDAY

TRUTH: JOHN 5:10-18

Are religion and a relationship with Christ the same thing? ■ **YES** ■ **NO** ■ **UNSURE**

JOHN 5:10

Define *Legalism*:

- ■ Dependence on moral law rather than personal religious faith
- ■ Perfectly obeying all laws the way that God commanded us to
- ■ Ranking all the laws by importance and following them in order
- ■ Purposely breaking every rule that is set before you

JOHN 5:11

Does the relationship that this man had with Jesus trump the religious rules that the Jews were enforcing? ■ **YES** ■ **NO**

Where and when have I seen people choosing to follow rules just because they are the religious rules that they have been taught? ______________________________

JOHN 5:13

Does Jesus only heal people who know Him?

- ■ Yes, today Jesus will only heal those who already know Him and ask Him the right way.
- ■ Sort of, Jesus will heal someone who is not yet a Christian at the moment that they decide to believe in Him.
- ■ No, Jesus heals and some people will accept Him and some will choose to reject Him.

A time that I have seen Jesus heal someone as a way of teaching that person about Himself was ______________________________.

When is a time in my life that I felt Jesus' healing power? ____________________

JOHN 5:14

What did Jesus say to the man when He saw him later?

- ■ "Tell everyone about me."
- ■ "Sin no more."
- ■ "Live however you want to live now."

JOHN 5:15

Do I ever give God credit for healing me? ■ **YES** ■ **NO, I DON'T THINK TO.**

SHARE IT

My personal relationship with Jesus trumps all other religious rules.

SATURDAY WEEK 9

TRUTH: JOHN 5:19-29

People have all kinds of opinions about who Jesus was. Some say He was a great teacher, some say He was one of many good prophets, some say He is the actual Son of God.

Who do I say that He is?

- ☐ Great teacher
- ☐ One of the great prophets
- ☐ Inspiring civil rights activist
- ☐ Actually the Son of God
- ☐ Other ______________________________

JOHN 5:19-20

How is my relationship with my father like or not like the relationship Jesus has with His Father? ______________________________

How much does a person's relationship with their own father impact their relationship with God?

- ☐ It is impossible to have a good relationship with God if you don't have a good relationship with your father.
- ☐ A healthy relationship with your earthly father can be a great illustration to teach you a lot about your Heavenly Father.
- ☐ A bad relationship with your earthly father can make it difficult to truly understand your Heavenly Father's true character.
- ☐ There is no correlation between the two.

These 3 words best describe my father:

______________ ______________ ______________

I will spend a few minutes right now praying for my father. ☐ **YES** ☐ **NO**

I will talk to my father and thank him for what he means to me. ☐ **YES** ☐ **NO**

If my relationship with my father is fractured, I will pray for God's healing. ☐ **YES** ☐ **NO**

JOHN 5:24

"…he who hears my word and believes him who sent Me has______________ ."

In my own words, this verse means: ______________________________

____

SHARE IT

"A good father will leave an imprint on his daughter for the rest of her life." ~ Dr. James Dobson

WEEK 10 SUNDAY

TRUTH: JOHN 5:30-47

JOHN 5:32

"There is another that bears witness about me..." Who is Jesus speaking of?

☐ Peter ☐ Moses ☐ John ☐ Muhammad ☐ Caesar

JOHN 5:35

What were their thoughts about John for a while?

☐ They had always been against him.
☐ They were willing to rejoice with him for a while in his light.
☐ They never noticed him.

JOHN 5:38

What is the first step to getting God's Word abiding in me? ______________________

____

What is the value of spending time reading God's Word daily? ______________________

____

Read **Psalm 119:9** and answer this question: "How can a young man cleanse his way?"

____

JOHN 5:39

The Bible testifies (witnesses) about Jesus.
Am I familiar enough with the Bible to find a verse that testifies about Jesus?
Verse: ______________ ; (says) ______________________

____

JOHN 5:42

What are some ways that I can tell that the love of God is within someone? __________

____

Can the same be said of me? ☐ **YES** ☐ **NO** ☐ **UNSURE**

JOHN 5:43

Jesus said that when He came in His Father's name:

☐ They did not receive Him. ☐ They received Him right away.
☐ They received Him after a little while.

What about me?

☐ I have not received Him. ☐ I received Him right away.
☐ I received Him after a little while.

SHARE IT

"Abide in me, and I will abide in you." ~ **John 15:4**

MONDAY WEEK 10

TRUTH: PSALM 119:81-88

PSALM 119:81-82

Do I have passion and desperation for God's Word? ▢ **YES** ▢ **NO**

Think about some of the things I am passionate about, things I just cannot go without:
▢ A Certain Friend ▢ Instagram, Snapchat Streak, Facebook, Twitter
▢ A Sport or Hobby ▢ Drugs or Alcohol ▢ Health/Exercise
▢ Other ______________________________

Are these things more important than God's Word in my life? ▢ **YES** ▢ **NO**
Most likely the answer is yes by the way I live.

If I were on trial accused of being desperate for Jesus would I be convicted? ▢ **YES** ▢ **NO**

I realize that my behavior shows that I value ______________________ more than my relationship with God.

PRAY: *God, please help me to balance my time better and spend more time with You. Give me a hunger and thirst for You that I have never experienced. In Jesus' Name, Amen.*

Do any of these worldly things that I spend so much time on really give me peace or contentment? ▢ **YES** ▢ **NO**

Am I easily distracted from my quiet time? ▢ **YES** ▢ **NO**

Am I determined to put my relationship with Christ first? ▢ **YES** ▢ **NO**

I will list some ways that I am going to do this:_________________________________

____

PSALM 119:83-86

Am I willing to walk through the smoke to go deeper into truth? ▢ **YES** ▢ **NO**

Difficulties will come. I will stay faithful to God and His Word.
What two words does the Psalmist cry out in **verse 86**? ________________________ !

Call out to God! He is my salvation. He is my Hope. He is my Help.

PSALM 119:88

Sometimes I need God to ______________________________ so I can keep His Word.

PRAY: *God, please revive me; breathe life into me so I will obey You today.*

SHARE IT

God is my Salvation, my Hope, and my Help.

WEEK 10 TUESDAY

TRUTH: PSALM 119:97-104

PSALM 119:97

Oh, how (my name)______________________________ loves Your law!
Can I honestly say that? ☐ **YES** ☐ **NO**

PSALM 119:98-100

What three groups will God's Word make me wiser than?
1)________________ 2) ________________ 3) ________________

How does God's Word help me against my enemies? ________________________

____

What does **1 Timothy 4:12** say? Let no one despise (look down upon) your

________________.

You can still gain wisdom even if you are young or a new Christian.

PSALM 119:101

I have restrained (***held back, kept***) my feet from every __________________ way, that I may keep Your _______________.

How hard have I been working at keeping/obeying God's Word?

Not At All 0 1 2 3 4 5 Real Hard

PSALM 119:102

When God Himself teaches me, I won't want to depart from His ________________.

Who is my favorite Bible teacher/speaker? ____________________________
I will drop them a note to thank them for teaching me God's Word. ☐

PSALM 119:103

Do I find God's Word to be **sweet** or **sour** ? (Circle)

PSALM 119:104

According to this verse what do I get from God's precepts (commands)? ____________

____

What do I hate because of God's precepts? ____________________________

____

SHARE IT

Loving God's Word keeps me from sin.

WEDNESDAY WEEK 10

TRUTH: PSALM 119:113-120

PSALM 119:113

Am I living double-minded? YES NO
Am I the same person at church that I am at school? YES NO
Am I the same person at home that I am at work? YES NO
Do I say that I love God and yet love other things more? YES NO
Do I use inappropriate language with some but talk another way at church or at home? YES NO

Do I go to youth group and church on one day, yet live differently during the rest of the week? YES NO

Do I say I love God's Word yet have questionable relationships? YES NO

A double-minded person will not love God's Word.
A double-minded person will not have hope in difficult times.
A double-minded person does evil.
A double-minded person rejects God's truth.

What is the opposite of double-minded? ______________________________

How can I remain firm in the faith? ______________________ God's Word.
Do not just read it. Study it. Memorize it. Pray it. Share it.

PSALM 119:114-117

When I stand firm, my God will be a S__________ to me. (**v. 114**)
When I stand firm, my God will be my ________________. (**v. 114**)
When I stand firm, my God will ______________ me in hard times. (**v. 116**)
When I stand firm, my God will keep me ______________. (**v. 117**)

PSALM 119:118-120

What does God do with the wicked? ______________________________

Albert Barnes defines the fear of God as reverence for God; *respect for His law, His will, His government, Himself; the fear of offending Him, which will lead us to do right. This fear is not that of a slave; it is not mere dread; it is not terror. It is consistent with love, and springs from it...it does not produce terror, but rather delivers from it, and preserves the mind from alarms.*

Do I have a healthy fear, respect of God? YES NO
Do I respect His power, authority, and rule over my life? YES NO

SHARE IT

The only God-ordained fear is the fear of God, and if we fear Him, we don't have to fear anyone or anything else.
~ Mark Batterson

WEEK 10 THURSDAY

TRUTH: PSALM 119:121-128

PSALM 119:121, 126

What right thing have I done today? ______________________

Do I have anyone in my life that has oppressed/wronged me? ☐ **YES** ☐ **NO**

Will I trust God to act on my behalf regarding this? ☐ **YES** ☐ **NO**

How do I feel when someone just ignores God's laws? ______________________

____

PSALM 119:122-123

What is one of my favorite promises/righteous words in God's Word?

____

☐ I will share this with someone today.

PSALM 119:124

I need God to teach me His ______________________.

One thing God has been teaching me lately is: ______________________

______________________.

PSALM 119:125

How am I currently serving God? ______________________

What area would I like to serve God in someday? ______________________

____

I need God to give me ______________________ so that I may know His Word/testimonies.

One area God has given me understanding is: ______________________

______________________.

PSALM 119:127-128

Who or what do I love? Make a list. ______________________

____

____

____

According to **Psalm 139**, the thoughts and reasons God loves me are too numerous to count; yet my thoughts of God, if I am honest, fall short.

When I love God's Word, I will hate (**v.128**) ______________________.

SHARE IT

A life that loves God will love His Word and hate every false way.

FRIDAY WEEK 10

TRUTH: PSALM 119:137-144

PSALM 119:137-138

MATCH THE WORDS WITH THEIR DEFINITIONS.

Virtuous	**Eternal**
Honorable	**Righteous**
Loyal, Constant, Steadfast	**Upright**
Lasting forever	**Pure**
Wholesome and untainted by immorality	**True**
Dependable, reliable, trustworthy	**Faithful**

Do I ever just thank God for WHO HE IS?

Try this: for every letter of the alphabet, praise God for His character.
Ex. A-awesome. B-Beautiful. Z- zealous.

A ____________	**I** ____________	**Q** ____________	**Y** ____________
B ____________	**J** ____________	**R** ____________	**Z** ____________
C ____________	**K** ____________	**S** ____________	
D ____________	**L** ____________	**T** ____________	
E ____________	**M** ____________	**U** ____________	
F ____________	**N** ____________	**V** ____________	
G ____________	**O** ____________	**W** ____________	
H ____________	**P** ____________	**X** ____________	

PSALM 119:139

Zeal is defined as *eagerness and ardent interest in pursuit of something.*

What am I excited about pursuing right now? What am I passionate about?

____

PRAY: *Lord, give me a passion for Your Word today. May I not just read it, but help me to hunger and thirst for more of it. I want to serve You and others with an excitement for the eternal. In Jesus' Name, Amen.*

PSALM 119:140

How am I a servant in the body of Christ? ______________________

If I am not serving in any capacity, how can I get involved today? ____________

____

SHARE IT

"All other passions build upon or flow from your passion for Jesus…the most crucial danger to a Christian, whatever his role, is to lack a passion of Christ." ~ Wesley L. Duewel

WEEK 10 SATURDAY

TRUTH: PSALM 119:153-160

PSALM 119:153-154

God does not promise an easy path. When I stand for truth there will be opposition, but Who will plead my cause? (**v. 154**) ______________________________

Think of those who are less fortunate than I am. Who pleads for them? ____________
Who is God bringing to mind that I can plead for? ______________________________
How can I serve and help those in need? ______________________________

____

PSALM 119:155

PRAY: *Thank You, Jesus, for revealing Your truth to me when there are so many who have rejected Your truth. Thank You for my salvation. There are many in my own life who are far from Your salvation. I sometimes lose hope that they will ever trust in You, but I know that all things are possible with God.*

Today I am praying for ______________________________ to come to know You. Give me opportunities to share Your love with them. In Jesus' Name, Amen.

PSALM 119:156-157

Great are God's ____________________. As, I look for ways to serve the less fortunate, as I remember to love my enemy, and as I pray for those who do not know Jesus, I need to never turn from God's ______________________________.

Someone who has shown me mercy is: ________________________.

PSALM 119:158

Have I kept God's Word today? ☐ **YES** ☐ **NO**

PSALM 119:160

How much of God's Word is true? ______________________________
How many of His righteous judgments will last forever? ____________________

Since all of God's Word is true, can I trust Him with my life? ☐ **YES** ☐ **NO**

SHARE IT

"The entirety of Your word is truth, and every one of Your righteous judgments endures forever." ~ **Psalm 119:160**

SUNDAY WEEK 11

TRUTH: PSALM 119:169-176

PSALM 119:169-172

I choose what comes out of my mouth.

What will I use my tongue for today?

Will I: (Circle)

Complain or Pray?
Curse or Praise?
Gossip or Build up?
Criticize or Encourage?
Despise or Forgive?

PSALM 119:173-176

God is my H____________________.
God has helped me recently by: ____ .

Today I need God's help in this area: ____ .

PRAY: *God, I confess that I have not kept my mouth pure. I am calling out to You for help in using my mouth as a tool to praise You and share of Your goodness as long as I live.*

I have messed up; I have sinned. I believe in Your truth and Your Word. Forgive me and guide my every step to stay on the path of righteousness. Help me.

I need to tell ________________________ today about you. Help me to be brave, to be unashamed of the Gospel, and to have courage to speak truth.

God, ________________________ needs some encouragement today. I will write, call, or text words of truth to them today.

God, I have hurt ____________________________ with my tongue. Help me to admit I was wrong and ask them for their forgiveness today.

In Jesus' Name, Amen.

PSALM 119:176

A verse I am memorizing right now is: ____ .

SHARE IT

"I am profitably engaged in reading the Bible…it is the best book which God has given to man." ~ Abraham Lincoln

WEEK 11 MONDAY

TRUTH: JOHN 6:1-14

JOHN 6:2

Why were the people following Jesus?

- They saw Him healing the sick.
- They wanted to learn the secrets of the universe.
- They recognized that He is the Savior, and they wanted to put their faith in Him.

JOHN 6:6

What is the difference between testing and tempting? ________________________________

____

JOHN 6:9

The boy had 5 loaves and 2 fish, but what is more important is that he was willing to share it. Obviously, it was not enough to feed that entire crowd, but he offered it to the disciples anyway.

A time that I saw someone offer themselves to be used by God even though they logically were not going to be the whole answer to the problem: ________________________________

____

How often am I willing to share with others? ☐ Not often ☐ I love to share!!

JOHN 6:12

"When they were filled..." shows that when Jesus provides for us He often provides above and beyond our needs.

I have seen God provide for me above and beyond my needs.

☐ **YES** ☐ **NO** ☐ **NEVER NOTICED**

List 3 areas of your life where God has come through for you over and above the necessary means:

____

____

____

There are some people who teach that after the boy was willing to share his food, others then dug into their bags and pulled out food, so this was actually an exercise in community sharing, not a Jesus miracle.

After reading today's verses, how would you respond to this thought? ________________

____

SHARE IT

"The funny thing about the boy who gave away his fish and the loaves is that he, too, ended the day with a full stomach."
~ Mark Hart

TUESDAY WEEK 11

TRUTH: JOHN 6:15-21

JOHN 6:15

Jesus knew He had a mission, but He recognized that the people were about to try to make Him king. How much would I be tempted to be the king, justifying that maybe being the king was the method God wanted me to use?

Not too much 1 2 3 4 5 Very tempted

JOHN 6:18

Why a strong wind? Sometimes things happen that just seem to not make sense to me: sports injury, forgot my homework, lost my voice on a big day… why do these things need to happen?

Do I feel that they are **just by chance, a consequence of my actions, or always something strategically designed by God… or maybe a combination of some of those?**

A time recently where something happened that just didn't make sense, which made me wonder why God would let that thing happen to me: ______________________________

____.

JOHN 6:19-20

How did the disciples react when they saw Jesus walking on the water to them?

____

Later in this story, Jesus made the boat get to land instantly. Why did He not use that trick to get Himself onto the boat instantly? Why go through the trouble of walking on the water? ____

I have a friend named ______________________________ that really needs to see God's power in their life.

I will commit to praying for my friend every day for one week that God would show up in their life in a big way, and they would notice it.

☐ YES ☐ NO

I will commit to following up in a week to tell that friend that I prayed about this for them.

☐ YES ☐ NO ☐ THAT SOUNDS REALLY AWKWARD BUT I WILL TRY.

SHARE IT

"God, Your plan is perfect. Bewildering. Puzzling. Troubling. But perfect." ~ Max Lucado

WEEK 11 WEDNESDAY

TRUTH: JOHN 6:22-34

JOHN 6:22

The people came to look for Jesus but didn't find Him because He was in:

- The hull of a ship
- Capernaum
- The basement of His friend's house
- Nineveh

JOHN 6:25-26

Why did Jesus say that they were seeking Him?

- They wanted to hear His teachings.
- They wanted Him to train them to go into all the world.
- They wanted some more free bread.

Do all that seek Jesus really know what they are getting themselves into? **YES** **NO**

Do all that seek Jesus do so for the right reasons? **YES** **NO**

A time that I was seeking Jesus for all the wrong reasons was: ____.

Am I currently seeking Jesus for the right reasons? **YES** **NO**

JOHN 6:29

What did Jesus say is the work of God? ____

Do I believe in Him Whom God sent? **YES** **NO** **NOT SURE**
(If I'm not sure, I will ask God to help me and I will talk with a trusted friend).

JOHN 6:33

What kind of bread was Jesus describing here? ____

SHARE IT

"I love those who love me, and those who seek me diligently will find me." ~ **Proverbs 8:17**

THURSDAY WEEK 11

TRUTH: JOHN 6:35-40

JOHN 6:35

Jesus said, "He who comes to Me shall never ______________________, and he who believes in Me shall never ____________________."

In my own words, what Jesus was saying here is: ____.

JOHN 6:37

When will Jesus cast me out?

- After I have sinned 70 x 7 times
- After a reasonable amount of chances
- Never
- If I give up on Him

JOHN 6:38

Jesus was here to do Whose will? ▢ His ▢ God's ▢ Ours

JOHN 6:40

"And this is the will of Him who sent Me, that everyone who sees the Son and believes in Him may have everlasting life; and I will raise him up at the last day."

I will take the challenge to memorize this verse this week.

- Yes, I will try my best.
- No, I just won't have the time.
- I have already memorized this verse.
- Reading the Bible is a big commitment for me; memorizing it sounds really difficult, but I will give it a try.

This is the story of when I gave my life to Jesus or the story of where I am at right now in my walk with Jesus (could be just interested and not committed yet, could be committed to Christ since early memories): ____

____

____

____

____

SHARE IT

If you know Jesus, you'll never walk alone.

WEEK 11 FRIDAY

TRUTH: JOHN 6:41-51

JOHN 6:41-42

The people had a hard time accepting Jesus as amazing because:

- They saw Him grow up, and they didn't expect God's Chosen One to be someone that they saw grow up.
- They were used to seeing Him sin, and they questioned why He was saying He was good now.
- They had never heard of Him before.
- They had just started following His ministry and hadn't been impressed by Him yet.

I find it hard to do things in my own town or in my own family because people don't expect great things from me since they already know me.

AGREE **DISAGREE**

A time that I felt like people overlooked me simply because they already knew me and didn't expect that I was capable of great things: ______________________________

This made me feel: ____.

It encourages me to know that Jesus knows what it feels like to be overlooked and underestimated. **AGREE** **N DISAGREE**

JOHN 6:44

"No one can come to Me unless the Father who sent Me draws him; and I will raise him up at the last day."

The circumstances/people that God used in my life to draw me to Himself were:

____

____

____.

JOHN 6:47

How much do I agree with Jesus' statement about Himself: "I am the Bread of Life"?

- I guess I am like the people in His town that don't believe yet.
- Not only do I agree, but I trust my life to Him daily.
- I think He is making this whole thing up.
- I am so lost right now; I have no idea what He is talking about and what bread has to do with anything.

SHARE IT

The Bread of Life never gets stale.

SATURDAY WEEK 11

TRUTH: JOHN 6:52-59

First things first; in this passage, is Jesus speaking literally or figuratively about eating His body and drinking His blood?

☐ Literally ☐ Figuratively

I know that Jesus used imagery and figurative speech often in His teaching, but If I had been there hearing Jesus say these things about eating His flesh and drinking His blood, how would I have reacted to what He was saying that day? Would I have understood His intention?

____

____

____

JOHN 6:54

Have I really accepted Jesus for who He is and what that means? Am I halfway in following Jesus? Do I follow Him when things are going well, or am I all in with following Jesus? Do I follow Him even when I know it may not be easy?

- ☐ Yes, I am committed to following Christ no matter what it takes.
- ☐ No, I am interested only in the good He can bring me, but I am not on board with the difficult stuff.
- ☐ I haven't made up my mind yet, but I am honestly searching and trying to understand what all this means. I am honestly asking Jesus to make Himself clear to me.

Some of the things that Jesus knew He would be facing in the rest of His short physical life on earth: (Circle what applies)

Fame **Pain** **High Status** **Rejection** **Abandonment**
Government Office **Riches** **Death** **Happiness**
Sadness **Friendship** **Denial** **Anger** **Hatred** **Betrayal**
Doubt **Love** **Humiliation** **Unjust Treatment**

Knowing that I may face these same types of hardships (if I haven't already), will I still commit to following Jesus no matter what? ☐ **YES** ☐ **NO**

SHARE IT

"Jesus of Nazareth always comes asking disciples to follow Him—not merely 'accept Him,' not merely 'believe in Him,' not merely 'worship Him,' but to follow Him: one either follows Christ, or one does not." ~ Lee C. Camp

WEEK 12 SUNDAY

TRUTH: JOHN 6:60-71

JOHN 6:60

Many of those who were following Jesus decided that it would be too hard to stick with Him so they decided not to follow Him anymore. In my life, I have seen some people who started following Jesus but then chose not to follow Him anymore. It really hurt to see the people below choose to not follow Jesus:

____________________ ____________________

____________________ ____________________

I am going to commit to pray for each of these people at least 3 different times today. (Come back tomorrow and fill in.)

- I prayed for them once.
- I prayed for them twice.
- I prayed for them 3 times.

I am going to contact one of these people on my list and show them one act of kindness today: maybe a note, maybe I can buy them a snack, a smile across the cafeteria, etc. (Come back tomorrow and fill in.)

Yes, I decided to show an act of kindness toward: ____________________.
Yesterday I chose to ____.

- I am praying that they will see the love of Christ in me.

JOHN 6:67-69

When Jesus asked, "Do you want to go as well?" Peter answered: ____

Do I have a backup plan if this Jesus thing gets too difficult for me?

- Yes, I am good with Jesus right now because things are good in life and Jesus hasn't hurt my reputation or let me down, but the moment I suffer for Jesus, I'm out.
- Yeah, I'd like to say I'm "all in," but honestly I have one foot in and one foot ready to run for safety if this gets too hard.
- Not really, I don't have a plan… but sometimes I drift, and it takes a while to get back to Jesus. Sometimes it gets hard to follow Him, but something always happens that brings me back to Him, I think.
- Lord, to whom would I go? Why would I want to go anywhere He's not? He's my Best Friend.

SHARE IT

A rich man without God is just a poor man with money.

MONDAY WEEK 12

TRUTH: JOHN 7:1-13

JOHN 7:1

Sometimes Jesus was bold right in the face of danger, while other times He stayed back to avoid trouble.

In my life I have been bold and stood up for my faith while other times I have laid low to look for the best opportunity.

☐ Yes, that has happened to me. ☐ No, I think that is wrong.

JOHN 7:5

It is really hard when your own family does not know Christ or understand why He is so important to you. The family members that I pray to come to Christ are:

____.

Which represents me best?

- ☐ Most of my family have a relationship with Jesus and are committed to Him.
- ☐ Some of my family are committed to Christ and others are less committed.
- ☐ I often feel alone in my commitment to Christ; many in my family believe but are not as committed to Christ.
- ☐ I do feel alone; so far others in my family do not know Christ and do not understand why I am so committed to Him.

JOHN 7:10

Did Jesus go to the feast?

☐ No, He stayed home. ☐ Yes, but He went privately without attention.

JOHN 7:12-13

Why would the people not speak publicly about Jesus? ______________________________

____

The word for what the Jewish leaders were doing is:

☐ Acceptance ☐ Oppression ☐ Tolerance ☐ Accountability

I have seen oppression in my own life when ______________________________

____.

SHARE IT

"You are not alone. I'll be with you day after day after day."
~ *Jesus* (**Matthew 28:20** paraphrased)

WEEK 12 TUESDAY

TRUTH: JOHN 7:14-24

JOHN 7:14-16

The Jewish leaders wondered how Jesus could be teaching since He did not study under them. I imagine that the teaching of the Jewish leaders would have focused on: (circle)

Knowing the Laws. **Knowing God**

It is easy to point the finger at the Jewish leaders who were missing the point, but where in my life have I been guilty of missing the point by focusing too much on the law/rules than on knowing God Himself?

____

JOHN 7:18

Jesus spoke on Whose authority? ____________________________

Whose glory was He seeking? ____________________________

A time that I was guilty of speaking on my own authority, when really I was just seeking my own glory: ____________________________.

The person I know who is the best at doing things seriously for the glory of God is:

____.

Today, I will write them a quick note and let them know that I have noticed this quality in them; not to give them the glory, but to remind them that they are making a difference because they are allowing God to use them.

☐ **YES, I WILL WRITE THAT NOTE.** ☐ **NO, I DO NOT INTEND TO DO THIS.**

JOHN 7:24

Has someone ever judged me based on my appearance? ☐ **YES** ☐ **NO**

If yes, how did that make me feel? ____________________________

Have I ever been guilty of judging someone based on appearance? ☐ **YES** ☐ **NO**

Will I commit to stop judging others based on their appearance? ☐ **YES** ☐ **NO**

SHARE IT

"I give all the glory up to God; it's kind of a win-win situation. The glory goes up to Him and the blessings come down on me." ~ *Gabby Douglas*

WEDNESDAY WEEK 12

TRUTH: JOHN 7:25-29

JOHN 7:25

The people were asking questions about Jesus' origin because they thought that they would not know where the Messiah came from.

I have run into people who have asked me questions about Jesus.

- Yes, people have asked me sincere questions about my faith and Jesus.
- Yes, people have challenged me because they do not believe in Jesus, and they wanted to argue with me.
- No, people haven't really challenged me; they know I am a Christian, and they are ok with that.
- No, I keep it a secret that I am a Christian so I don't have to face questions.

I like it when people ask me questions about my faith:

- It gives me a chance to argue with people and show that I am smarter than they are.
- It gives me a chance to see where they are at and recognize what answers would make a difference in their lives.
- I actually don't like it when people ask me questions about my faith.

The last question that I was asked about Jesus is:

____

JOHN 7:28

Jesus answered the questions that they were asking.

How confident am I at answering questions that people have about Jesus?

Not so confident 1 2 3 4 5 Very confident

Sometimes I get asked questions about God that I don't know the answers to; what do I do with that? ____

____

____

(Hint: a great response would be, "I'm not sure about that, but I will check into it and get back to you." Just make sure you follow through!)

SHARE IT

"Great moves of God are usually preceded by small acts of obedience." ~ Steven Furtick

WEEK 12 THURSDAY

TRUTH: JOHN 7:30-39

JOHN 7:30

They were seeking to arrest Him, but they didn't because His time had not yet come. Basically it is saying that things don't happen unless God says it is time for them to happen. Do I agree with this statement?

- **YES, THAT IS HOW IT IS.**
- **NO, I DO NOT AGREE.**
- **ACTUALLY, I THINK IT'S A LITTLE DIFFERENT THAN THAT…**

Here is my explanation for the answer I chose above: ______________________________

____.

JOHN 7:31

What is the reason many people gave for believing Jesus here? ____________________

____

What is a real-life sign or miracle that I have seen Jesus do in my life or the lives of people I know recently? ______________________________________

____

Jesus chose to do these signs and miracles because:

- He loved attention.
- People were sick, and it was His job to heal them, all of them.
- To draw attention to who He was as the Son of God.

JOHN 7:34

Jesus talks about going somewhere that others cannot go. Many times He speaks in a way that people simply don't understand. I choose to follow Jesus even though there are things that I don't understand. Here are a few things that I just don't understand about Jesus and the life He asks me to live:

____

____

____

____

SHARE IT

"He performs wonders that cannot be fathomed, miracles that cannot be counted." ~ **Job 5:9** (NIV)

FRIDAY WEEK 12

TRUTH: JOHN 7:40-53

JOHN 7:40

The people had a hard time deciding Who Jesus really was. They thought He was a prophet, the Christ, etc. I have heard people offer different suggestions for Who Jesus might have been; some of the ideas I have heard are: ______________________

____

I believe that Jesus is actually ______________________, and the reason I believe this is ______________________________.

JOHN 7:45

The Pharisees were so against Jesus.

In my life I find:

- Most people are actively against Jesus and all He stands for.
- Some people do have a strong dislike for Christians but for the most part they leave me out of it.
- Most people say they are Christians, but I don't think they really know what it means.
- Most people in my life are excited and encouraging to me about my faith.

JOHN 7:46

"No man ever spoke like this man."
Some of my favorite things that Jesus has said are:

____

____

____

If people were accusing Christians in my school or group of friends of being Christ-followers, how likely would I be to be found "guilty"?

Not guilty 1 2 3 4 5 Obviously guilty

SHARE IT

"Your life as a Christian should make non-believers question their disbelief in God." ~ Dietrich Bonhoeffer

WEEK 12 SATURDAY

TRUTH: JOHN 8:1-11

JOHN 8:1-5

The Pharisees brought a woman to Jesus who had been caught in the very act of adultery. (Mark which best describes me.)

- ☐ I sometimes tend to judge those who I find out are guilty of "big" sins.
- ☐ I am pretty good at loving the sinner and hating the sin.
- ☐ I will always look the other way when I see sinful behavior.
- ☐ Other ______________________________

Some people try to distract me from following Jesus by suggesting impossible scenarios to test me like this one: ______________________________

When this happens I usually:

- ☐ Ignore them because they are trying to get me off my mission.
- ☐ Engage with them and argue until I win.
- ☐ Have an awesome comeback ready to go that will win the argument.
- ☐ Try to bring them back to the main topic of Who Jesus truly is and why they need Him.
- ☐ Other ______________________________

JOHN 8:6

Many people have speculated what Jesus bent down and wrote in the dirt. There really is no answer; we will never know this side of Heaven. But my guess is that He wrote:

______________________________.

JOHN 8:7

There is no denying that the Pharisees were very good at trying to follow the rules, but why did Jesus' response turn them away one by one? ______________________________

____

Lately I have been guilty of judging ______________________________ when I know that I am not without sin. Right now, I will spend a few minutes praying for that person.

☐ **YES, I DID THAT.** ☐ **NO, I DID NOT.**

CHALLENGE – Do you have the courage to apologize to that person? God will give you the strength to do it.

SHARE IT

"He who is without sin among you, let him throw a stone at her first." ~ **John 8:7**

SUNDAY WEEK 13

TRUTH: JOHN 8:12-20

JOHN 8:12

"I am the __________ of the world. Whoever ________________ Me will not walk in ____________________ but will have the light of _____________."

WORD BANK: **Darkness** **Life** **Light** **Follows**

Jesus is the light in the darkness which to me means: ________________________

____

A time recently that Jesus proved Himself to be the light in my life was: ____________

____

JOHN 8:13

It is frustrating to me when people will not take me at my word:

- ☐ My parents/authority always trust everything that I say right when I say it.
- ☐ My parents/authority never trust anything that I say.
- ☐ My parents/authority will listen to me but wait to see if what I claimed is true or not.
- ☐ My parents/authority give me the benefit of the doubt, but if I get caught lying the consequences are more severe.

What is one thing I personally do to improve my credibility with my parents or other authority figures in my life? ________________________

____

JOHN 8:19

The Pharisees didn't know who Jesus meant by His Father. Am I able to explain to someone the basic facts of the Bible if they were interested and asked me about it?

☐ Yes, I would be ready to do that. ☐ No, I would not be able to do that.

If not, will I ask my youth leader or pastor to help me with this? ☐ **YES** ☐ **NO**

SHARE IT

We are indeed the light of the world, but is your switch turned on?

WEEK 13 MONDAY

TRUTH: JOHN 8:21-30

JOHN 8:22

Someone I have tried to talk to about Jesus, but they really just don't understand what I am talking about, is: ____.

When I encounter someone who just doesn't understand the truth about Jesus and God, I:

- ☐ Leave them alone because they don't want me bothering them with my ideas and my religion.
- ☐ Pick a fight with them so that I can show off my vast knowledge and Biblical expertise.
- ☐ Pray for them, asking God to show me ways that I can get through to them.
- ☐ Tell them my life story and all about Jesus, whether they want to hear about it or not!
- ☐ Other ______________________________________

Am I confident in my own ability to share my own personal story about my relationship with Jesus? ☐ **YES, I CAN DO THAT.** ☐ **NO, I CAN'T DO THAT.**

This is how I started my relationship with Jesus and what He means to me today:

____

____

____

____

____

____

____

____

____

____

____

Note: If I do struggle with sharing my story about my relationship with Jesus, I will talk with someone who can help me with this. ☐ **AGREE**

SHARE IT

Your story is the key that can unlock someone else's prison. Share your testimony.

TUESDAY WEEK 13

TRUTH: JOHN 8:31-38

JOHN 8:32

What do I need to be set free from today? ______________________________

____

What will set me free? ____

"And you shall ________ the ________, and the truth shall make you ________ ."

WORD BANK: **truth know free**

Today I will take the challenge to memorize this small verse. ☐ **YES** ☐ **NO**

Jesus is the Truth. To let His truth set me free, I will write down the lies I have been believing and write down the truths I am choosing to believe instead. ____________

____

____

____

Why would I not choose to let Jesus set me free today? (Circle any that apply.)

SHAME PRIDE ANGER RESENTMENT FEAR INDIFFERENCE

JOHN 8:34

When I choose not to let go of what I am holding on to, I am choosing to live in slavery to it. Have I chosen today to live in slavery or freedom?

☐ Slavery ☐ Freedom

I will explain the difference for me between Freedom and Slavery. ______________

____

____

I will write a prayer to Jesus thanking Him for being the Truth and asking Him to help me to choose daily to live in His truth and freedom.

____

____

____

____

SHARE IT

"Believing a lie will put you in bondage. Believing the truth will set you free." ~ Nancy Leigh DeMoss

WEEK 13 WEDNESDAY

TRUTH: JOHN 8:39-47

JOHN 8:40

Have I ever been in a situation where people were accusing me of doing something wrong, but they themselves were doing things that were just as wrong?

- Yes, I have been in a situation like that.
- No, I have never been in a situation like that.

If yes, how did I deal with it at the time? ____________________________________

____

Now that I am out of that situation what would I do differently? ________________

____

The person who seems to be accusing me the most these days is ________________.

I know that it is wrong for me to pray for bad things to happen to that person; I will choose to pray that others will see my accusers for who they really are.

- Yes, I will commit to praying that instead of hoping they get punished.
- No, I am not going to pray that about them.

Here is one positive thing that I can do to or for my accusers that will help me to start to see them the way that Jesus sees them: ____________________________________

____

I will commit to pray every day for one week for the person who accuses me the most.

- Yes, I will make that commitment.
- No, I will not make that commitment.

JOHN 8:42

Jesus says, "If God were your Father, you would ______________________________."

Many people claim to view God as their Father. According to this passage, how can I actually know if they really do have God as their Father?________________________

____

SHARE IT

"Forgiveness doesn't excuse their behavior. Forgiveness prevents their behavior from destroying your heart."
~ Author Unknown

THURSDAY WEEK 13

TRUTH: JOHN 8:48-59

JOHN 8:48-49

The Jewish leaders who are questioning Jesus are not understanding what He is getting at. He is claiming to be the actual Son of God, but they are not hearing Him say that, mostly because they are underestimating Him because He appears to be just a man like them.

Have there been times in my life where I underestimated Jesus? ☐ **YES** ☐ **NO**

If so, what was I wrongly thinking about Jesus? ______________________________

____

Take those wrong thoughts about Jesus and turn them into truth.

____

____

____

JOHN 8:51

Does Jesus literally mean that those who follow Him will never die?

- ☐ Yes, He is literal.
- ☐ No, He is being figurative.
- ☐ Actually, He is speaking truth, but He means something different than what they picture when they hear, "death."

What does He really mean when He says that they will never taste death? ____________

____

JOHN 8:58

Why did the Pharisees want to stone Jesus right away when He said, "Before Abraham was, I am"? What does that even mean?

____

____

____

What does it mean to me to know that Jesus has always existed?

____

____

SHARE IT

"Let's offer grace in the place of judgment." ~ Wendy Pope

WEEK 13 FRIDAY

TRUTH: PSALM 107:1-16

PSALM 107:1-2

Who are three people I am thankful for?

____________________ ____________________ ____________________

God loves me. Do I believe God's love is for me? ☐ **YES** ☐ **NO**

I am redeemed (***set free from the penalty of sin by the payment of Christ's death on the cross***) spiritually and eternally from sin's grip.

Do I live like I'm redeemed? ☐ **YES** ☐ **NO**

PSALM 107:4-16

These verses describe two groups of people who are not living in this freedom: the Wanderers and the Prisoners.

Am I wandering around in this life without purpose or meaning? ☐ **YES** ☐ **NO**
People who live apart from God are lost and wandering.

Have I called out to Jesus to save me? ☐ **YES** ☐ **NO**

What is my purpose in this life?
How can I serve God faithfully in my:
School? ____
Home? ____
Church? ____
Friendships? ____

Living in obedience to God creates purpose and meaning and keeps me from wandering in this world.

Who do I know that is lost and needs to hear about God's Love? ____________________

A prisoner lives in disobedience to God's Word. Sin is deceptive. The very thing that looks fun and cool actually leads to bondage.

Am I living in **obedience** or **disobedience** to God's Word? (Circle)

God allows the wanderers and the prisoners to go through these trials to bring them to Himself. According to **verse 13** what did they do about their problem? ________________

____

Each of these people humbled themselves, cried out to God, and He answered them. He wants me to do the same. When I have a problem I will pray, believing God will provide.

☐ Yes, I will do this. ☐ No, I will not do this.

SHARE IT

"Living in obedience to God creates purpose and meaning and keeps me from wandering lost in this world."
~ Angelina Hartzler

SATURDAY WEEK 13

TRUTH: PSALM 107:17-32

Write out three things I am thankful for.

______________________ ______________________ ______________________

In these verses, there are two more kinds of people who need God's steadfast, loyal, undeserving love: the Sick and the Overwhelmed.

PSALM 107:17-22

What caused the sickness? (**v. 17**) ________________________________

Sickness is not always caused by sin, but in this case it was.

TRUE OR FALSE.

T F I can live how I want without consequence.
T F Rebelliousness and disobedience can lead to illness.
T F People who live in sin do not deserve God's grace.

What sin in my life do I need to confess today? ________________________

There is no sin so deep that God will not heal or forgive (**vv. 19-20**).
Cry out to God! He will answer.

Am I overwhelmed by a circumstance in my life right now? ▢ **YES** ▢ **NO**

Is there a situation that seems out of my control? Journal some thoughts here:

____

____

____

TRUE OR FALSE.

T F I can handle life's problems on my own.
T F I am in control of my life.
T F I do not need help from anyone.
T F I cannot do this on my own and need God's help.

Which group do I relate to the most? Circle one.

WANDERERS PRISONERS SICK OVERWHELMED

Fill in the blanks with these words: **Provide, Praise, Problem, Pray** .
When I have a ______________, I will not depend on myself, but I will __________. I know God will __________________ an answer, and I will ___________ Him for how He continually shows me His steadfast love.

SHARE IT

There is no sin so deep that God will not heal or forgive.

WEEK 14 SUNDAY

TRUTH: PSALM 107:33-43

PSALM 107:33-34

What happens to rivers, water springs, and a fruitful land where wickedness dwells?

____

PSALM 107:35-37

What does God do to the wilderness and dry land for the hungry? ____________

"Blessed are those who hunger and thirst for righteousness, for they shall be filled." **Matthew 5:6**

Do I hunger and thirst for **righteousness** or **other things** to satisfy the emptiness in my heart? (Circle)

PSALM 107:39-43

TRUE OR FALSE.

T F God doesn't care when I am oppressed, afflicted, or needy.
T F Life is perfect for those who love God.
T F I should rejoice when I see God take care of people who are in need.

I will be ____________ if I observe/take heed/attend to the way God deals with the wicked and the needy (**v. 43**).

How observant am I?

Oblivious 0 1 2 3 4 5 Super Observant

Today, I will observe how God is working in the lives of those around me and come back and write some observations here. ______________________

____

Someone I know who is in need right now: ______________________

As I pray for their need, is God putting on my heart a way I can help them with this need?
☐ **YES** ☐ **NO**

If yes, how can I help? ______________________

What do I feel is my greatest need?
I will call out to God right now. I will write out a prayer to God for help in my need.

____

____

____

____

SHARE IT

The wanderers, the prisoners, the sick, and the overwhelmed all need God's grace.

MONDAY WEEK 14

TRUTH: EZEKIEL 1:1-14

EZEKIEL 1:1-2

Ezekiel was one of the Israelites that was taken captive by Babylon. To me, captivity would be: (circle)

DEPRESSING SCARY FRUSTRATING EASY STRESSFUL

If I found myself in a situation like Ezekiel and the Israelites, I would:
- Blame God for the situation.
- Lose faith in God.
- Trust God throughout the situation.
- Not think about God at all.

EZEKIEL 1:3-4

Ezekiel saw a vision of the majesty of God's glory; what were some ways he described the coming whirlwind? ____

____

When I try to picture God in His glory, what do I picture? ______________________

____

EZEKIEL 1:5-14

All of a sudden, Ezekiel saw several incredible things.
What stands out most about his vision? ______________________________

Sometimes in difficult situations, God shows Himself to His people in a special way.
Have I ever seen this truth in my life? **YES** **NO**

In the space below, what are some special ways I have seen God reveal Himself in my life?

____

____

____

Did this happen during a difficult time for me? **YES** **NO**

God reveals Himself during difficult times so that I will: (check any)
- Know He is there.
- Trust Him more.
- Not be scared/discouraged.
- Something else: ______________________

SHARE IT

Even in the tough times, I know God is with me.

WEEK 14 TUESDAY

TRUTH: EZEKIEL 1:15-28

EZEKIEL 1:15-25

As Ezekiel continued to describe the vision God gave him, he regularly used the words "like" and "likeness" because:

- ☐ He did not know what he was talking about.
- ☐ The vision was so unique and hard to describe.
- ☐ The vision was simple.

Have I ever tried to imagine or describe to someone else what God, angels, and Heaven are like? ☐ **YES** ☐ **NO**

Was that a simple or difficult task? ______________________________

EZEKIEL 1:26-28

Ezekiel had seen the creatures and now had a glimpse at the glory of God and His throne. How did he describe this? ____

____

When Ezekiel recognized he was in the presence of God and His glory, how did he respond?

- ☐ Jumped for joy
- ☐ Stood quietly
- ☐ Fell on his face

By falling on his face, Ezekiel was showing God what?

- ☐ Dishonor
- ☐ Honor and reverence
- ☐ Sleepiness

Ezekiel struggled to describe God's glory, and he fell in the presence of that glory. What does that say to me about God?

- ☐ He is mean.
- ☐ He is incredible.
- ☐ Nothing

Have I ever been so overcome by being in God's presence (in prayer, worship, or Scripture) that I fell on my face to worship Him? ☐ **YES** ☐ **NO**

Take some time to consider God's glory and praise Him for who He is.

SHARE IT

"Isn't it a comfort to worship a God we cannot exaggerate?"
~ Francis Chan

WEDNESDAY WEEK 14

TRUTH: EZEKIEL 2:1-3:7

EZEKIEL 2:1-3

Israel was in captivity for living in disobedience toward God.
Had captivity changed their actions toward God? ☐ **YES** ☐ **NO**

When I face consequences for sin, do I continue in sin or return to God?

____ .

EZEKIEL 2:4-3:3

God told Ezekiel hard times would come but told him not to be afraid. What could Ezekiel find courage in during those times?

- ☐ His own strength
- ☐ The hope Israel would eventually listen
- ☐ In the God who sent him

Have I ever been scared to be outspoken for God in the world? ☐ **YES** ☐ **NO**

According to Jesus (**John 16:33**), how can I find courage and cheer despite tribulations/ difficult times? ____ .

Although Israel was living rebelliously, Ezekiel was to be faithful to God. When have I found it hard to be faithful to God when no one else was? ____________________

____ .

EZEKIEL 3:4-7

God was not sending Ezekiel to a foreign people, but to his own nation Israel. Why was this a benefit for Ezekiel? (Check any)

- ☐ There was no language barrier.
- ☐ The people would have been more receptive to another Israelite.
- ☐ He knew what the people were going through.
- ☐ Something else: ________________________

Who is God leading me to share Him with in my circle of influence…
Among friends: ______________________________
Among relatives: ______________________________
Anywhere else: ______________________________

What makes me uniquely suited to reach the above individuals? ________________

____ .

SHARE IT

"And how shall they believe in Him of whom they have not heard? And how shall they hear without a preacher?"
~ **Romans 10:14b**

WEEK 14 THURSDAY

TRUTH: EZEKIEL 36:1-15

EZEKIEL 36:1-5

Ezekiel now turned his prophecy toward: (check one)
- ☐ Israel
- ☐ Babylon
- ☐ Creation (Mountains)

TRUE OR FALSE.

T F Ezekiel's prophecy toward creation was a result of God's anger toward the disregard Israel's captors had toward the land.

T F God's words show that He cares for creation.

Match the following passages with the truths they teach about God and nature/creation.

God controls the weather.	**Colossians 1:16**
God has a future plan for the earth.	**Matthew 5:45**
God created everything, including nature.	**Romans 8:19-21**

Am I reading any of the above truths for the first time? Which sticks out most to me?

____

EZEKIEL 36:6-15

The fact that God cares even for the hills, rivers, and valleys shows me that He must care so much more for me.
- ☐ I agree with this statement.
- ☐ I disagree with this statement.
- ☐ I have never thought about this.

How often do I thank God for His blessings in nature, whether it is the rain He sends, the seasons He brings, the beauty of the hills, etc.?

Never Sometimes Regularly Daily

Because God cares for His created work, I will respond by:
- ☐ Being a good steward.
- ☐ Not taking His creation for granted.
- ☐ Praising Him for His creation.

SHARE IT

Since God cares for His creation—He definitely cares for me!

FRIDAY WEEK 14

TRUTH: EZEKIEL 36:16-25

EZEKIEL 36:16-19

Why did God allow Israel to face captivity?

- ☐ As a consequence for sin
- ☐ He gave up on Israel
- ☐ Just to be unkind

TRUE OR FALSE.

T F Because God is just and holy, He will always punish sin.

What are some ways I have faced God's discipline for sin in my life? ____________________

____

EZEKIEL 36:20-21

Israel's rebellion against God resulted in consequences, and one major consequence was what? (Check one)

- ☐ People did not like them as much.
- ☐ Israel did not believe in God.
- ☐ Israel's actions profaned God's name.

Instead of being a witness of God to the world, Israel's sin hurt the testimony they were supposed to have. How does sin hurt my ability to share God with others? ______________

____

EZEKIEL 36:22-25

TRUE OR FALSE.

T F Although Israel had sinned, God had not abandoned them, and they would still be able to be an example to the nations.

T F In the same way, although I may be facing consequences for my sin, I trust that God has not abandoned me.

Where am I at right now? (Check one)

- ☐ I have a faithful testimony toward others.
- ☐ I am facing consequences for my sin.
- ☐ I am simply not being an effective witness.

If I have hurt my testimony, what are some practical steps I can take?

- ☐ Repent and return to God
- ☐ Begin living righteously again
- ☐ Something else: ____

SHARE IT

Sin hurts. God forgives.

WEEK 14 SATURDAY

TRUTH: EZEKIEL 36:26-38

EZEKIEL 36:26-28

God told Ezekiel that the day would come where Israel would walk in line with His commandments because He would:

- Force them to.
- Make them perfect.
- Give them His Spirit.
- Give them more commands.

What does this say about the Holy Spirit? (Check one)

- He helps God's people to live righteously.
- Everyone has the Spirit.
- It says nothing important about the Spirit.

This same promise is true for believers today because, as Christians, the Holy Spirit lives in all of us and allows us to overcome sin if we do what? (**Galatians 5:16**)

____

What does it mean to "walk in the Spirit"? (Check one)

- To surrender to Him obediently with His guidance and help
- To be perfect
- To be slightly less sinful

EZEKIEL 36:29-32

In this future day where Israel would walk in the Spirit, how would they respond to their sin?

____

Do I loathe (detest/hate) sin in my life? **YES** **NO**

EZEKIEL 36:33-38

God also told Ezekiel that when these things came to pass the other nations would take notice. Why does it matter that the nations recognize it is God who does these things?

______________________________.

When people see my life and how God is working in me, it can change how they think about God. How will this truth affect how I live this week? ______________________________

______________________________.

SHARE IT

"The Spirit-filled life is not a special, deluxe edition of Christianity. It is part and parcel of the total plan of God for His people." ~ A.W. Tozer

SUNDAY WEEK 15

TRUTH: EZEKIEL 37:1-14

EZEKIEL 37:1-3

How would I have answered God's question (**v. 3**)? ______________________________

The dry bones represented death, and for many people death seems:

- Exciting
- Hopeless
- Promising

EZEKIEL 37:4-6

God told Ezekiel to prophesy that the bones would be brought to life. What would I have thought in this moment? ______________________________

TRUE OR FALSE.

T F Because God is the God of creation, I should trust that nothing is impossible for Him, including raising the dead to life.

EZEKIEL 37:7-10

What awesome displays of God's power have I seen in my life? ______________________________

EZEKIEL 37:11-14

The bones represented the broken hope of Israel in their captivity.

Do I ever feel broken in my situation, cut off from hope? **YES** **NO**

Who do I look to for help in difficulties?

- Friends
- Family
- God
- Others: ______________________________

Israel needed to put their faith in God that He would restore them in their helplessness.

Have I been facing similar moments recently? **YES** **NO**

Have I been putting my faith in God? **YES** **NO**

Despite what happens in life, can anything separate me from God? (**Romans 8:38-39**) **YES** **NO**

SHARE IT

"Jesus gives us hope because He keeps us company, has a vision, and knows the way we should go." ~ *Max Lucado*

WEEK 15 MONDAY

TRUTH: EZEKIEL 37:15-28

EZEKIEL 37:15-22

Before their captivity, the nation of Israel had been divided. Here God shows them through Ezekiel that one day they will:

- Be destroyed.
- Be further divided.
- Be united again.

As Israel faced division and captivity, they may have felt abandoned by God. Was this feeling right? Why or why not? ______________________________

____

When was there a time I felt like God may have given up on me? ______________________________

____

EZEKIEL 37:23-25

How do you think the Israelites felt when hearing they would be ruled by a descendant of David (Jesus Christ, the Messiah)? ______________________________

EZEKIEL 37:26-28

Israel rebelled against God, was scattered to different nations, and was no longer prominent. Here we learn that God:

- Does not give up on His people.
- Will move on to better nations.
- Is indifferent to what we do.

If God does not give up on His people, then that means He does not give up on me.

- I agree with this statement.
- I disagree with this statement.
- I need to think some more.

In light of God's faithfulness to His people (including me), what are some practical ways I will respond?

- Be faithful to Him
- No longer doubt His faithfulness
- Something else: ____________________

SHARE IT

"Being confident of this very thing, that He who has begun a good work in you will complete it..." ~ **Philippians 1:6a**

TUESDAY WEEK 15

TRUTH: EZEKIEL 38:1-12

EZEKIEL 38:1-6

Who were some of Israel's many enemies? ______________________________

____

Having so many enemies would make me feel: (circle)

Scared. Bold. Anxious. Confident. Something else: ____________________.

Are there times when it feels like everyone/everything is set against me? ☐ **YES** ☐ **NO**

What do I put my hope in during those times?

- ☐ My friends
- ☐ My family
- ☐ God
- ☐ Myself

Who was on Israel's side (**v. 3**)? ______________.
How would I respond if I knew God was on my side?

____.

According to **Psalm 118:6-9**, what should my attitude be since God is on my side?

____.

Based on the above truth, whom should I put my confidence in when trouble surrounds me?

- ☐ My friends
- ☐ My family
- ☐ God
- ☐ Myself

EZEKIEL 38:7-12

Sometimes others may devise wicked plans, but my response will always be to hope in the Lord.

- ☐ I agree with this.
- ☐ I disagree with this.
- ☐ I am still trying to trust God.
- ☐ I need to spend more time thinking about this.

SHARE IT

"What then shall we say to these things? If God is for us, who can be against us?" ~ **Romans 8:31**

WEEK 15 WEDNESDAY

TRUTH: EZEKIEL 38:13-23

EZEKIEL 38:13-23

What was going to happen to Israel's enemies?

- Israel's army would defeat them.
- God would defeat them.
- They would overthrow Israel.

Have I been trusting God in any difficult situation(s) I have been facing? **YES** **NO**

God said that all these things would happen "on that day" (**v. 14**), but did He specifically say when that day would come? **YES** **NO**

God was promising to deliver Israel, but He did not tell them when. Would this bring me encouragement or discouragement?

- Encouragement
- Discouragement
- Neither

When was there a time I was discouraged because God's timing did not seem to be the same as mine? ______________________________.

How did I choose to respond when I realized God's timing was different?

- With impatience
- With anger
- With trust
- A different way: ______________________________

TRUE OR FALSE.

T F Based on the truth of **Isaiah 55:8-9**, because God's ways and thoughts are higher than mine, I should trust His timing.

In the space below, write down some ways God might be working "behind the scenes" when I am going through situations.

____

____

____

After saving Israel, God would be glorified (**v. 23**). Will I glorify (praise and honor) Him when He delivers me from difficult times? **YES** **NO**

SHARE IT

"God can. God will in His own timing and plan. Just have faith." ~ Crystal McDowell

THURSDAY WEEK 15

TRUTH: EZEKIEL 39:1-16

EZEKIEL 39:1-6

How many of the people in the army of Gog would be defeated (**v. 4**)? ______________

EZEKIEL 39:7-9

How many people would hear of what had happened?

- Just Israel
- Just Gog
- All the nations

All the weapons left would provide fuel for fires for how many years?

- 1 year
- 7 years
- Less than a year

EZEKIEL 39:11-16

How long would the defeat of Israel's enemies take to clean up in the land?

____

Based on the above facts, what would be a good word to describe God's judgment? (Check any)

- Thorough
- Insignificant
- Adequate

Based on this passage of Scripture, what word best describes God?

- Just
- Patient
- Gentle

According to **Hebrews 9:27**, although some may escape judgment on earth, what will happen when this life is over? ______________________________

____

TRUE OR FALSE.

T F Although sin is present in this world, because God is just I trust that His proper and thorough judgment will come in the right time.

T F In light of these truths, I will trust that because God is just, He will always deal with evil in the right way and at the right time.

SHARE IT

"For all His ways are justice, a God of truth and without injustice; righteous and upright is He."
~ **Deuteronomy 32:4b**

WEEK 15 FRIDAY

TRUTH: EZEKIEL 39:17-29

EZEKIEL 39:17-24

Who were the different groups of people mentioned?

- The nation of Israel
- The Gentiles
- All the nations
- Gog

TRUE OR FALSE.

T F When this prophecy is fulfilled, all people and nations will recognize God as ruler and Lord of Israel.

Who are some people I know that do not recognize God in their lives?

Have I shared the truth about God with the above individuals? **YES** **NO**

EZEKIEL 39:25-29

When God restores Israel, they will rejoice in seeing Him and will repent of their sins. Why is sin such a big deal? (Check one)

- It separates us from God.
- It's not that big of a deal.
- Because my pastor says it is.

Although one day every knee will bow and recognize God as ruler (see **Romans 14:10-12**), the ones who will do so and rejoice are the ones who have received salvation.

- I agree with this statement.
- I disagree with this statement.
- I need to think some more.

Do I already recognize Jesus as Ruler of my life because I have put my faith in Him and received salvation from my sins? **YES** **NO**

Do I desire that others would recognize Jesus Christ as their King of kings and Lord of lords in this life? **YES** **NO**

In light of this truth, will I share the good news of salvation with others?
YES **NO** **I NEED TO PRAY ABOUT THIS**

SHARE IT

"That at the name of Jesus every knee should bow, of those in heaven, and of those on earth, and of those under the earth." ~ **Philippians 2:10**

SATURDAY WEEK 15

TRUTH: EZEKIEL 43:1-9; 44:1-4

EZEKIEL 43:1-5

If I had to use one word to describe what it would be like to see God's glory, that word would be: ____________________.

EZEKIEL 43:6-9

In the day when He dwells in the midst of Israel, God said Israel must be sure to put what far away from them (**vv. 7, 9**)?

- Doubt
- Divisiveness
- Sin
- Happiness

Ezekiel was learning that sin cannot enter God's presence.

Why is it important for people to know this truth? (Check one)

- So that we would know our sin separates us from God
- So that we would feel helpless
- So that we would have more knowledge about God

What does this truth say about God? (Check one)

- He is angry.
- He is unfair.
- He is holy.

Although sin separates all people from God, what did God do that we might have a relationship with Him? (see **Romans 5:8-9**) ____________________________________

____

EZEKIEL 44:1-4

Not only is God's presence absent of sin, but it is also full of ____________________ (**v. 4**).

Have I ever thought about what it will be like to be in God's presence some day?

YES **NO**

When I think about God's glory, it makes me want to respond by:

- Praising Him
- Thanking Him
- Looking forward to it
- Another response: ______________________________

SHARE IT

"Happy the soul that has been awed by a view of God's majesty." ~ A.W. Pink

WEEK 16 SUNDAY

TRUTH: EZEKIEL 47:1-12

EZEKIEL 47:1-9

What are some of the things Ezekiel saw in this future kingdom ruled by God?

____

____

When I think of being with God one day, I imagine it will be:

- ☐ A time to sit on a cloud and play the harp.
- ☐ A long boring time of only singing songs.
- ☐ A constantly exciting time.
- ☐ Something else: ____________________

Based on what I normally consider being with God to be like, does it make me **excited** or **disinterested** ? (Circle)

EZEKIEL 47:10-12

In addition to trees, water, and fish, what else was shown to be present in this future kingdom?

- ☐ Food
- ☐ Medicine
- ☐ Fishing
- ☐ Animals

Although this future kingdom (called the Millennial Kingdom) is not yet here, does this glimpse of God ruling make me excited to be with Him for all eternity in Heaven?

☐ **YES** ☐ **NO**

What do I look forward to most about being with God for all eternity?

____

Peace, health, and healing will all be present in this future time, but today I can also look to God for these same things even in the difficulties of life.

- ☐ I agree with this statement.
- ☐ I disagree with this statement.
- ☐ I need to think some more.

Spend some time in prayer today, thanking God for the blessing of being with Him forever someday, and rejoicing in the excitement of eternity. ☐

SHARE IT

"I would not give one moment of Heaven for all the joy and riches of the world, even if it lasted for thousands and thousands of years." ~ Martin Luther

MONDAY WEEK 16

TRUTH: 1 KINGS 1:15-18, 29-37

Being the king is a big deal. In Israel it was a very big deal. In Israel the king was to be an earthly representation of the rule and reign of God over His people. Today's passage records the transition of the throne from David to his successor as he dies of old age. Let me see if I can match all the characters.

Bathsheba	**Son of Jesse, slayer of Goliath, king of Israel**
David	**Son of David and Bathsheba**
Abishag	**Son of the Priest Jehoiada and head of the kings' bodyguard**
Solomon	**The prophet of God who tried to keep David on track**
Adonijah	**The high priest of Israel**
Zadok	**A young woman who cared for David in his old age**
Nathan	**Son of David and Haggith**
Benaiah	**One of David's wives, acquired by adultery and murder**

1 KINGS 1:36-37

After Bathsheba intervened on her son's behalf, David very publicly proclaimed that Solomon was to become king after his death. At this moment, Benaiah made an awesome statement in **verse 37**, "As the __________ has been with my lord the king, even so may He be with ____________________, and make his throne greater than the throne of my lord King ___________."

Who did Benaiah hope would establish Solomon as a great king? ____________________

If I am honest, who do I want to be in charge of my life right now?

- ☐ God
- ☐ Myself
- ☐ My Parents

Who, ultimately, is in charge of my life? ____

"The steps of a man are established by the LORD, when he delights in his way." **Psalm 37:23** (ESV)

Have I been letting God establish my steps lately? ☐ **YES** ☐ **NO**

Have I been delighting in **God's way** or **my way** lately ? (Circle)

Take some time to journal a prayer to surrender to God's way and God's leadership in your life.

____

____

____

SHARE IT

"For God is my King from of old, working salvation in the midst of the earth." ~ **Psalm 74:12**

WEEK 16 TUESDAY

TRUTH: 1 KINGS 2:1-12

1 KINGS 2:1-3

God made a promise to David before he died, but there were requirements for David's heirs to follow. They were to:

Walk in Whose ways? ______________________

Keep His? ______________________

Keep His? ______________________

Keep His? ______________________

Keep His? ______________________

If David's descendants would do this, then God would never take the throne away from David's family. David passed this challenge and promise along to Solomon as he was dying.

I am not Solomon or an offspring of David, but God has made promises to me too.

In **Romans 10:9**, what does God ask of me? ______________________

In **Romans 10:9**, what does God promise me? ______________________

Have I done what God asks of me in **Romans 10:9**? ☐ **YES** ☐ **NO**

If no, will I do that right now? ☐ **YES** ☐ **NO**

☐ I will talk with someone about making this decision.

How am I doing with walking in God's ways?

Not so good 1 2 3 4 5 Great

How am I doing with keeping God's statutes, commandments, judgments, and testimonies?

Not so good 1 2 3 4 5 Great

1 KINGS 2:10-12

As David died, Solomon took the throne with these instructions still ringing in his ears. If I was Solomon, could I do it?

☐ **YES** ☐ **NO** ☐ **MAYBE**

Do I try to do what God has asked me to do in my life?

☐ **YES** ☐ **NO** ☐ **SOMETIMES**

SHARE IT

"Smart men walked on the moon, daring men walked on the ocean floor, but wise men walk with God."
~ Leonard Ravenhill

WEDNESDAY WEEK 16

TRUTH: 1 KINGS 3:1-15

1 KINGS 3:1-5

Solomon got married and was faithful to God! God was pleased with Solomon and told him to ask for anything he wanted. To be honest, if God told me that, I would ask for

____.

1 KINGS 3:9

What did Solomon ask for from God? (Circle the correct answer.)

To live a long time

To be crazy rich

For his enemies to die

An understanding heart to be able to discern good and evil

1 KINGS 3:10

Solomon's request pleased God so God granted him this ability along with a bunch of other stuff he didn't ask for. This is an incredible ability Solomon asked for, and God has actually told me I can have the same ability. (**Hebrews 5:14**)

What are some ways I can develop this ability?
(Check the ones that would help.)

- [ ] Watching popular TV shows/movies
- [ ] Talking to Christians
- [ ] Reading popular magazines
- [ ] Listening to popular music
- [ ] Paying attention to sermons
- [ ] Talking to my friends
- [ ] Reading the Bible
- [ ] Listening to godly music
- [ ] Prayer

I'm going to pray right now and ask God to develop this ability in me and journal my prayer here.

____

____

____

____

SHARE IT

"But what is liberty without wisdom and without virtue? It is the greatest of all possible evils; for it is folly, vice, and madness without tuition or restraint." ~ Edmund Burke

WEEK 16 THURSDAY

TRUTH: 1 KINGS 3:16-28

In these verses I see Solomon putting to use the wisdom that he was given by God. In the midst of a tragic situation, he had to decide who was telling the truth.

Have I ever had to decide who was telling the truth in the midst of a difficult situation?

YES **NO**

What happened? ______________________________

____

1 KINGS 3:23-26

Sometimes justice is hard to find. Solomon proposed to the two women that they could have fairness, but it would cost the life of the living child.

How did the two mothers react? (Draw a connecting line.)

The False Mother	**Chose fairness instead of the life of the child**
The True Mother	**Chose the life of the child instead of fairness**

Solomon knew the true mother would sacrifice her own desires to save her child, so he observed their behavior in order to determine who was telling the truth.

When I have to determine who is telling the truth, would observing behavior help me?

YES **NO**

What kind of behaviors might indicate that someone is lying? ______________________________

____

Do I value truth in my life?	**YES**	**NO**	**SOMETIMES**
Do I speak truth even if it hurts me?	**YES**	**NO**	**SOMETIMES**
Do I lie to get what I want?	**YES**	**NO**	**SOMETIMES**
Do I hang out with people that lie?	**YES**	**NO**	**SOMETIMES**
Do I want justice based on truth?	**YES**	**NO**	**SOMETIMES**
Do I want justice based on fairness?	**YES**	**NO**	**SOMETIMES**

How can I be more truthful this week?

____

SHARE IT

"It is highly convenient to believe in the infinite mercy of God when you feel the need of mercy, but remember also His infinite justice." ~ B. R. Haydon

FRIDAY WEEK 16

TRUTH: 1 KINGS 4:20-34

1 KINGS 4:20-34

Solomon was actually keeping the charge that his father David gave him.

1 Kings 3:3 says, "Solomon loved the LORD, walking in the statutes of his father David." These verses from **chapter 4** show the result of the king of Israel walking with the Lord, but what was it that people came to see and wonder at in Israel? (Only check one.)

- ☐ Israel's huge population growth
- ☐ Israel's peaceful geographical expansion
- ☐ Israel's abundant natural resources
- ☐ Israel's excessive food & livestock reserves
- ☐ Israel's astonishing peace with all its neighbors
- ☐ Israel's impressive army
- ☐ Solomon's wisdom

All of Israel's success and prosperity came from Solomon's wisdom which he received because he followed God so closely. This was the true treasure in Israel.

Do I think I can be wise like Solomon? ☐ **YES** ☐ **NO**
Why or why not? ______________________________

What can I do to find that kind of wisdom? ______________________________

____

What does **James 1:5** tell me to do? ______________________________

____

If I get God's wisdom, will I be rich and famous like King Solomon?

- ☐ Yes, God wants me to be rich and famous.
- ☐ No, God didn't make me king of Israel.
- ☐ Maybe, but I don't know what God's plan is for me yet.

Right now, I need to ask God to give me wisdom. I need to learn to determine right and wrong by walking closely with Him.

- ☐ Yes, I'm going to do that right now.
- ☐ No, I'm good on my own.

SHARE IT

"But the wisdom that is from above is first pure, then peaceable, gentle, willing to yield, full of mercy and good fruits, without partiality and without hypocrisy." ~ **James 3:17**

WEEK 16 SATURDAY

TRUTH: 1 KINGS 6:1-14, 38

1 KINGS 6:1

How long were the Israelites living in the Promised Land before they got around to building a temple for God? ______________________________

How long was Solomon king before he got to work on building the temple? __________

Having the temple was significant for a lot of reasons; it provided the following: (circle the true statements, cross out the false)

A place for God's Spirit to physically reside on earth

A place for people to transport to and from Heaven

A place for sacrifices to be made properly

A place for God's people to come together and worship

A place for the Israelite army to sleep

A physical symbol of Israel's devotion to God

When Jesus came to earth, He changed all of that.

Where does God's Spirit reside now? (**1 Corinthians 6:19**)

____

Do we still make sacrifices? (**Hebrews 10:10-14**) ____________________

Where do we come together for worship? (**Acts 2:47; Matthew 18:20**)

____

What is the symbol of our devotion to God? (**Matthew 5:16; John 13:35**)

____

1 KINGS 6:38

It took 7 years for Solomon to finish building God's temple.

How am I doing? Do I consider myself a temple of God? What parts do I still need Him to work on? ______________________________________

____

SHARE IT

"Jesus lifts us beyond the building and pays the human body the highest compliment by making it His dwelling place, the place where He meets with us. Even today He would overturn the tables of those who make it a marketplace for their own lust, greed, and wealth." ~ Ravi Zacharias

SUNDAY WEEK 17

TRUTH: 1 KINGS 11:1-13

1 KINGS 11:1-8

Solomon's kingship had been awesome…up until this point. These verses are the record of Solomon falling away from his true King. Let me see if I can put these in order: (1-4)

___ As Solomon grows old, he lets his wives lead him into idolatry. (His original sin leads him into worse sin.)

___ Solomon breaks God's law and has 700 wives and an additional 300 concubines. (He takes what is forbidden.)

___ Solomon builds altars for his wives' false gods in the land of Israel. (He starts leading other people into sin as well.)

___ Solomon allows himself to love/desire many women from many nations. (He wants what he knows he shouldn't.)

1 KINGS 11:9-13

The result of Solomon's progression into sin is that God followed through on His promise and would remove the kingdom of Israel from Solomon's family (**1 Kings 2:4**). Every sin has a consequence and when you're the king of Israel, it's a really big consequence. I need to realize that the same thing can happen to me.

Am I going through a progression of sin in my life? ☐ **YES** ☐ **NO**

Is there something I let myself desire/lust for that I know God doesn't want for me? ☐ **YES** ☐ **NO**

If so, what is it? ______________________________

Do I commit sin as I pursue that thing? ☐ **YES** ☐ **NO**
If so, how? ____

Is this sin leading me into deeper sin? ☐ **YES** ☐ **NO**
If so, how? ____

Am I leading other people into sin? ☐ **YES** ☐ **NO**
If so, how? ____

I need to remember that Solomon did not start out planning to worship false gods; he was just too obsessed with women. I will pray now and ask God to help me avoid falling into the traps of sin as well. ☐

SHARE IT

"Temptation usually comes in through a door that has deliberately been left open." ~ Arnold Glasow

WEEK 17 MONDAY

TRUTH: 1 KINGS 11:41-12:15

1 KINGS 12:4, 14

After being king for 44 years, Solomon died and the kingdom of Israel passed on to his son Rehoboam. However, we know that God was going to divide the kingdom and take some of it away from Rehoboam as a part of God's judgment on his father's sin. This is the beginning of that story.

If I was suddenly made the king of a nation and I wanted to establish a strong kingdom, what would I do first?

- ☐ Do something to make everyone like me
- ☐ Do something to make everyone respect/fear me
- ☐ Do something to make everyone worship me

Which one did Rehoboam choose? ______________________________

1 KINGS 12:6-11

When faced with this difficult decision (how to treat the people), who did Rehoboam go to get advice? (Select any correct answer.)

- ☐ He went to the older men who had advised his father.
- ☐ He went to his young friends whom he'd grown up with.
- ☐ He went to God in prayer.
- ☐ He went to God through one of God's prophets.

Who gave him the best advice? ______________________________
Who should he have gone to? ______________________________

Has anyone come to me for advice when they were making a difficult decision?
☐ **YES** ☐ **NO**

If yes, did I give them wise, biblical advice? ☐ **YES** ☐ **NO** ☐ **NOT SURE**
Who do I consider my best human advisors? Why? ______________________________

____

Do my friends who are my age generally make good decisions or bad decisions? Why?

____

Who do I need to be going to when I have an important decision to make? __________

Do I have a difficult decision to make in the near future? ☐ **YES** ☐ **NO**
If yes, where will I go for advice? ______________________________

SHARE IT

"Trust in the LORD with all your heart, and lean not on your own understanding; in all your ways acknowledge Him, and He shall direct your paths." ~ **Proverbs 3:5-6**

TUESDAY WEEK 17

TRUTH: 1 KINGS 12:16-30

1 KINGS 12:16-20

God's judgment on Solomon came to pass. Solomon's son had made a terribly unwise decision, and the people of Israel rebelled because of it. Let me see if I got all the details right.

(Fill in the blank using the word bank.)

WORD BANK: Rehoboam Jeroboam two ten north Judah

Israel split into ________ separate nations.

________ tribes of Israel rejected Rehoboam as king.

The ten tribes lived in the __________ and became known as Israel.

Two tribes of Israel remained loyal to ________________________.

The two tribes lived in the south and become known as ______________.

The ten tribes proclaimed _______________________ as their new king.

1 KINGS 12:21-24

Rehoboam started to put an army together to go make Israel follow him as king (basically start a civil war), but God sent him a message.

What was the message?

- Don't go to war; this is all part of My will.
- Go to war; you have to prove yourself to Me.
- You are a wise man; do what you think is best.

1 KINGS 12:25-30

While Rehoboam is listening to God's will down in Judah, Jeroboam is up to something in Israel.

What is Jeroboam doing?

- Building a big wall to separate the Northern Kingdom from the Southern Kingdom.
- Building two golden idols that Israel can worship instead of traveling to Jerusalem (which is in Judah) to worship God.
- Building a statue of himself to remind Israel who is really king.

In the midst of all this mess, at least Rehoboam listened to what God told him to do. (Circle) Do I **do what God tells me to do** or do I **worship things other than God**?

SHARE IT

"You will certainly carry out God's purpose, however you act, but it makes a difference to you whether you serve like Judas or like John." ~ C.S. Lewis

WEEK 17 **WEDNESDAY**

TRUTH: 1 KINGS 13:1-10

1 KINGS 13:1-3

God hates it when His people worship false gods. In the Northern Kingdom of Israel, King Jeroboam had instituted the worship of false gods by burning incense and sacrifices upon altars. God would not remain quiet about this.

TRUE OR FALSE.

T F God sent a man to prophesy a judgment upon the idol worship.
T F The man prophesied that a child named Samuel would come.
T F This child would be a descendant of David.
T F This child would burn up all the sheep of Israel on the false altars.
T F This child would burn up the false prophets on the false altars.
T F The man said that to confirm this prophecy the altar would be miraculously split in half before everyone.

1 KINGS 13:4-6

King Jeroboam did not like this prophecy. I am going to put what happened next in my own words: ______________________________

____

____

In the middle of His judgment on Jeroboam, God still had mercy on him. This is just another reminder of how awesome and merciful God is. Sin always has consequences, but God is always looking to give mercy. When I'm caught in sin and its consequences, I can call out to God and ask for His mercy.

I will describe a time that I called out to God for His mercy. ______________________________

____

____

Do I need to ask God for mercy right now? ☐ **YES** ☐ **NO**

If yes, I will write a prayer here. ______________________________

____

If no, I will write a note to thank God for His mercy in your life. ______________________________

____

SHARE IT

"Embrace in one act the two truths--thine own sin, and God's infinite mercy in Jesus Christ." ~ Alexander Maclaren

THURSDAY WEEK 17

TRUTH: 1 KINGS 13:11-25

I can really learn a lot from this passage of Scripture. It is really rather simple. A godly person is tricked by another person into disobeying God. Sounds familiar.

1 KINGS 13:15-17

What did God tell the man not to do?
"You shall not ______________________ nor ______________________ there, nor return by going the way you came." (**v. 17b**)

What did the old prophet ask the man to do?
"Come home with me and ____________________." (**v. 15b**)

Initially the man of God declined the offer, but then the old prophet lied and said that God said it was ok for him to come and do the opposite of what God had originally told him.

What do I think the man should have done? ______________________________

____

Has there ever been a situation where I thought God wanted me to do (or not do) something but someone else said it would be ok? What happened? ______________

____

Have I ever told someone that they could do something that God didn't want them to do?
☐ **YES** ☐ **NO**

Describe what happened. ______________________________________

____

The truth is that some people pretend to represent God in order to trick me.
What can I do to prevent myself from being tricked? ________________________

____

SHARE IT

"What would you expect? Sin will not come to you, saying, 'I am sin.' It would do little harm if it did. Sin always seems 'good, and pleasant, and desirable,' at the time of commission." ~ J.C. Ryle

WEEK 17 FRIDAY

TRUTH: 1 KINGS 16:29-17:7

1 KINGS 16:29-30

It's been about 50 years since Israel divided, and there have been several new kings in each, but the current kings in this passage are King Asa in Judah (South) and King Ahab in Israel (North).

What was Ahab remembered for in **verse 30**?

- Ahab built a temple better than Solomon's.
- Ahab wrote the book of **1 Kings**.
- Ahab did more evil than all the kings who came before him.

1 KINGS 16:30-17:7

Ahab married a foreign woman who brought with her the worship of a false god named Baal. Baal worship was particularly despicable to God due to its sexual perversions and child sacrifice. As Ahab was setting up this false worship in the land of Israel, God began to set up His prophet Elijah for a showdown.

What was Elijah's first task?

- To declare a drought
- To multiply bread and fish
- To anoint Ahab with oil

Pastor James MacDonald once said, "Idolatry is when anything takes God's place in your life – including you."

As I am reading about Israel falling into idolatry, I need to ask myself:

Do I have any idols that I serve?	**YES**	**NO**	**MAYBE**
Is there anything I want more than I want God?	**YES**	**NO**	**MAYBE**
Is there anything I serve more diligently than God?	**YES**	**NO**	**MAYBE**
Is there anything I value more than my relationship with God?	**YES**	**NO**	**MAYBE**
Is there anything I would sin to get?	**YES**	**NO**	**MAYBE**

Idols come in all shapes and sizes; who or what is my idol today? ____________________

What is something I will do today to get rid of this idol? ____________________

____

SHARE IT

"What each one honors before all else, what before all things he admires and loves, this for him is God." ~ Origen

SATURDAY WEEK 17

TRUTH: 1 KINGS 17:8-24

Before God used men to write down His word in the Bible, God would give His word to men and have them proclaim it. Usually, when God did this, He would also have the men perform miracles to prove that their message from God was legitimate.

1 KINGS 17:16-24

Today's passage had two major miracles recorded. Who benefitted from each one? (Draw a connection.)

A supernaturally bottomless bin of flour and jar of oil

A miraculous healing and resurrection from death

Elijah the Prophet
The Widow
The Widow's Son
The Widow's Family

These miracles proved that Elijah was a messenger of God, but they also showed how much God cared for Elijah, this widow, and her family. God loves to answer prayer and provide for His people.

I will write an answer to prayer God has given to me. ______________________________

____

I will write a thank you note to God listing specific things He has provided for me. _____

____

____

Where do I need a miracle right now in my life? What do I need God to provide or heal for me? ____

____

I know that God may not always give me what I ask for, but I know He loves me and is capable of far more than I could ever ask or think, so I am going to journal right here and ask God to provide a miracle for me in this way: ______________________________

____

____

____

____

____

____

____

____

____

SHARE IT

"But without faith it is impossible to please Him, for he who comes to God must believe that He is, and that He is a rewarder of those who diligently seek Him." ~ **Hebrews 11:6**

WEEK 18 **SUNDAY**

TRUTH: 1 KINGS 18:1-16

1 KINGS 18:1-4

God was finally ready to have His showdown with the wicked King Ahab using His prophet Elijah. God sent Elijah to King Ahab, and on his way, Elijah met a man named Obadiah.

Who was Obadiah?

- ☐ A criminal hiding from the king
- ☐ A high-ranking official working for Ahab
- ☐ An enemy of Ahab trying to start a rebellion

Verse 3 says that Obadiah "feared the Lord"; how did he prove that?

- ☐ He prayed three times a day.
- ☐ He refused to eat unclean meat.
- ☐ He rescued 100 of God's priests from execution.

Who massacred the priests of God?

- ☐ King Ahab
- ☐ King Ahab's wife, Jezebel
- ☐ Elijah

1 KINGS 18:12

Obadiah was in a difficult position; he worked for a king who was evil and a queen who was even more evil. Yet, he says in **verse 12**, "I have feared the Lord from my youth."

Have I ever had to work for or serve an evil person?	☐ **YES**	☐ **NO**
If I worked for Ahab, would I have remained faithful to God?	☐ **YES**	☐ **NO**
If I worked for bad people, would I turn bad?	☐ **YES**	☐ **NO**
When I work for people, do I use my position to do good?	☐ **YES**	☐ **NO**
Do I think I could be like Obadiah?	☐ **YES**	☐ **NO**

Because Obadiah remained faithful to God, he was able to use his position to save lives. Sometimes God puts us in difficult positions because He wants us to do something good there.

Am I currently in a difficult position where I could do some good? ☐ **YES** ☐ **NO**

What can I do today to prepare myself in case I am ever in a situation like Obadiah?

____

SHARE IT

"Brave men are all vertebrates; they have their softness on the surface and their toughness in the middle."
~ G.K. Chesterton

MONDAY WEEK 18

TRUTH: 1 KINGS 18:17-29

1 KINGS 18:17-18

Ahab called Elijah the "troubler of Israel" because of Elijah's preaching and the drought that had come to the land. Elijah responded that it was actually Ahab who caused the trouble when he turned away from God and brought idol worship into Israel.

What trouble do I have in my life?

Where do I think that trouble comes from?

Three days ago, in Quiet Time, I asked myself if I have any idols in my life. What do I think today?

1 KINGS 18:20-24

Elijah threw down the gauntlet for all of Israel. They needed to decide who they thought was the true God, and who they would follow, either Baal or the God of Abraham.

What did Elijah challenge the prophets of Baal to do?

1 KINGS 18:25-29

After hours of Baal's prophets calling out for their god to send fire, there was still no response, and Elijah started making fun of them. The fact is, idols/false gods will never respond because they are not real and therefore cannot actually care about their followers. The only reason idols exist is to steal people from worshiping the true God.

Who/What do I really think God is?

Who/What do I really follow with my life?

SHARE IT

"No one ever lost out by excessive devotion to Christ."
~ Harry Ironside

WEEK 18 TUESDAY

TRUTH: 1 KINGS 18:30-40

1 KINGS 18:30-40

Now that the prophets of Baal had failed to call down fire from the heavens, it was Elijah's turn. Elijah wasn't going to let anyone question God's power though, so he made things a little more intense.

What did Elijah do to make God's power more impressive?
(Fill in the blanks.)

He built a large ________________ around the altar. He put the ____________ and the ____________ on the altar. He dumped _____ pots of water on the altar _______ times, soaking everything and filling the trench with water.

What did God do to prove His power and presence?
(Select the correct answer.)

- ☐ God sent down fire from Heaven.
- ☐ The fire consumed the entire bull offering.
- ☐ The fire consumed all the wood.
- ☐ The fire dried up all the water.
- ☐ The fire consumed the altar itself, all the stones, and dust.
- ☐ All of the above.

1 KINGS 18:40

For Elijah, for King Ahab, and for all the people of Israel, there was no question that something incredibly supernatural had just happened. God had proven Himself as the one true God. The people immediately worshiped God.

What did Elijah do next?

- ☐ He led everyone in a song of recommitment to God.
- ☐ He threw a party!
- ☐ He rounded up the false prophets who had deceived all of Israel and executed them.

God doesn't mess around when His people follow false gods. He will prove His superiority, and He will ultimately always destroy the false gods.

How should I respond when I see followers of God giving into and serving false gods/idols? ____

How will I respond if one of God's followers calls me out about a false god/idol in my life?

____

SHARE IT

"Courage is contagious. When a brave man takes a stand, the spines of others are often stiffened." ~ Billy Graham

WEDNESDAY WEEK 18

TRUTH: 1 KINGS 18:41-19:7

1 KINGS 18:41-45

Elijah had just experienced a major spiritual victory for God! God had responded to Elijah's prayers by sending fire down from Heaven, and Elijah had led the people in rejecting false gods and choosing the one true God. Now, God was going to return His blessing to the land of Israel by ending the drought.

TRUE OR FALSE.

T F Elijah had his son keep watch for rain while he prayed.
T F Elijah prayed seven times for rain before he saw the first cloud.
T F Elijah warned King Ahab to return to Jezreel before he could get caught in flash flooding.
T F Ahab got caught in the flooding and drowned.
T F The rain never came.

1 KINGS 19:1-3

When Ahab's wife, Jezebel, found out what Elijah had done and how all the prophets of her god had been killed, she declared that she would hunt down Elijah and kill him as well. How did Elijah respond when he heard this? (Select the right answer.)

- ☐ He ran away and went into hiding.
- ☐ He went into serious suicidal depression.
- ☐ He felt like he was a failure and nothing he did mattered.
- ☐ All of the above

1 KINGS 19:4-7

Elijah found himself at a real low-point in life, and it was at that moment God came to him providing comfort. Sometimes eating a good meal and getting a good night's rest is exactly what one needs most.

Have I ever felt like running away/hiding? ☐ **YES** ☐ **NO**
Have I ever fallen into serious depression? ☐ **YES** ☐ **NO**
Have I ever felt like a failure at life? ☐ **YES** ☐ **NO**
Do I believe I can bring my low-points to God? ☐ **YES** ☐ **NO**

Right now, today, I need to bring my low-points to God in prayer.
Will I do that? ☐ **YES** ☐ **NO**

Do I have a friend that I know is going through a low-point? ☐ **YES** ☐ **NO**

Will I pray for that friend right now? ☐ **YES** ☐ **NO**

☐ I commit to going to a trusted adult when I am struggling with depression.

SHARE IT

"I know the sorrow and I know the hurt would all go away if You'd just say the word, but even if You don't, my hope is You alone." ~ MercyMe (Lyrics from "Even If")

WEEK 18 THURSDAY

TRUTH: 1 KINGS 19:8-21

1 KINGS 19:8-10

In the midst of his depression, God fed Elijah and supernaturally empowered him to travel far away from everyone and everything before they had a heart-to-heart conversation. (Fill in the blanks.)

What did Elijah tell God was his problem? (**1 Kings 19:10**)
I have been ____________________ for You.
Israel has broken their ____________________ with You.
Israel has __________________________ their altars to You.
Israel has killed the ________________________ You have sent.
I am all ____________________.
Israel wants to _________________ me.

1 KINGS 19:11-12

God could have responded to Elijah in a lot of ways, but what did He do? (Place in the correct order.)
_____ Spoke in a still small voice
_____ Sent an earthquake to shake the mountain
_____ Sent fire down on the mountain
_____ Sent a wind powerful enough to break rocks off of the mountain

1 KINGS 19:15-21

In that small voice God answered all of Elijah's fears and frustrations. He would deal with Israel's lack of faithfulness, and He would show Elijah that he was not alone.

Who are the three men that God would use to kill off the sinful Israelites?

________________________ ________________________ ________________________

How many faithful people were there left in Israel that had never worshiped the false god Baal? ____________________

What was the name of the young man who became Elijah's servant and "prophet-in-training"? ___________________

PRAY: ***Dear God, when I feel at the end of myself, I need to remember that You are in control and I am not alone. I will always be in the minority, but there will always be people like me, being faithful to You.***
In Jesus' Name, Amen.

SHARE IT

"We overcome, not because we're a moral majority or a righteous remnant, but because we're blood-covered sinners who know that if the gospel can change us, it can change anyone." ~ Russell Moore

FRIDAY WEEK 18

TRUTH: 1 KINGS 21:1-16

1 KINGS 21:1-16

Ahab was still the king of Israel (the northern tribes), and he was still evil. I would think that watching God send down fire and rain from Heaven at Elijah's request might have set Ahab on a godly path, but it did not. In today's passage I see just how corrupt and evil Ahab was.

Ahab wanted something that was not his.
What did he want? ______________________________

Ahab tried to get what he wanted legally but could not.

How did he respond to being told no? ______________________________

____

Ahab's wife, Jezebel, told him to stop being a baby, and she took matters into her own hands. What did Jezebel do? ______________________________

____

____

In the end, Ahab got what he wanted, but he let his wife use his power and authority to kill a guy and take his property. What kind of a man was Ahab? How would I describe him?

____

How does all this make me feel about Ahab? ______________________________

Has there been a time recently where I really wanted something that belonged to someone else? If so, what was it? ______________________________

How do I respond when someone tells me I cannot have what I want? ______________

____

Do I let other people talk me into sin when I feel upset about something?
☐ **YES** ☐ **NO**

Is there anyone I need to apologize to for acting sinfully when I did not get my way? If so, who? ______________________________

If there is something I need to return or if there is someone I need to make things right with, will I do it today? ☐ **YES** ☐ **NO**

SHARE IT

"Where do wars and fights come from among you? Do they not come from your desires for pleasure that war in your members? You lust and do not have. You murder and covet and cannot obtain. You fight and war. Yet you do not have because you do not ask. You ask and do not receive, because you ask amiss, that you may spend it on your pleasures." ~ **James 4:1-3**

WEEK 18 SATURDAY

TRUTH: 1 KINGS 21:17-29

Nothing that Ahab had done had been kept secret from God. God sent Elijah to Ahab to deliver a prophecy of judgment upon Ahab and his household.

What was the prophesied fate for Ahab? (Circle)

a. He would be killed by a lion.

b. After his death, dogs would lick up his blood.

c. Calamity would come upon Ahab's whole family.

d. All of the above

e. Only b and c

What was the prophesied fate for Jezebel?

- She would be publicly executed by decapitation.
- She would die in Babylon.
- She would be eaten by dogs.

Through Elijah, God specifically stated what Ahab's sin was:

Ahab committed ____________________. (**v. 19**)

Ahab ____________________ the land from Naboth. (**v. 19**)

Ahab ______________ himself to do wickedness. (**v. 25**)

Ahab let his wife ______________________ .(**v. 25**)

Ahab behaved abominably by following _____________. (**v. 26**)

How did Ahab respond when he received this prophecy from Elijah?
God said, "See how Ahab has __________ himself before Me…" (**v. 29**)

Because of Ahab's humility before God, God had mercy on him. The prophecies would still all come true, but God would delay some of it to extend mercy to Ahab.

Mercy is defined as ***the act of withholding punishment or condemnation that is deserved.***

God always responds to humility with mercy. When I am honest and broken about my sin, He responds with grace and mercy. That is the Gospel.

Is there anything I need to humbly bring to God? **YES** **NO**

Is there an area of my life where I need His mercy? **YES** **NO**

- I will talk to God right now about needing His mercy.

SHARE IT

"A man does not get grace till he comes down to the ground, till he sees he needs grace. When a man stoops to the dust and acknowledges that he needs mercy, then it is that the Lord will give him grace." ~ D.L. Moody

SUNDAY WEEK 19

TRUTH: 1 KINGS 22:29-40

God always keeps His word and as Ahab was about to find out, that is not always a pleasant thing. King Ahab (king of Israel) and King Jehoshaphat (king of Judah) decided to work together to attack the king of Syria. Ahab was warned by God he would not survive the battle (**1 Kings 22:1-28**), but he went for it anyway. What tactic did Ahab try to avoid dying in battle? ______________________________

____

Because of Ahab's deception, Jehoshaphat was almost killed, but God had other plans. How was Ahab killed? ______________________________

____

God keeps His word even down to the detail of dogs licking up Ahab's blood. Do I really believe that God keeps His word? Why or Why not? ______________________________

____

In **Matthew 25:31-46**, Jesus promised that He would return one day and judge the world. The righteous will be sent into eternal life and the unrighteous into eternal punishment.

Do I really believe that Jesus will return one day? ☐ **YES** ☐ **NO** ☐ **SOMETIMES**

Do I really believe that Jesus will judge the world? ☐ **YES** ☐ **NO** ☐ **SOMETIMES**

Do people try to avoid God's judgment? ☐ **YES** ☐ **NO** ☐ **SOMETIMES**

Do I want God to keep His word? ☐ **YES** ☐ **NO** ☐ **SOMETIMES**

Am I ready for God to keep His word and judge me? ☐ **YES** ☐ **NO** ☐ **SOMETIMES**

Jesus came to earth to take God's judgment for me, so that I will not have to face the punishment for my sin. Jesus took my punishment for me and offers to stand in my place on my day of judgment.

Do I believe that? ☐ **YES** ☐ **NO**

Do I admit I have sinned and deserve punishment? ☐ **YES** ☐ **NO**

Have I asked Jesus to take my punishment for me? ☐ **YES** ☐ **NO**

Do I live my life like I believe all that? ☐ **YES** ☐ **NO**

SHARE IT

"In Jesus Christ on the Cross there is refuge; there is safety; there is shelter; and all the power of sin upon our track cannot reach us when we have taken shelter under the Cross that atones for our sins." ~ A.C. Dixon

WEEK 19 MONDAY

TRUTH: JOHN 9:1-12

JOHN 9:2-3

When something bad happens:

- I often assume that there had to be a reason for this to happen: that I earned it in some way because of a sin I committed.
- I always think that it is just random and my actions had no bearing on this event.
- I think it through to see if this could be a logical consequence to a bad choice that I made somewhere along the way.

What did the disciples assume was the reason for this man's blindness? ____________

____

Jesus' answer was:

- That the works of God would be displayed in him.
- It was a warning for those around him to do good.
- That his ancestors' sin would be carried out upon him.

Something that I have observed in someone else's life that was clearly an opportunity for God to show His great and powerful works was:

____

____

Can I identify a time in my life when God chose to use me and my life as an example to others of what He alone can do? ____

____

How do I feel when God chooses to use me as His example for others to see the great things that God alone can do? ____

____

JOHN 9:9

Some people thought this man just looked like the one who was blind. I have noticed that some people really have a hard time just accepting that God is the One Who is responsible for doing something. An example of this from my own life is: ____________________

____.

SHARE IT

"We are changed not by being told what we need to do for God, but by hearing the news about what God has done for us." ~ *J.D. Greear*

TUESDAY WEEK 19

TRUTH: JOHN 9:13-23

JOHN 9:16

Why did the Pharisees have a problem with Jesus curing this blind man?

- ☐ Jesus never filled out the paperwork for a permit to perform miracles.
- ☐ Jesus did this miracle on the Sabbath.
- ☐ The man was supposed to stay blind.

TRUE OF FALSE.

T F Many of the Pharisees were upset, not because Jesus healed a blind man, but because He did not do it according to their rules.

I have experienced that in my own life; I did something right, but others were upset because I didn't do it the way that they wanted me to do it.

☐ **AGREE** ☐ **DISAGREE**

Explain: ______________________________

Some of the Pharisees questioned if Jesus could be the Messiah because they didn't think a sinner could do such signs. I have seen God work in my own life, and if I could only tell about ______________________________ ______________________________ from my own life, I believe that other people today would be more likely to give the credit to Jesus.

Right now, I am going to pray for the opportunity to share that story of Jesus working in my own life with someone within the next 24 hours.

☐ **YES, I WILL PRAY FOR THAT.** ☐ **NO, I WILL NOT BE PRAYING FOR THAT.**

JOHN 9:22

The blind man's parents were afraid to answer because the Jewish leaders had consequences for people who were following Jesus. The leaders were using fear to gain followers. Was that Jesus' style of leadership? If not, what does Jesus use to gain followers? ______________________________

I have seen examples of religion led by fear in my own life when ______________________________ ______________________________

The area that I am most tempted to be more focused on the rules than on the spirit of what is being done is: ______________________________ ______________________________

SHARE IT

Share your story with someone. You never know how one sentence of your life story could inspire someone to rewrite their own.

WEEK 19 WEDNESDAY

TRUTH: JOHN 9:24-34

JOHN 9:24

Before I met Christ, I wasn't physically blind, but these characteristics did describe me (3 things that I was before I met Christ):

____

____

____

After meeting Jesus, my life has been different in these ways (3 ways that my life is different because of meeting Jesus):

____

____

____

Virgin birth, walking on water, healing blind men: people tell me that these things are hard to believe in because they have not seen them, but if my life is different, then they may see a reason to believe God is real.

- ☐ I try to share my story often, of who I used to be and who I now am.
- ☐ I don't really notice much of a difference since I met Jesus. I still struggle with the same things; I haven't changed much.
- ☐ I can't remember before I knew Christ so my story is not super dramatic.
- ☐ I have never really tried to share who I used to be and who I am today after meeting Christ.

JOHN 9:27

A person I have told how God has changed my life, but they just aren't listening is:

____.

Today I am going to pray for a chance to share my story with them again, specifically who I used to be and how I am different now that I have met Jesus.

☐ Yes, I will pray that. ☐ No, I will not pray that.

I can tell a difference between my life today and my life before I met Jesus.

☐ **AGREE** ☐ **DISAGREE**

SHARE IT

There is much I don't know about God, but what I do know has changed my life.

THURSDAY WEEK 19

TRUTH: JOHN 9:35-41

JOHN 9:35

Jesus is not interested in simply seeing someone become a follower of Him and then moving on to the next person. He cares about each of us individually; that is why He followed up with the blind man.

In my own life I believe:

- Jesus was more interested in seeing me become His follower.
- Jesus pursued me before I became His follower, then moved on to the next person.
- Jesus pursued me before I became His follower, rejoiced when I became His follower, and continues to pursue me to help me grow.

Looking back, it is easier to see that Jesus was at work all along. Here are some examples from my life in regard to my relationship with Christ.

Before I became a Christian, Jesus was pursuing me in this way: ______________________

____

When I finally trusted Christ, it was because of Jesus doing this: ______________________

____

Jesus has been helping me grow in this way: ______________________

____

JOHN 9:39

Why does Jesus say that He came into the world for those who can't see to be able to see and that those who think they see to be made blind? ______________________

____

Something in my life that I used to be blind to before Jesus helped me to see: __________

____

JOHN 9:40

Who else was listening to the conversation? ______________________

Some people in my life who are spiritually blind that are listening in and watching me as a follower of Jesus: ______________________

____

SHARE IT

"I am a little pencil in the hand of a writing God."
~ Mother Theresa

WEEK 19 FRIDAY

TRUTH: JOHN 10:1-13

JOHN 10:1

I have seen some "robbers" trying to get to the sheep by some way other than through the door; someone or something that I have seen trying to take people away from following Christ: ____.

JOHN 10:3

The Good Shepherd calls us out by name and leads us.

Some people I have seen Jesus call out by name and lead are:

____________________ ____________________

____________________ ____________________

But I have seen friends and loved ones follow the robbers astray. Some people that I have seen leave the flock and follow someone or something other than the Good Shepherd are:

____________________ ____________________

____________________ ____________________

JOHN 10:4

How do I know that it's the voice of the Good Shepherd that I am hearing?

- It is a voice that speaks the truth from Scripture.
- It is a voice that always challenges authority and begs me to go my own way.
- There is no one way to know for sure.

JOHN 10:5

Whose voice should I never follow? ____________________

JOHN 10:11

"I am the ____________________. The Good Shepherd __________ down his __________ for the____________________."

WORD BANK: **sheep lays Shepherd life**

In what ways has Jesus been the Good Shepherd in my life? ____________________

____

SHARE IT

"My sheep hear my voice, and I know them, and they follow me." ~ **John 10:27**

SATURDAY WEEK 19

TRUTH: JOHN 10:14-21

JOHN 10:14

Jesus knows His sheep (His true followers), and His sheep (His true followers) know Him.

How do I know Jesus? How do I know that something is from Jesus?

List 6 characteristics that help me recognize when something is from Jesus.

1.______________________ 4. ______________________
2.______________________ 5. ______________________
3.______________________ 6. ______________________

JOHN 10:15

What does it mean to me that Jesus laid down His life for His sheep? ______________

____

JOHN 10:16

Jesus says that He has other sheep that are not of this fold; who does He mean? (Circle)

Animals **Gentiles (non-Jews)**

It will be hard for the Jews to hear that Jesus also died for the Gentiles (the non-Jews). Although I know it is wrong to judge anyone, if I am honest, it is hard for me to know that Jesus also died for ______________________________

____

I know that I am not supposed to judge these people (those listed above), but it is difficult for me. Today instead of hating them, I choose to pray for them.

☐ Yes, I will pray for them. ☐ No, I will not be doing that.

"Don't judge others because they sin differently than you."
How should that statement change my outlook on life and the people I interact with?

____

JOHN 10:17-18

What power does Jesus have over His life? ______________________________

____

How does His statement make me feel? ______________________________

____

SHARE IT

"Greater love has no one than this, than to lay down one's life for his friends." ~ **John 15:13**

WEEK 20 SUNDAY

TRUTH: JOHN 10:22-30

JOHN 10:22

I have people in my life that just don't get it…I feel like I tell them what I believe, but they simply don't understand what I am saying. Someone who this is true about is:

____

A recent example of someone just not understanding what I believe: ________________

____

JOHN 10:25

When Jesus talked about His works that bore witness for Him, He was referring to:

- ☐ The miracles that are listed in the Bible.
- ☐ Things in the Bible and things in our lives today.
- ☐ A collection of writings that Jesus left for us after He penned them.

JOHN 10:27

"My ____________ hear my voice, and I __________ them, and they __________________ me."

Since I am not texting Him regularly and hanging out face-to-face after school, how do I get to know Jesus so that I recognize His voice?

____

____

JOHN 10:28-30

Jesus talks about eternal life and that no one will ever take His flock away from Him.

- ☐ I sometimes struggle believing that Jesus' forgiveness is eternal and that I can't mess that up at all.
- ☐ Sometimes I don't always feel saved because I have unconfessed sin in my life, but I know my salvation is eternally secure.
- ☐ I know that Jesus has me safely in His hands, also in the Father's hands, and no one will take me away from Him. Even if it is hard to believe it sometimes – I know that it is true.

SHARE IT

"We are his people and the sheep of his pasture."
~ **Psalm 100:3**

MONDAY WEEK 20

TRUTH: JOHN 10:31-42

JOHN 10:30-31

Jesus said, "I and My Father are one," and the religious leaders picked up stones to stone Him (again). He knew that this would make them want to stone Him again. What have I done when I knew that answering with the truth was going to cause someone to be upset? When do I speak the truth boldly, and when do I use discretion to not cause an argument?

Did I **speak the truth boldly in love / not say anything at all** ?

JOHN 10:32-33

There are times in my life when I know that I am doing the right thing but my accusers are still saying I am wrong. When that happens:

- I tend to get defensive and fight back.
- I find fault in them and point that out to whoever will listen.
- I pray for my accusers and choose to forgive them no matter what they say about me.
- I ignore them, pretend it doesn't hurt, then cry myself to sleep at night.

JOHN 10:37

Jesus said, "If I do not do the works of My Father, then do not believe Me." Jesus was without sin; He was perfect. However, this passage points out to me that it is important to be consistent in my walk with God, so that what I do backs up what I am telling other about Him.

Here is my response to that statement: ____________________

____

____

When it comes to being consistent in following Jesus, the thing I struggle with the most is:

____

____

SHARE IT

"Decide what you are going to decide before you have to decide." ~ Susan Davis

WEEK 20 TUESDAY

TRUTH: JOHN 11:1-13

JOHN 11:1

If I was Mary and Martha having seen Jesus heal complete strangers, what would I expect to happen after I sent word to Jesus that my brother (a close friend of Jesus) was sick?

- Jesus to take His time and come visit when it fits His schedule.
- Jesus to drop everything and come heal my brother.
- Jesus to at least say the words that will heal my brother if He can't make it here in person.

JOHN 11:4

What did Jesus say was the reason for this sickness? ______________________________

____

JOHN 11:5

How did Jesus feel about Mary, Martha, and Lazarus? ______________________________

____

JOHN 11:6

What does it say that Jesus did when He heard about Lazarus' illness? _______________

How would I feel if I were begging Jesus to save my brother, and I find out that He was just choosing not to come for two extra days? ______________________________

____

It has been said that when we pray, God always answers our prayers, but He has 3 answers: Yes, No, and Wait.

Here is my response to that statement: ______________________________

____

Which statement is true?

- No one controls Jesus; He will let us suffer just to prove that point.
- He has it all in control. We may not like the plan He has, but we can trust that it is for our good and for His glory.
- We need to work harder to impress Him if we want quick answers.

This is a time that I thought that Jesus was absolutely going to do what I asked (told) Him to do, simply because I thought I had earned it: ______________________________

____

- I realize now that this was wrong thinking because God is in control and will answer me according to His loving plan.

SHARE IT

"The only way God shows us He is in control is to put us in situations we can't control." ~ Steven Furtick

WEDNESDAY WEEK 20

TRUTH: JOHN 11:14-29

JOHN 11:14

I have prayed hard for God to heal ____________________ , but He chose not to. When that happened I ____ .

JOHN 11:16

The disciples questioned whether Jesus really wanted to go back to Judea again because the last time they were there, the Jews wanted to stone Jesus. Jesus assures them that He is going back to Judea. What is Thomas' response?

- "I think I'm going to sit this one out."
- "Let us also go, that we may die with Him."
- Trick question – Thomas had already doubted and disappeared.

What would my response to Jesus be if He was determined to go back to Judea, the place where they wanted to stone Him? ____

JOHN 11:25-27

Because Jesus is the Resurrection and the Life, what did He say would happen to those who believe in Him even if they die? ____

____

JOHN 11:29

Martha rose quickly and went to Him. She went back and told her sister, Mary, that the Teacher was looking for her. Mary and Martha both thought that Jesus could and would have saved their brother, but He chose not to. Yet they both went to Him right away. When God answers "No" or "Wait" to my prayers, am I quick to run back to Him? Would I be so faithful to go to Jesus right away even after He let my loved one die?

- Yes, I have full confidence in Jesus and my confidence surpasses my emotions even if it had been my brother's death that we are talking about.
- No, I would not go to Jesus because I would still be mad at Him and unable to trust Him.
- It's complicated, and here's why: ____

  ____

SHARE IT

Keep praying, but be thankful that God's answers are wiser than your prayers.

WEEK 20 THURSDAY

TRUTH: JOHN 11:30-37

Is it ever OK to question God? ☐ **YES** ☐ **NO** ☐ **NOT SURE**

JOHN 11:32

Notice the way that Mary questions Jesus. She is pointing out that if He had been there, He could have kept her brother from dying. But look closely: what is the first word that she says to Jesus? ________________

She still calls Jesus, Lord. She knows that He is Who He says He is and that He is in control. She just didn't understand the plan that He had for this situation, so she openly questioned Jesus – and it's ok.

When I find myself in situations where I don't understand why God is doing what He is doing:

- ☐ I question Him. I ask Him to show me why He is doing this, but I am willing to trust Him, answers or not.
- ☐ I would never question God. That is disrespectful, and I have no place to question Him.
- ☐ I walk away. If God can't do things the way that I want things done, then I have no time for Him.
- ☐ Other ________________________________

Something that God has done or is doing that I question is: ________________

____

Am I secure enough in my relationship with Jesus to question Him but still trust Him? Explain. ________________________________

____

JOHN 11:35

Jesus wept. He got emotional.

When is the last time I got emotional and wept for something or someone? ____________

____

____

I will spend some time now praying and thanking Jesus for His compassion for me and asking Him to give me that same compassion for others.

____

____

____

____

____

SHARE IT

"I thought faith would say, 'I'll take away the pain and discomfort," but instead it said, 'I'll sit with you in it.'"
~ Brene Brown

FRIDAY WEEK 20

TRUTH: JOHN 11:38-44

JOHN 11:38

If this was my brother that had died, 3 emotions that I would be feeling would be:

____________________, ____________________, ____________________.

JOHN 11:39

I do trust Jesus with my life, but if I were standing there and He said to roll back the stone:

- I would be so nervous that Jesus would be embarrassed.
- I would be angry that He was desecrating my brother's tomb.
- I would wait to see what would happen.
- Other ____

How did Martha respond? ______________________________

____

JOHN 11:44

Sometimes God comes through for us in ways that we would never have even imagined! In the space provided, I will write about a time that God came through for me in a way that I never thought was possible. ____________________________

____

____

Jesus did a lot of things for the sake of those who would see it and those who would one day hear about it. Someone I know who really needs to hear the story that I just wrote is:

____

Today I will pray for an opportunity to share this story with that person. I will pray that God works it into a conversation somehow, and if I need to, I will go out of my way to start a conversation with that person.

- Yes, I will pray that it comes up.
- No, I can't do that.
- Yes, I will pray that it comes up, and I will go out of my way to spend time with that person soon so I can talk with them.

SHARE IT

It may look like your situation is never going to change, but in a split second God can completely resolve it.

WEEK 20 **SATURDAY**

TRUTH: JOHN 11:45-57

JOHN 11:45-46

If I had been on the fence about Who Jesus was, but I was there and I saw Jesus bring Lazarus back from the dead I would:

- Finally believe that He really is Who He says He is.
- Need more proof.
- Be scared and run the other way.
- Other ______________________________

JOHN 11:46-48

Some of those who actually saw this happen went to the Pharisees to tell them what they saw. Why would they still side with the Pharisees over Jesus? They were so focused on their religion that they forgot that they had been looking for the Messiah.
What were they afraid of? (**v. 48**) ______________________________

____

Am I more in love with **Jesus** or **my religion** ? (Circle)

JOHN 11:49-52

What had the high priest Caiaphas prophesied about that year?

- The Son of God coming to earth and the Pharisees stopping Him
- One man dying for the sake of bringing the Jews together
- Someone trying to overthrow him as high priest
- Someone coming in as a political leader to overthrow Rome

JOHN 11:53

Sometimes people are against me even though I am doing the right thing. Sometimes it seems like they are so focused on bringing me down that they don't even see the good I am trying to do.

In the space below I will write out a prayer to God to help me deal with these situations when they arise. ______________________________

____

____

____

____

SHARE IT

"Blessed are you when they revile and persecute you and say all kinds of evil against you falsely for My sake."
~ **Matthew 5:11**

SUNDAY WEEK 21

TRUTH: JOHN 12:1-11

JOHN 12:3

Mary made a huge sacrifice to anoint Jesus with the oils that she used. Why did she not think twice about this action? ______________________________

____

JOHN 12:4-5

Judas points out that the value of this oil is what?

- ☐ 1000 Lyra
- ☐ 300 Denarii (Pence) (A Year's Wage)
- ☐ 600 Yen

Why did Judas get upset about this? ______________________________

____

A denarius is about a day's wages, so 300 of them is about a year's worth of wages… think about that.

Do I have anything in my life worth that much money?

- ☐ No, not a chance.
- ☐ Yes, but it's taken me forever to save it.

If I were in this situation that Mary was in:

- ☐ I would give the gift to the disciples and Jesus so that they could use it for their living expenses.
- ☐ I would have sold it and used the money to buy something for Jesus.
- ☐ I would have done exactly what Mary did and poured it out as an offering over Jesus' feet.
- ☐ I would have done something completely different (explain). ______________________________

____

I don't have money or valuable things like that, but here is what I will do for Jesus:

____

____

SHARE IT

"And though she spoke no words, everything she said was heard, as she poured her love for the Master from her box of Alabaster." ~ *CeCe Winans (Lyrics from "Alabaster Box")*

WEEK 21 MONDAY

TRUTH: JOHN 12:12-19

JOHN 12:12-15

How do I handle praise when people throw it my way?

- Gracefully; I humbly accept all praise and never let it go to my head.
- I make a show of how good I am at giving the glory back to God.
- I downplay the praise by pointing out what I am not good at.
- I feel super awkward and want to crawl into a hole and die.

If I had been one of the disciples watching the way the crowd was honoring Jesus, I would be thinking: ______________________________

____

____

The crowd would soon turn on Jesus; was their praise of Him on this day authentic?

- Yes, but they didn't really know Him (by faith) so they were genuinely happy with Him that day but would give up on Him in a week.
- No, most of them followed the Pharisees and were waiting for their chance to turn Jesus in.
- No, if they were authentically happy, their mood couldn't change that quickly when a week later they would be calling for His death.

JOHN 12:16

The disciples didn't understand at that moment that prophecies were being fulfilled, but they recognized it later as they thought about it. I tend to be able to see ways that God provided for me much better when I am looking back at a situation rather than when I am in the middle of the situation. One specific situation that I can look back and clearly see God's provision is: ______________________________

____

____

JOHN 12:19

Why is this so upsetting for the Pharisees? ______________________________

____

SHARE IT

"Hosanna! Blessed is He who comes in the name of the LORD! The King of Israel!" ~ **John 12:13**

TUESDAY WEEK 21

TRUTH: JOHN 12:20-26

JOHN 12:24

What do I think Jesus' illustration about a grain of wheat must fall and die for it to be effective means? ____

____

JOHN 12:25-26

He who __________ his life, will __________ it, and he who hates his __________ in this world will keep it for eternal life. If anyone __________________ Me, let him ____________________________ Me, and where I am, there my servant will be also. If anyone serves Me, him My Father will honor.

WORD BANK: serves loves life loses follow

The person who comes to mind most when I think about these verses is

______________________________.

The reason that I think about this person is ____

____.

Today I will take the time to connect with that person by text, email, letter, etc., to let them know how much I appreciate the way they live for God.

☐ Yes, I will do that. ☐ No, I am not going to do that.

I have been able to serve God by ____

____.

What is an area that I would like to be able to serve God in? ____________________

____

I will spend some time praying today that God will open some opportunities for me to serve in this way. ☐ **YES** ☐ **NO**

SHARE IT

"Life's most persistent and urgent question is, what are you doing for others?" ~ Dr. Martin Luther King Jr.

WEEK 21 WEDNESDAY

TRUTH: JOHN 12:27-43

JOHN 12:27

Jesus shows a raw moment between Him and His Father where He asks:

____.

Does this make Jesus any less powerful in my mind? ☐ **YES** ☐ **NO**

How does this show of His humanity make me feel? ______________________

JOHN 12:28-30

In what ways am I able to glorify God's name in my life?

1. ____
2. ____
3. ____

Did God the Father need to speak out loud for Jesus to know what He was saying?

☐ No, God did that for the sake of the people who were gathered.

☐ Yes, God always speaks with a loud, booming, audible voice.

JOHN 12:42-43

What was the reasoning behind people believing but not admitting it?

☐ Afraid to embarrass their families

☐ Afraid that the Jewish leaders would put them out of the synagogue

☐ Afraid that Jesus would make them sell everything they owned

☐ Afraid their friends would laugh at them

They loved ______________________________ more than the praise of God.

Do I love the praise of men more than the praise of God?

☐ Yes, it's something I struggle with every day.

☐ No, God's praise is all that matters to me.

Someone I know who has been offered a relationship with Jesus but simply chooses not to accept Him for their own reasons is ______________________________.

I believe the reason that they choose not to accept Christ is ____________________

____.

Today I will spend time praying for that person. ☐ **YES** ☐ **NO**

SHARE IT

"It's pride, plain and simple, that keeps me from giving God all the glory and keeping some of it for myself. It is a battle we all fight in some form or another, some of us daily or even hourly." ~ Francis Chan

THURSDAY WEEK 21

TRUTH: JOHN 12:44-50

JOHN 12:44

Jesus is once again redirecting the focus from Himself to the One who sent Him. I have noticed that ______________________ is very good at redirecting the glory that people give them back to God the Father.

A good example of this is: ____

____

____

I want to be better at redirecting the glory to God, but my pride often gets in my way. My pride is most tempting to me when this happens: ______________________

____

Three things that I can personally do to help my battle against this pride:
1. ____
2. ____
3. ____

JOHN 12:46

Jesus said, "I have come as a light into the world, that ______________"

- when believers need the light, I will be there."
- whoever believes in Me should not abide in darkness."
- I can expose the darkness that is created by the Pharisees."
- all will be able to see."

JOHN 12:47

Jesus did not come into the world to judge it, but to ______________ it.

Where would I personally be if Jesus had come into the world simply to judge those who sinned? ____

JOHN 12:48

What did Jesus say would judge those who reject Him? ______________________

____

Am I daily spending time in God's Word, believing and applying what it has to say to me personally? **YES** **NO**

SHARE IT

"Not unto us, O Lord, not unto us, but to Your name give glory, because of Your mercy, because of Your truth."
~ **Psalm 115:1**

WEEK 21 FRIDAY

TRUTH: PSALM 114:1-8

PSALM 114:1-6

Israel went out from Egypt, from a strange and foreign place, a place that they did not belong, and they entered into the presence of God. The whole earth moved at His presence.

Have I ever felt as if I did not belong? ☐ **YES** ☐ **NO**

What does it feel like? ____

____

Have I ever been in a place that I should not have been? ☐ **YES** ☐ **NO**

How did this make me feel? ____

Read **1 Corinthians 3:16**.

Where is God's dwelling place today? ____

God dwells within me. God lives in me. Think about that for a minute. How does knowing this make me feel? ____

____

What are some characteristics of a life marked by the presence of God? ______________

____

____

Do my actions reflect God's presence in my life? ☐ **YES** ☐ **NO**

What specifically is God bringing to mind right now that I need to stop? ______________

____

When God is present in my life, I will love others.

How well am I doing at loving other people?

Not so good **0** **1** **2** **3** **4** **5** **Great**

What is something I will do today to show someone God's love? ______________

____

PSALM 114:7

Does knowing that God dwells within me 24 hours a day, 7 days a week change the way I want to live? ☐ **YES** ☐ **NO**

What are those changes that need to be made? ____

____

____

SHARE IT

Practice His Presence.

SATURDAY WEEK 21

TRUTH: PSALM 115:1-18

God's presence in my life should change the way I live.

PSALM 115:1

What phrase is repeated in this verse? ______________________________

Who should get the glory? ______________________________

It is not until I take my eyes off of myself and focus on God that He can fully get the glory in my life.

TRUE OR FALSE.

T F I like being praised.
T F There are times I steal the glory from God.
T F I want all the attention for things I have accomplished.
T F It is easy for me to take the attention off of myself and give it to God.

I will write down some things to give God the glory (***credit, praise***) right now. ______________________________

____

____

____

PSALM 115:9-11

What phrase is repeated in these verses three times? ______________________________

____

To give God glory, I have to TRUST in Him at all times.
Is there any situation in my life right now where I need God's help? ______________________________

____

What do I need God to shield me from today? ______________________________

PSALM 115:12-15

As I give God the glory by living in obedience to Him and His Word, what does God want to do in my life? (One word repeated 5x in **vv. 12-15**) ______________________________

God wants to bless me as I trust Him.

TRUE OR FALSE.

T F I trust God with my life.
T F It is hard for me to trust God.
T F I have been hurt too many times, and I do not trust anyone.

SHARE IT

It is not until I take my eyes off of myself and focus them on God that He can fully get the glory in my life.

WEEK 22 SUNDAY

TRUTH: PSALM 116:1-14

PSALM 116:1-8

Write out the first four words of this Psalm. ______________________

Why did the writer of this Psalm love God? ______________________

____

Can I say with confidence, "I love the Lord"? ■ **YES** ■ **NO**

Why do I love God? ______________________

____

Now read and write out **Deuteronomy 6:5**. ______________________

____

In what three areas of my life am I to love God?

______________ ______________ ______________

HEART. What action do I need to take to write God's law on my heart?

____

SOUL. The soul includes my heart, my thoughts, my desires, my actions, the way I talk, and the talents God has given me. When I think about this, am I loving God with my whole being? ■ **YES** ■ **NO**

What area(s) of my life need to change today? ______________________

____

STRENGTH. Using my whole strength is doing everything in my means to glorify God and serve Him faithfully. What resources do I have that I can use to further the kingdom of God?

____

____

Does my life show an authentic love for my God? ■ **YES** ■ **NO**

Am I living a life that's the same at school, at home, and at church? ■ **YES** ■ **NO**

Are my desires and thoughts pleasing to God? ■ **YES** ■ **NO**

Do the ways I dress and talk show God that I love Him above all else? ■ **YES** ■ **NO**

SHARE IT

A life that reflects my love for God will be seen by the way I behave, the things I look at, the music I listen to, the way I talk, and the things I think about.

MONDAY WEEK 22

TRUTH: PSALM 116:15-117:2

PSALM 116:16

This verse says, "I am Your ______________."

Am I willing to show merciful kindness to others by serving? **YES** **NO**

What are some ways I can get involved in serving others? ______________________

____

PSALM 116:17-19

For what or whom am I thankful? ______________________

I will write a praise to God about how He is working in my life. ______________________

____

____

I can call on God for my every need. I will list some of my prayer requests here.

____

____

____

I commit to living a life of obedience to the Lord. **YES** **NO**

If yes, I will ask ______________________ today to help hold me accountable.

PSALM 117:1

Mercy has been described as God not giving us what we do deserve. Grace on the other hand is God giving us what we do not deserve.

How does God's merciful kindness make me feel? ______________________

____

How has He shown compassion, pity, love, and patience toward me even though I do not deserve this? ______________________

____

Is there anyone from whom I have been withholding mercy who needs my forgiveness today? **YES** **NO**

If yes, who? ______________________

SHARE IT

When I choose to love God with all my heart, soul, and strength, others will see kindness, thankfulness, praise, prayer, and obedience in me.

WEEK 22 TUESDAY

TRUTH: PSALM 118:1-14

PSALM 118:6-13

God can save me in my greatest need, trial, or circumstance here on this earth.

Who is on my side? (**v. 6**) ______________________________

Who is my helper? (**vv. 7-13**) ______________________________

Who is my trust/refuge? (**vv. 8-9**) ______________________________

When I have a problem, who is that one person I turn to? ____________________

TRUE OR FALSE.

T F Prayer and faith in God need to be my first response in trouble.

T F God is good even in difficult times.

T F God is on my side, fighting for me when I am in a trial.

T F It is better to trust in God alone than in any help man can give me.

PSALM 118:14

The Lord is my ____________________, ____________, and my ____________________.

God can save me eternally. I am one breath away from eternity.
Have I accepted this free gift from God? ☐ **YES** ☐ **NO**

Have I admitted I am a sinner, believed that Jesus died, was buried, and rose again for my sin? ☐ **YES** ☐ **NO**

Have I confessed Him as Lord of my life? ☐ **YES** ☐ **NO**

Have I thanked Him for my salvation lately? ☐ **YES** ☐ **NO**

I will journal here about the time I asked Jesus to save me. (If I have just now asked Jesus to save me, I will tell a trusted friend, pastor, or parent.) ____________________

____

____

____

____

____

____

____

____

SHARE IT

God can save me in my greatest need, trial, or circumstance here on this earth.

WEDNESDAY WEEK 22

TRUTH: PSALM 118:15-29

PSALM 118:14-15

A person who has experienced true salvation will be filled with unexplainable joy.
Am I full of joy? **YES** **NO** **SOMETIMES**

If not, what is keeping me from having true joy found only in Christ? ______________________

____

What things in this life give me joy? ______________________________________

____

PSALM 118:16-17

A person who has experienced true salvation will tell others!
Who have I told about Christ lately? ______________________________________

Who have I shared my quiet time with recently? ____________________________

I shared my quiet time with ______________________________________ today.

I will pray for an opportunity to share God's salvation with ______________________ .

PSALM 118:19-21

A person who has experienced true salvation will worship in holiness.
Is my heart right before God? **YES** **NO**

According to **Psalm 139** nothing is hidden from the Lord.
What have I been trying to keep secret? ____________________________________

Is there anything I need to confess before the Lord that has been hindering my relationship with Him? ____

____

PSALM 118:22-29

A person who has experienced true salvation will be characterized by rejoicing, thankfulness, and praise.

I will spend some time here rejoicing in my salvation and this day that God has given me!

Write out and memorize **Psalm 118:24**. ____________________________________

____

____

SHARE IT

A person that has experienced true salvation will be characterized by rejoicing, thankfulness, and praise.

WEEK 22 THURSDAY

TRUTH: EXODUS 1:1-14

EXODUS 1:1-7

God's chosen people, Israel, were in the land of Egypt and they were being blessed by God as seen by:

- Their great wealth.
- The land they owned.
- Their growth from a small group to a mighty nation.

Sometimes God blesses me, and I do not even realize it. One way God has blessed me is

____.

EXODUS 1:8-10

The new king of Egypt feared the Israelites because of God's blessing toward them. When was a time someone was jealous or angry with me because of something God blessed me with? ____

EXODUS 1:11-14

Because of his fear, what did the king of Egypt do to the Israelites? ____________

____

Sometimes the world responds in hostility toward those who follow after God (**John 15:18-19**). This makes me feel: (Circle)

SCARED **ANGRY** **CONFUSED** **NERVOUS**

OTHER: ____

The reason I feel this way is because ______________________________

____.

Even though the world may hate those who believe in Jesus, **John 15:26** reminds me that I am not alone because I have:

- The Holy Spirit.
- Good friends.
- Friendly neighbors.

The same way that God was with Israel, He is with me even when the world is against me.

- I agree with this statement.
- I disagree with this statement.
- I need to think some more.

SHARE IT

I serve a God who will never leave me nor forsake me!
(See **Hebrews 13:5**.*)*

FRIDAY WEEK 22

TRUTH: EXODUS 1:15-22

EXODUS 1:15-16

The king of Egypt saw that afflicting the Israelites was not enough, so he ordered the midwives to do what? ____________________

The midwives knew that the king's order was wrong in God's sight. When has someone told me to do something that I knew would not please God? ____________________

____

Did I go along with what that person told me to do? ☐ **YES** ☐ **NO**

EXODUS 1:17

How did the midwives respond to the order? ____________________

____

For believers in Christ, to fear God does not mean to be scared of Him, but to have such great reverence and awe for Him that it results in our obedience and worship. Do I fear God?
☐ **YES** ☐ **NO** ☐ **NEVER THOUGHT ABOUT IT BEFORE**

Do I believe that God is worthy of my obedience, reverence, and worship? ☐ **YES** ☐ **NO**

What are ways I can better fear God in how I act and live:
At School? ____________________
At Home? ____________________
With Friends? ____________________

According to **Proverbs 9:10**, what is another result of the fear of the Lord?

____

EXODUS 1:18-22

Obedience to God was dangerous for the midwives, but what was the result of that obedience? (Check any that apply.)

☐ God blessed them.
☐ Israel grew mightier.
☐ They were put in prison by Pharaoh.

SHARE IT

"(The fear of God) is consistent with love, and springs from it... it does not produce terror, but rather delivers from it, and preserves the mind from alarms." ~ Albert Barnes

WEEK 22 SATURDAY

TRUTH: EXODUS 2:1-10

EXODUS 2:1-2

Why did the mother hide her child (look back at **Exodus 1:22**)? ____________________

____

This would be a scary time to have a child. Scary situations sometimes cause believers to question God.

Have I ever questioned God? ☐ **YES** ☐ **NO**

How did I respond to a situation when I did not understand what God was doing?

- ☐ I prayed about it.
- ☐ I sought advice from others.
- ☐ I shut God out.
- ☐ Something else: ____

EXODUS 2:3-4

The time came when the mother's only option was to send the baby off and trust God to be with him. That would have made me feel: (Circle)

NERVOUS SCARED ANGRY HOPEFUL CONFIDENT

EXODUS 2:5-10

The child was rescued by ________________________________, and the Hebrew nurse was the child's ______________________.

God provided for Moses and his mother, even though she did not know what would happen. How strong is my faith in God?

Weak 1 2 3 4 5 Very Strong

What situation am I facing right now where I can trust God more? ____________________

____

Sometimes God allows believers to go through difficult times so that they will grow in their faith. What else does this testing result in according to **James 1:3-4**?

____

Spend some time in prayer now, asking God to strengthen your faith in whatever situation He is allowing you to face. ☐

SHARE IT

"To trust God in the light is nothing, but trust him in the dark—that is faith." ~ C.H. Spurgeon

SUNDAY WEEK 23

TRUTH: EXODUS 2:11-25

EXODUS 2:11-15

What did Moses do when he saw an Egyptian beating one of his fellow Hebrews?

____

When Moses realized his actions were known, how did he respond?

- ☐ He was scared and ran away.
- ☐ He freed the Israelites from slavery.
- ☐ He faced Pharaoh for what he did.

How do I respond when I commit sin?

- ☐ I deny it.
- ☐ I own up to it and ask for forgiveness.
- ☐ Something else: ____________________________

EXODUS 2:16-22

Although Moses was in a strange land, God was still providing for him. What are some of the ways God provided for Moses? ____________________________

____

EXODUS 2:23-25

Eventually, the bondage of the Israelites caused them to ________ out to God (**v. 23**) and God ____________________ (**v. 24**) their groaning.

Have I ever cried out to God because of a difficult situation? ☐ **YES** ☐ **NO**

It was many years of bondage before all of Israel cried out to God for deliverance. Why is it that sometimes I wait to ask God for help?

- ☐ I think I can solve the situation myself.
- ☐ I blame God for what I'm going through.
- ☐ Some other reason:____________________________

Do I trust that God can help me through any situation I face? ☐ **YES** ☐ **NO**

Match the truth of Scripture that applies to Moses' and Israel's situation.

Moses	**Psalm 34:17**
Israel	**Proverbs 28:13**

Which of the above verses most applies to me? ____________________________

SHARE IT

No matter what comes my way, I will look to God!

WEEK 23 MONDAY

TRUTH: EXODUS 3:1-12

EXODUS 3:1-6

How would I feel if I heard God speak to me? (Circle)

AFRAID **EXCITED** **SHOCKED** **NERVOUS** **JOYFUL**

OTHER: ______________________________

I would feel this way because ______________________________

______________________________.

Do I feel the same way about the Bible, which is God's Word? ☐ **YES** ☐ **NO**

EXODUS 3:7-11

What was God calling Moses to do? ______________________________

Moses' objection showed that he thought what about God's command?

- ☐ He felt he was unworthy
- ☐ It was an impossible task
- ☐ He did not believe God was serious

EXODUS 3:12

God responded to Moses by saying, "I will certainly ______________________________ you."

How would that response have made me feel? ______________________________

____

Which commands in God's Word do I feel unworthy/unable to accomplish? (Check any)

- ☐ Sharing the Gospel (**Matthew 28:19-20**)
- ☐ Loving my enemies (**Matthew 5:44**)
- ☐ Living a life of prayer (**1 Thessalonians 5:17**)
- ☐ Another command: ______________________________

What makes me feel unworthy to do God's commands and whatever else He is calling me to?

____

God promised Moses He would be with him. What does God promise me in **Matthew 28:20b**?

____

If God says He will be with me to the very end of the age, how will that affect how I respond to His commands and call in my life? ______________________________

____

____

SHARE IT

"God's present is His presence. His greatest gift is Himself."
~ Max Lucado

TUESDAY WEEK 23

TRUTH: EXODUS 3:13-22

EXODUS 3:13-15

God revealed Himself as "I Am Who I Am," a name that signifies His eternal self-existence. What are some other names in Scripture that are used of God? (Match the name with the verse.)

"Abba, Father"	**Genesis 17:1**
"LORD, my Rock"	**Galatians 4:6**
"Almighty God"	**Psalm 28:1**

EXODUS 3:16-22

God told Moses that the Israelites would ________________________ his voice (**v. 18**), but Pharaoh would ____________ let them go (**v. 19**). God would respond with wonders after which Israel would be set free. While leaving they would _____________________ (**v. 22**) the Egyptians.

If God gave me the entire plan of what was about to happen, I would ________________ ____.

God is omniscient, which means that He is all-knowing.

- ☐ I believe this statement.
- ☐ I do not believe this statement.
- ☐ I need to think about this some more.

If God is all-knowing, then did Moses need to worry? ☐ **YES** ☐ **NO**

If God is all-knowing, then is there anything I need to worry about? ☐ **YES** ☐ **NO**

Not only is God all-knowing, but He told Moses that He would perform wonders (miracles). This is because God is also omnipotent, which means He is all-powerful.

- ☐ I believe this statement.
- ☐ I do not believe this statement.
- ☐ I need to think about this some more.

Even though God told all this to Moses, Moses still needed to trust God. Where are some areas in my life where I need to trust in God's power?

____

____

____.

SHARE IT

"God's part is to put forth power; our part is to put forth faith."
~ Andrew Bonar

WEEK 23 WEDNESDAY

TRUTH: EXODUS 4:1-17

EXODUS 4:1

Despite all that God told Moses, he still made excuses. What excuse did Moses make this time?

- That God did not know all things
- That the people might not believe God sent him

What was the first excuse Moses had made? (**Exodus 3:11**) ______________________

____

EXODUS 4:2-9

How did God respond to Moses' excuse? ______________________________

____

TRUE OR FALSE.

T F God's answer to Moses showed that God is powerful.

EXODUS 4:10

What was the next excuse Moses made? ______________________________.

EXODUS 4:11-13

After God overruled Moses' last excuse, Moses finally gave up and asked God to just do what?

- Leave him alone
- Leave Israel where they were
- Send someone else

What are some excuses I make toward God and His commands? __________________

____

God was showing Moses that He would help him with the task God was calling him to do. Do I believe that God will help me too? **YES** **NO**

EXODUS 4:14-17

In the end, God brought Aaron to help Moses. Who has God brought into my life that has helped me in following Christ? ______________________________

Have I ever considered that person to be a blessing from God? **YES** **NO**

Am I willing to trust that whatever God commands or calls me to, He will also give me all I need to accomplish it? **YES** **NO**

SHARE IT

"The reality is that the Lord never calls the qualified; He qualifies the called." ~ *Henry Blackaby*

THURSDAY WEEK 23

TRUTH: EXODUS 4:18-31

EXODUS 4:18-23

God refers to Israel as His son (**v. 22**), and today God continues to refer to those who believe in Him as His children (**1 John 3:1**). Being a child of God matters to me because

____ .

EXODUS 4:24-26

Although Moses was obedient to God's commands to go to Egypt, what command had he not obeyed? (**Genesis 17:9-11**)

____

Do I ever obey some of God's commands while ignoring others? ☐ **YES** ☐ **NO**

Before Moses could lead Israel, he had to be right before God.
What is an area in my life I need to get right in God's sight? __________________________

____

EXODUS 4:27-31

When Moses and Aaron went to the Israelites, the people responded by: (Check one)
☐ Believing, bowing, and worshiping God.
☐ Rejecting Moses and Aaron.

When Moses obeyed God by going to Egypt and then circumcising his son, God blessed him. God also blesses me when I am obedient to Him.
☐ I agree with this statement. ☐ I disagree with this statement.
☐ I need to think some more.

Moses responded to God in obedience, and Israel responded in worship.

When I obey God, it will lead others to worship Him.

Do these two things (obedience and worship) describe my walk with God? ☐ **YES** ☐ **NO**

Today I will obey and worship God by ____

____ .

SHARE IT

"True worship is obedience to God for no other reason than that you delight in God." ~ J.D. Greear

WEEK 23 FRIDAY

TRUTH: EXODUS 5:1-12

EXODUS 5:1

As soon as Moses finished meeting with the Israelites, he immediately began the mission God gave him. Am I doing what God has called me to do right now in my life?

- **YES**
- **NO**
- **STILL FIGURING THIS OUT**

What makes me most afraid about following God's plan for me?

- Persecution
- Rejection
- I am not afraid to follow His plan.
- Something else: ______________________

EXODUS 5:2

Pharaoh did not know God. Who is in my life that does not know God? ______________

TRUE OR FALSE.

T F I believe God put the above person(s) in my life so I could share the Gospel with them.

EXODUS 5:3-5

Pharaoh responded to Moses' and Aaron's request to worship God with disbelief and then by claiming that they were lazy.

When people criticize my worship of God, it makes me:

- Feel like keeping my faith a secret.
- Get defensive, and I begin arguing with them.
- I have never been criticized for my worship of God.

EXODUS 5:6-12

Pharaoh reacted to the faith of the Israelites by giving what command (**vv. 7-8**)?

____

God's people have always faced persecution for their faith in Him.
Have I ever been persecuted for my faith? **YES** **NO**

How should I respond to those who persecute me for my faith? (**Romans 12:14**)

____

What are practical ways I can bless those who persecute me? ______________

____

____

SHARE IT

"No healthy Christian ever chooses suffering; he chooses God's will, as Jesus did, whether it means suffering or not."
~ Oswald Chambers

SATURDAY WEEK 23

TRUTH: EXODUS 5:13-23

EXODUS 5:13-19

Sometimes the first thing God's people find when they are obedient to Him is opposition from others. Have I found this to be true at any point in my life? ☐ **YES** ☐ **NO**

TRUE OF FALSE.

T F When opposition comes into my life, I still trust God with the situation.

EXODUS 5:20-21

The Israelites were angry with Moses and Aaron, but what reasons had the Israelites been given to trust them? (**Exodus 4:29-31**)

____

The Israelites should have remembered how God worked through Aaron and Moses instead of doubting!

What are ways I have seen God work in my life? ______________________________

____

EXODUS 5:22-23

How did Moses react to what the Israelites said?

- ☐ He got angry with them.
- ☐ He prayed to God.
- ☐ He blamed Aaron.

Although Moses was right to pray, his prayer showed that he had begun to doubt God and doubt God's plan for him. Moses needed to learn to:

- ☐ Pray less.
- ☐ Trust God more.
- ☐ Be more patient.

Sometimes when difficult times come, it is hard to trust God even though I have seen Him work in my life. When this happens, how do I respond?

- ☐ By doubting God like Moses did
- ☐ By asking God to help me trust Him more
- ☐ By ignoring the entire situation
- ☐ By talking to friends about what is going on

Because God has worked in my life, I will commit to trust Him even when I face opposition. ☐ **YES** ☐ **NO**

SHARE IT

"And those who know Your name will put their trust in You; for You, Lord, have not forsaken those who seek You."
~ **Psalm 9:10**

WEEK 24 SUNDAY

TRUTH: EXODUS 6:1-13

Am I working on trusting God more based on Saturday's commitment? ☐ **YES** ☐ **NO**

EXODUS 6:1

God responded to Moses saying, "Now you shall see what ____ will do to Pharaoh." Moses needed to realize God was in control.

TRUE OR FALSE.

T F Sometimes I try to fix things instead of letting God be in control.

EXODUS 6:2-4

God first reminded Moses of the past. Why is it important that I remember God's promises and position in my life? ____

____

EXODUS 6:5-6

Next, God reminded Moses what He was about to do.

TRUE OR FALSE.

T F Sometimes I need to be reminded of God's promises.

Where should I turn to be reminded of God's promises?

- ☐ Scripture
- ☐ My Pastor
- ☐ Prayer

EXODUS 6:7-8

God then told Moses the ways He would bless them in the future.

Do I believe God has my future in mind as well? ☐ **YES** ☐ **NO**

EXODUS 6:9-13

Unfortunately, the people of Israel did not listen to Moses.
Why did they struggle to believe him? (Check one.)

- ☐ They did not trust him.
- ☐ Their circumstances made belief difficult.
- ☐ They wanted to stay in Egypt.

Sometimes I get focused on my circumstances, like those going on…

At School ____.

At Home ____.

With my ____.

Instead of focusing on these, I will focus on Christ. ☐ **YES** ☐ **NO**

SHARE IT

"We have to pray with our eyes on God, not on the difficulties." ~ Oswald Chambers

MONDAY WEEK 24

TRUTH: EXODUS 6:28-7:13

EXODUS 6:28-7:2

What was God's command to Moses now? ______________________________

____

EXODUS 7:3-5

In the end, everyone would know that the God of Moses was the one true God Almighty. This shows that God's plan had:

- ☐ A chance of working.
- ☐ A purpose.
- ☐ Nothing to show for it.

Do I believe God still has a plan and a purpose for my life and the world? ☐ **YES** ☐ **NO**

EXODUS 7:6

How do I respond to God's commands?

- ☐ I hesitate to follow them.
- ☐ I obey fully, like Moses and Aaron did.
- ☐ I do not listen to God's commands.

The most difficult command from God for me to follow is... ______________________

____.

EXODUS 7:7-13

TRUE OR FALSE.

T F When Moses and Aaron obeyed God, everything went just as God had said it would.

If God always keeps His word, why do I sometimes struggle to follow His commands?

- ☐ I do not like being told no.
- ☐ Obedience is too difficult.
- ☐ I feel stuck in sin sometimes.
- ☐ Because it seems like no one else follows His commands

What is a practical way this week that I will fully respond to God's commands the way that Moses and Aaron did? (**v. 6**) ______________________________

____

Spend some time now in prayer, asking God to help you follow through on your above commitment. ☐

SHARE IT

"There will be no peace in any soul until it is willing to obey the voice of God." ~ D. L. Moody

WEEK 24 TUESDAY

TRUTH: EXODUS 7:14-25

EXODUS 7:14

Pharaoh's heart was ______________________. This means his heart was disobedient, unrepentant, and set against God.

Some people I know who have set their hearts against God include: ______________ ______________________________.

Have I tried to share the Gospel with the above person(s)? ☐ **YES** ☐ **NO**

What are some other practical ways I can reach those individuals?

- ☐ Pray for them
- ☐ Be loving toward them
- ☐ Something else: ______________________________

EXODUS 7:15-21

Seeing this miracle would have made me:

- ☐ Freak out
- ☐ Believe in God
- ☐ Do nothing different

EXODUS 7:22-25

Pharaoh was looking for an excuse to doubt Moses, Aaron, and the God they served. What excuse did he find? (**v. 22**)______________________________

____

Although Pharaoh chose to harden his heart, God was going to give him more chances to repent. What does this say about God?

- ☐ He is patient.
- ☐ He is loving.
- ☐ He is gracious.

How does **2 Peter 3:9** apply to Pharaoh in his situation here? ______________

____

How does this apply to those I know with hardened hearts? ______________

____

Because God loves people this much, I will find a way this week to share the love of Christ with the individual(s) I mentioned. ☐ **YES** ☐ **NO**

SHARE IT

I'm so glad I serve a patient and loving God!

WEDNESDAY WEEK 24

TRUTH: EXODUS 8:1-15

EXODUS 8:1-2

God warned Pharaoh what would happen if he refused to let the Israelites go?

____

What is the purpose of warnings? ______________________________

____

Is a warning helpful to those who never hear it? ☐ **YES** ☐ **NO**

All throughout Scripture God warns ungodly individuals of the consequences for their disobedience. What does this tell me about God?

- ☐ He cares for the ungodly.
- ☐ He is unfair by judging the ungodly.
- ☐ Nothing

What is one of God's warnings to the ungodly today? (**Romans 6:23a**)? ____________

____

Who is supposed to share this warning, and the good news of the Gospel, with the world? (**Matthew 28:18-20**)

- ☐ Only the disciples
- ☐ All Christians
- ☐ The Holy Spirit

Is the warning of **Romans 6:23a** helpful if the world does not hear it? ☐ **YES** ☐ **NO**

EXODUS 8:3-15

In the end, the warning God gave came true. This shows me that:

- ☐ God is serious when He warns.
- ☐ God is unkind.
- ☐ Pharaoh was treated unfairly.

God gave Moses the warning to share with Pharaoh, just like He has given me the warning to share with those who do not believe in Jesus.

- ☐ I agree with this statement.
- ☐ I disagree with this statement.
- ☐ I need to think some more.

SHARE IT

"For the wages of sin is death, but the gift of God is eternal life in Christ Jesus our Lord." ~ **Romans 6:23**

WEEK 24 THURSDAY

TRUTH: EXODUS 8:16-32

EXODUS 8:16-19

The third plague was an infestation of ______________.

Despite their attempts to duplicate the miracle as before, even the magicians admitted to Pharaoh, "This is the ____________________ of God."

The magicians surrendered and admitted that God's power was beyond them. How did Pharaoh react?

- By accepting God's power
- By rejecting them and hardening his heart
- By letting Israel go

What is going on in my life where I need God to work in a powerful way?______________

____

Do I believe God has the power to do this? **YES** **NO**

EXODUS 8:20-24

Having shown His power to be far greater than the Egyptian magicians, God now shows Pharaoh another act of His might. The flies that would infest the land would:

- Be on the Egyptians only.
- Cover the Egyptians and Israelites.

The thing that is most impressive to me about these miracles is:__________________

____.

EXODUS 8:25-32

There are two responses to God's power: to deny and reject Him, or to submit and worship Him. Which did Pharaoh choose?__________________________________

Which of the above responses is true in my life?______________________________

What must be present if I want God to move powerfully in my life? (**Mark 11:22-24**)?

____

I will seek God's will and trust in His power in my life. **YES** **NO**

SHARE IT

"Evil is real – but so is God's power and love." ~ Billy Graham

FRIDAY WEEK 24

TRUTH: EXODUS 9:1-12

EXODUS 9:1-7

The more Pharaoh hardened his heart, the more severe the plagues became. This next plague resulted in what?

- ☐ The death of all Egyptians
- ☐ The death of all Egyptian livestock
- ☐ The death of all livestock

Once again, Pharaoh refused to submit to God's correction. When was the last time I was punished but still repeated the same sin later? ______________________________

____

Did I receive a greater punishment for continuing in that sin? ☐ **YES** ☐ **NO**

This newest plague was a reminder that God is the ultimate ruler of all animal life.

☐ **I AGREE.** ☐ **I DISAGREE.**

EXODUS 9:8-12

The next plague resulted in painful boils on both the Egyptians and on animals. The last painful sickness I experienced was ______________________________ .

Did I turn to God for healing during that time? ☐ **YES** ☐ **NO**

When I am sick, I rely most on:

MEDICINE DOCTORS PARENTS GOD TIME

Even though Pharaoh tried to rely on himself and his magicians, who removed every plague that came?

- ☐ The magicians
- ☐ Moses
- ☐ God

Because God showed His power over the animals and people, this proves that He is:

- ☐ God over all creation
- ☐ Pretty important
- ☐ Nothing special

SHARE IT

God is the God of all creation.

WEEK 24 SATURDAY

TRUTH: EXODUS 9:13-26

EXODUS 9:13-17

God revealed to Pharaoh that despite his pride in continually rejecting God, what remained true?

- There was no one like God.
- Pharaoh only had power because God gave it to him.
- Pharaoh continued choosing to exalt himself.

Pharaoh's pride in refusing to submit to God had resulted in destruction already in Egypt. Has my pride ever led to destruction? **YES** **NO**

What is an area of my life where my pride gets the best of me?

- Sports
- Friends (popularity)
- Accomplishments
- Something else: ______________________________

I will stop and pray that God would help bring humility to that area of my life.

EXODUS 9:18-26

The plague of hail came just as God had warned: on all "who did not ______________ ______________________________." (**v. 21**)

Why do I disregard God's commands and warnings at times?

- I think I know better.
- I do not think there will be consequences.
- I would rather enjoy sin in the moment.
- Another reason: ______________________________

Sometimes, pride is seen not only in building myself up with my words and actions, but also as I intentionally disregard God's commands.

- I agree with this statement.
- I disagree with this statement.
- I need to think some more.

According to **Proverbs 16:18-19**, what does pride result in? ______________
____

According to the above passage, what should I desire instead of pride? ______________
____

SHARE IT

"You can have no greater sign of confirmed pride than when you think you are humble enough." ~ *William Law*

SUNDAY WEEK 25

TRUTH: EXODUS 9:27-35

EXODUS 9:27-28

What did Pharaoh do for the first time?
- Admit his sin
- Recognize God's righteousness
- Recognize the sinfulness of his people

What does it normally take for me to admit when I am wrong?
- Getting caught
- Facing consequences/discipline
- Something else: ______________________________

EXODUS 9:29-30

Moses knew that Pharaoh was not truly sorry for his sin.

How do I know when I am not truly sorry for my sin?
- When I repeat the same sin again
- When I say sorry only because I had to
- When I refuse to ask forgiveness no matter what

Moses knew that Pharaoh's repentance did not come from a changed heart toward God. What do I think true repentance is? ______________________________

____

Repentance is *a change of mind that results in a change of action*. Does this describe me when I repent of my sin to God? **YES** **NO**

EXODUS 9:31-35

Does the above description of repentance describe Pharaoh? **YES** **NO**

What truth is found in **1 John 1:9**?
- God forgives my sins when I confess my sin to Him.
- Because I am saved, it does not matter when I sin.

I commit from now on to respond to my sin by:
- Confessing my sin to God.
- Trusting God will forgive me.
- Changing my behavior.

SHARE IT

Repentance is a change of mind that results in a change of action.

WEEK 25 MONDAY

TRUTH: EXODUS 10:1-15

EXODUS 10:1-7

What had God's command been to Pharaoh all along?

- ☐ Stop making My people work
- ☐ Let My people go to serve Me
- ☐ Be kinder to My people

This was a hard command for Pharaoh to follow.

What is a command from God in Scripture that I find hard to follow? ______________________

____

EXODUS 10:8-11

TRUE OR FALSE.

T F Pharaoh was willing to give in completely to the request of Moses.

Pharaoh was not willing to fully obey God. Have there been times when I have not been fully willing to obey God? ☐ **YES** ☐ **NO**

What commands from God do I tend to obey half-heartedly?

- ☐ Sharing the Gospel (**Matthew 28:18-20**)
- ☐ Honoring my parents (**Exodus 20:12**)
- ☐ Watching my language (**1 Peter 3:10**)
- ☐ Something else:____

Why do I struggle to obey God fully sometimes?

- ☐ I feel trapped by sin.
- ☐ I think the sin will be better than obedience to God.
- ☐ I'm not sure why.

Although I may be tempted to disobey God and reject His commands, what promise does **1 Corinthians 10:13** tell me about temptation? ______________________________

____.

From now on, I am going to strive to fully obey God's commands. ☐ **YES** ☐ **NO**

Spend some time in prayer, asking God to make you willing and steadfast in your commitment to obey Him! ☐

SHARE IT

"Lord, whatever You want, wherever You want it, and whenever You want it, that's what I want." ~ *Richard Baxter*

TUESDAY WEEK 25

TRUTH: EXODUS 10:16-29

EXODUS 10:16-20

What was constantly happening with Pharaoh?

- ☐ He was kinder toward Moses.
- ☐ His heart grew harder.
- ☐ He was growing more powerful.

Although at first Pharaoh seemed to show remorse for his sin, his request was not that God soften his heart, but that God would "take away from me ______________." (**v. 17**)

Hard hearts regret consequences not the sin itself.
Have I ever confessed my sin only because I was sorry about the consequence?
☐ **YES** ☐ **NO**

EXODUS 10:21-24

Just like before, Pharaoh tried to bargain with God's command to let Israel go. What did he try to prevent Moses from taking this time? ______________________________

Hard hearts try to bargain with God. Have I ever tried bargaining with God in my sin, saying if God did one thing, I would do something in return? ☐ **YES** ☐ **NO**

What are some reasons bargaining with God is not right?

- ☐ It shows I think I know best.
- ☐ It is not full obedience.
- ☐ It lacks faith and repentance.
- ☐ Another reason: ______________________________

EXODUS 10:25-29

Another effect of a hard heart is pushing others away.
Who do I push away in my life when I'm not walking with God as I ought to?

____

Would I characterize myself right now as having a hard heart? ☐ **YES** ☐ **NO**

Why or why not? ______________________________________ .

Today I will ask God to soften my heart toward His commands. ☐ **YES** ☐ **NO**

SHARE IT

"Create in me a clean heart, O God, and renew a steadfast spirit within me." ~ **Psalm 51:10**

WEEK 25 WEDNESDAY

TRUTH: EXODUS 11:1-10

EXODUS 11:1-5

God knew that only one more plague would be necessary to break Pharaoh's hard and rebellious heart. What was this tenth plague? ______________________________

TRUE OR FALSE.

T F The plague would affect only Pharaoh and his house.

T F The plague would affect every Egyptian house.

Israel had been abused by all of Egypt, and now the sins of the nation of Egypt would be punished. What does this say about God?

- ☐ He will judge sin.
- ☐ He is unfair.
- ☐ He hates Egyptians.

The Egyptians thought there would be no consequences for their sins. Have I ever thought that about sin in my life? ☐ **YES** ☐ **NO**

What does Scripture say will be the result for the believer who sins? (**Hebrews 12:5-6**)

- ☐ God will discipline the believer.
- ☐ There will be no consequences for sin.

EXODUS 11:6-10

After the tenth plague came, what would be the response in Egypt? (**v. 6**)

____

Although the Egyptians would cry out in pain and sorrow after the tenth plague, they would not turn to God in repentance.

How do I usually respond after I sin?

- ☐ Get upset about the consequences
- ☐ Think how to not get caught next time
- ☐ Ask God for forgiveness

Because God takes sin seriously, I will take sin seriously also.

When I sin, I will respond by repenting of my sin.

- ☐ I agree with this statement.
- ☐ I disagree with this statement.
- ☐ I need to think some more.

SHARE IT

"He who covers his sins will not prosper, but whoever confesses and forsakes them will have mercy."
~ **Proverbs 28:13**

THURSDAY WEEK 25

TRUTH: EPHESIANS 1:1-6

Paul came to the city of Ephesus (in modern day Turkey) on his second missionary journey. He started a church that quickly grew into many house churches (**Acts 19, 20**). He is now imprisoned at Rome and writes the Ephesian people a special letter about Christian belief (**chapters 1-3**) and Christian behavior (**chapters 4-6**).

EPHESIANS 1:1-2

What two words does Paul use to describe the believers he is writing to?

______________________ ______________________

Can people describe me the same way? ☐ **YES** ☐ **NO**

What two blessings come from the Father and the Son?

______________________ ______________________

EPHESIANS 1:3

God's spiritual blessings to me cause me to give blessing (praise and thanksgiving) to God. My spiritual blessings are found where? ______________________

My spiritual new birth into God's family brings me into unique heavenly blessings that I can experience on earth.

I will list three blessings of salvation that I have received.

______________________ ______________________

____

EPHESIANS 1:4-5

God chose me in Christ before the world was created so I would be ______________ and ______________ before Him in love.

If I have placed my faith in Jesus to save me from my sin, God has ______________ me into His family.

EPHESIANS 1:6

For what reason did God choose me, adopt me, and make me acceptable in His beloved Son? ______________________

I truly want my life to be a testimony for God and His glory and grace.

☐ I agree with this statement. ☐ I disagree with this statement.

SHARE IT

I am blessed, chosen, adopted, accepted, redeemed, and forgiven by God.

WEEK 25 FRIDAY

TRUTH: EPHESIANS 1:7-14

EPHESIANS 1:7

Redemption (*the price paid for our sin and forgiveness, the losing and removal of our sin*) is only through Christ's ______________________________.

Have you been redeemed and forgiven for your sins? ☐ **YES** ☐ **NO** ☐ **NOT SURE**

Have you believed in Jesus and His payment on the cross for your sins? ☐ **YES** ☐ **NO**

If not, then you should do so right now! Write out **Romans 10:9**.

____

____

____

EPHESIANS 1:10

One day everything and everyone in ______________ and on __________ will be brought into submission and control of ______________________.

I can think of at least one area of my life that is not yet under the Lord's control which is:

______________________________.

I will spend some time right now talking with God about this and surrendering it over to His control.

☐ Yes, I will do this. ☐ No, I'm not ready to give this up.

EPHESIANS 1:11

God's counsel, God's will, and God's predestination have given me an ________________ (*great divine privileges, great spiritual possessions*) both now and forever.

EPHESIANS 1:12-14

When did I first remember hearing the Word of truth, the Gospel of salvation?

____

Every believer who trusts in Christ is sealed (stamped) with the Holy Spirit. The Holy Spirit within us is our guarantee of salvation, eternal life, and blessing.

What mark or stamp has the Holy Spirit left on my life? ______________________________

SHARE IT

I am sealed, signed, and delivered by God.

SATURDAY WEEK 25

TRUTH: EPHESIANS 1:15-23

EPHESIANS 1:17-19

Paul prays for God to give the Ephesian believers
W_______________, **R**______________________, **K** _____________________________,
I _________________________________.

Paul also prays for believers to see and experience three things.

1 The hope of His ____

2. The riches of His ____

3. The exceeding greatness of His ____

Who will I pray for right now who needs to see and know these things from God?

____

EPHESIANS 1:19-20

God's power has put Christ over and above all principality and power (***rulers and authorities***). These terms are used of holy angels, fallen angels, and human governments.

God's power enables me to live above and have victory over anything or anyone who tries to hinder my Christian life.

I need special power from God today for ____
____.

EPHESIANS 1:22-23

God's power is over His church (***all true believers in Jesus Christ***).

The church is His ____________________.

What is the church of Jesus Christ supposed to be doing according to **Acts 2:42**?

____

Am I a part of a church that worships and serves Jesus Christ? ☐ **YES** ☐ **NO**

How often do I attend church? ____

In what area of my church do I serve? ____

If I am not currently serving in my church, will I contact the pastor and ask him where I could serve? ☐ **YES** ☐ **NO**

SHARE IT

God's power enables me to have victory over anything or anyone who tries to hinder my Christian life.

WEEK 26 SUNDAY

TRUTH: EPHESIANS 2:1-7

EPHESIANS 2:1-3

Here is a sad description of our old life before we came to Jesus.

This is also a description of our family and friends who do not know the Lord.

Dead in ______________________________

Living like the ______________________________

Under the control of the ______________________________

Following the lusts and desires of the __________ **and the** __________

Naturally facing God's terrible ______________________________

EPHESIANS 2:4-5

BAD NEWS: My sins separated me from God and made me dead to God and His truth. I was like a walking dead person, alive in the flesh (body), but my soul and spirit were dead, unresponsive to God. Before surrendering my life to Christ, I was one of the living dead.

GOOD NEWS:
God is rich in M__________________.
He has shown me His great L__________________.
He has saved me by His G__________________________.

The Lord Jesus by God's grace has given me new life. My soul and spirit have been resurrected to life by God's great salvation. Someday my body will be resurrected (changed) into a new eternally living body.

I will list two people I know who are physically alive but dead to God, and pray for them now.

______________________________ ______________________________

EPHESIANS 2:6-7

God has rescued me and raised me up to sit with Christ in Heaven. I am still on earth but enjoy some of the blessings, benefits, and privileges of Heaven. One day, Jesus will come for me, and I will actually be with Him in Heaven.

Something I look forward to in Heaven: ______________________________

____

SHARE IT

"And when my days are done, I've got a Hope I am sure of, I'll be with You in heavenly places."
~ We Are Messengers (Lyrics from "Everything Comes Alive")

MONDAY WEEK 26

TRUTH: EPHESIANS 2:8-13

EPHESIANS 2:8-9

A gift is very special. Someone thought of you and something you needed and decided to pay a price and buy you that item so you would be helped and blessed. A gift comes from a heart of love.

What is the most recent gift you have received? ______________________________

What is the most recent gift you have given? ______________________________

Salvation is a ____________ of God's grace that we receive through faith in the death, burial, and resurrection of our Lord Jesus Christ.

To pay for or work for a gift that someone gives you would offend that person. Many think that we can try to buy or pay for salvation by our good deeds. But if we could work our way to salvation or into Heaven we would then be able to B__________________ (**v. 9**). We can only boast or brag or be proud of J______________.

Have I been trying to pay for my salvation by my own deeds? **YES** **NO**

Do I understand that there is no way that I could possibly earn God's free gift of salvation? **YES** **NO** **I AM NOT SURE.**

(If unsure, I will contact a trusted adult/friend about this.)

EPHESIANS 2:10

Our good works show that we are saved and are servants of the Lord. We are to surrender our lives to work for God in ways that will promote evangelism, discipleship, missions, church growth, worship, and holy living.

Yesterday I was able to do this good deed for someone ________________________.

EPHESIANS 2:11-13

Jews and Gentiles (people of other nations) whether circumcised or uncircumcised are now one people by faith in Christ.

Salvation by the blood of Jesus makes us all one as brothers and sisters in Christ.

Were you born with **a Jewish heritage** or **another national heritage** ?

SHARE IT

"We all bleed the same."
~ Mandisa (Lyrics from "Bleed the Same")

WEEK 26 TUESDAY

TRUTH: EPHESIANS 2:14-18

God's law of commandments and ordinances has been broken by mankind and has made all people enemies of God and often enemies of each other. Jesus paid for our transgressions of God's law and trespasses of God's Word so that all who believe are made new.

EPHESIANS 2:14-15

Jesus Christ is our P______________. (**v. 14**)
He is our peace through the shedding of His B____________ (**v. 13**) and the suffering of His body (flesh). (**v. 15**)

I have received Jesus as my Savior, I have been forgiven of all my sins, and I now am at peace with God!

☐ I agree with this statement. ☐ I disagree with this statement.

When did I become at peace with God? ______________________________
I will pray now for my friend ______________________________ and my family relative ______________________________ to also enter into peace with God.

EPHESIANS 2:16

Jews and Gentiles (***people of other nations***) are reconciled, united to God and each other by the ______________________________.

Jesus was put to death so that our sins and iniquities, our rebellion against God, would be put to death opening the door to a new relationship with God and each other.

TRUE OR FALSE.

T F Someone may make you their enemy, but do not make yourself someone else's enemy.

EPHESIANS 2:17-18

Jesus came to earth preaching peace in the Gospel to the Jews who thought they were near to Jehovah God and to the Gentiles who were content to be far from Jehovah God.

How many times is the word "peace" found in these verses? _______

Notice who Jesus is (**v. 14**) ______________________________
what He makes (**v. 15**) ______________________________
what He preaches (**v. 17**) ______________________________

Can I think of someone I should make peace with today? ☐ **YES** ☐ **NO**

☐ I will take care of this today.

SHARE IT

"He is our peace Who has broken down every wall."
~ Maranatha! Music (Lyrics from He Is Our Peace)

WEDNESDAY WEEK 26

TRUTH: EPHESIANS 2:19-22

EPHESIANS 2:19

Once I was a foreigner, alien, and exile from God and God's family. I did not know God or have a relationship with Him and His children.

Through the work of Christ in His death, burial, and resurrection and through faith in Christ, I am now adopted and accepted and am no longer a stranger but a fellow citizen with all the rights and privileges of citizenship.

The date I was born as a citizen of my country: ____________________

The date I was born again as a citizen of God's family and Heaven: ____________

EPHESIANS 2:20

God's family is like a household (**v. 19**) of people being brought together, being built up together, and prepared for our home in Heaven together. Our earthly families may end or be broken apart, but our heavenly family will enjoy life forever.

God's people, the church, are built upon the foundation of the ____________ and the ____________ (early Christian leaders).

Who is the Chief Cornerstone of this great church or family of people? ____________

EPHESIANS 2:21-22

God's great household of people, the church (God's family of believers) is being continually built up and constructed together by the Holy Spirit. Every believer is added to the church by the Holy Spirit, and every believer is being personally built up and developed to be a spiritually strong member of the church. This household or church of people is indwelt by the Lord Jesus Christ, and we are His temple (personally and corporately) through which He is worshiped and adored.

Am I growing spiritually to be a blessing to God and His family?

☐ **YES** ☐ **NO** ☐ **WANT TO**

SHARE IT

Jesus is the Rock of my salvation.

WEEK 26 THURSDAY

TRUTH: EPHESIANS 3:1-7

The mystery referred to in **verses three** and **four** was a wonderful secret that had been unknown in the Old Testament times of Israel and even in the gospels during the life of Jesus on earth. The mystery was fully revealed by the resurrected Lord Jesus Christ in the sending of His Holy Spirit so that Gentiles *(people of non-Jewish nations)* could become part of the family of God by faith in Jesus Christ.

EPHESIANS 3:1

Paul a prisoner of: ☐ the Romans ☐ the Lord ☐ the Jews

He knew that whatever happened to him, wherever he went, was part of God's plan for his life. He was a willing captive of the Lord Jesus Christ.

Have I made myself a prisoner of Jesus, and am I a willing captive under His control?

☐ **YES** ☐ **NO**

If not, why not? ____________________

EPHESIANS 3:2-4

God not only revealed Himself to Paul at his conversion on the Damascus road in **Acts 9**, but God also gave special revelations or revealing of truth to him to pass on to other believers in the Holy Scriptures.

Our Bible is a wonderful revelation from God to enable us to see wonderful mysteries, secrets, and truths that the world does not know or understand.

Write one biblical truth that I have learned: ____________________

____

EPHESIANS 3:5-7

The secret given to the apostles of Jesus and the prophets (preachers and teachers) of the early church (**v. 20**) was that Christ and His salvation was not just for the Jewish nation but the Gentile nations of the world. Paul was made a minister of the Gospel to the Gentiles by God's grace.

What country would I consider going to with the Gospel (good news of Jesus)?

____

☐ Spend time right now talking with God about this possibility.

SHARE IT

Put the GO in the GOspel!

FRIDAY WEEK 26

TRUTH: EPHESIANS 3:8-13

EPHESIANS 3:8

Am I also amazed that God has been so merciful, good, and gracious to me?

☐ **YES** ☐ **NO**

Paul thought of himself as the worst of ____________(**1 Timothy 1:15**) and the least of ____________(**v. 8**). This true humility allowed the Lord to use his life so wonderfully.

I believe that ______________________ is a very humble Christian, and I will pray for him/her now.

EPHESIANS 3:9

God created everything in the beginning. God also created a wonderful mystery of truth that He kept hidden in Christ until His resurrection from the grave and His ascension into Heaven: the truth that all nations, all languages, all colors, and all cultures of humanity can experience salvation and new life through faith in Jesus Christ.

What other languages would you like to learn so you could share the Gospel of Christ?

____

EPHESIANS 3:10

God wanted even the angels in Heaven (*principalities, powers, rulers, and authorities*) to see His glorious wisdom in building His church of believers on the earth in such a wonderful way.

Are angels watching us? ☐ **YES** ☐ **NO** ☐ **MAYBE**

EPHESIANS 3:11-12

God's eternal purpose for us is to have direct access, relationship, and fellowship with Him. We can boldly, with assurance and confidence, go to God anytime and anywhere.

Read **Hebrews 4:14-16**. ☐ I did. ☐ I didn't.

How often do I take advantage of going to God anytime and anywhere?

Not often 1 2 3 4 5 **All the time**

EPHESIANS 3:13

Don't faint or fall or give into suffering or problems in life. Go boldly to God in prayer!!

Take some time to journal a confident prayer to God right now about a problem you are having. ____

____

SHARE IT

I can boldly, with assurance and confidence, go to God anytime and anywhere.

WEEK 26 SATURDAY

TRUTH: EPHESIANS 3:14-21

Paul records his prayer in these verses for us to know how to pray and what to pray for.

EPHESIANS 3:14

Paul made this prayer on his ________________.
Sometimes the burdens of life cause us to simply fall on our knees or on our face to the Lord.
When was the last time I prayed on my knees? ______________________________

EPHESIANS 3:15

God's family of believers live in what two locations?
1.______________________________ 2. ______________________________

List two people who you believe are in Heaven because of their faith in Jesus to save them from their sins.
1.______________________________ 2. ______________________________

EPHESIANS 3:16

We should pray for strength from God for our inner person.

Jesus dwells in my heart because I have received Him by faith. ☐ **YES** ☐ **NO**

EPHESIANS 3:17-19

God's love gives us a secure foundation.
How does this thought make me feel? ______________________________

The love of God in Christ reaches up so very high, reaches down so very low, reaches out so very wide, and is so very complete.

I believe that God does fully love me all the time and will forever.
- ☐ Yes, I'm confident of God's love for me.
- ☐ I know God loves me, but sometimes I don't feel like He does.
- ☐ I'd like to learn more about God's love. (Talk to a trusted adult.)

EPHESIANS 3:20-21

What is my God able to do? ______________________________
His power is working where? ______________________________

I can ask for great things from God for His glory. ☐ **YES** ☐ **NO**

I am currently asking God for this great thing:______________________________
____.

SHARE IT

A big God can handle a big prayer!

SUNDAY WEEK 27

TRUTH: EPHESIANS 4:1-10

EPHESIANS 4:1-3

Christians are to walk (live) in a way that is worthy of the One who called us and the purpose He has for us.

How has my Christian life been lived in the last month?

Not well 1 2 3 4 5 Terrific

Am I satisfied with this? ☐ **YES** ☐ **NO**

How are we to treat other people? (**v. 2**) ______________________, ______________________, ______________________, and ______________________.

I am struggling to patiently love ______________________.
I will pray for him/her now. ☐ **YES** ☐ **NO**

I make every effort to keep unity with other believers.
☐ **YES**, most of the time. ☐ **NO**, it's way too hard.

EPHESIANS 4:4-6

God's church of believers is united in one __________, one __________, one __________, one __________, one __________, one __________, and one __________.

God is ______________ all, and __________ all, and ______________ all.

Don't let sin, Satan, or yourself break things up in the family of God.
Am I pushing someone away from God or from me for selfish reasons? ☐ **YES** ☐ **NO**

EPHESIANS 4:7-10

Every Christian has a special spiritual gift or gifts given to them at salvation by Jesus so that we can serve Him on earth. We need to discover our spiritual gift(s) and exercise and develop them for God.

My spiritual gift is ______________________________.

I will pray to discover my spiritual gift and talk with my youth leader more about this.
☐ **YES** ☐ **NO**

SHARE IT

Don't let sin, Satan, or yourself break things up in the family of God.

WEEK 27 MONDAY

TRUTH: EPHESIANS 4:11-16

There are many spiritual gifts given to believers in the church to enable them to serve the Lord effectively.

(**Romans 12:4-8; 1 Corinthians 12:1-11, 28-31; 1 Peter 4:8-11**)

EPHESIANS 4:11

Here is a list of leadership gifts to lead and build up the church.
Which of these gifts are evident in my church?

____

How would I feel if God has given me one of these gifts to use for His glory?

BLESSED **SCARED** **WILLING** **HESITANT**

EPHESIANS 4:12

Spiritual gifts help to mature and equip believers to minister to the church and build up the church.

CIRCLE: My church **seems to be growing spiritually** or **stays about the same**.

How could I get involved in my church to help it to grow?

____

EPHESIANS 4:13

God's goal for the church is to be united in faith, growing in the knowledge of Christ, and becoming more and more Christlike.

I believe I am more Christlike now than a year ago.

YES **NO** **NOT SURE**

Who do I know that is becoming more Christlike? ______________

EPHESIANS 4:14

Some Christians seem to remain as spiritual ______________.
They are not very stable and are easily confused and led away by false teaching.

Who do I know that continues to be an immature Christian? __________
I will pray and encourage them to grow. **YES** **NO**

EPHESIANS 4:16

The church body is like the human body. Each part of the body needs to properly fit together, work together, and minister together one to another, so the body will be healthy, strong, and effective.
I will pray now for the leaders of my church. **YES** **NO**

SHARE IT

A growing church is a going church.

TUESDAY WEEK 27

TRUTH: EPHESIANS 4:17-24

Paul describes the way unbelieving Gentiles live. He warns the Ephesian believers not to return to that lifestyle but to live new and godly lives for Christ.

EPHESIANS 4:17-21

Unbelievers are futile (empty, vain) in their ________________.
They are ____________________ from the life of God.
They are filled with blindness (hardness) in their ________________.
They have given themselves over to ______________________________.
Could a Christian live this way all of the time? ☐ **YES** ☐ **NO**
Write out **2 Corinthians 5:17**. ____

____

A true believer is someone who has learned of Christ and learned from Christ how to walk in truth.
Have I been living as **a true believer** or **an unbeliever** lately?

EPHESIANS 4:22

We need to put off/strip off our old way of living in sin and lust (just as we would take off clothes that become soiled, stained, and dirty).
By God's help I need to take this out of my life: ______________________________ .
I will ask this person to help me: ______________________________.

EPHESIANS 4:23

We need to have a renewal and a revival in our minds and our thought life every day.
If our thoughts go bad, so do our emotions, and then our actions.
What is one thought that often bothers me? ______________________________

Daily coming to God in His Word and prayer will help to cleanse and strengthen my mind.

I will put time in God's Word on my daily schedule and keep it a priority in my life.
☐ **YES**, I will do this. ☐ **NO**, I can't make time for this.

EPHESIANS 4:24

The *new man* refers to our new nature and our new life in Christ by His Holy Spirit. Daily I need to clothe myself with Christ. I need to surrender to the Holy Spirit to control me and renew me for righteousness and holiness.
I will yield myself all day to the Holy Spirit. ☐ **YES** ☐ **NO**

SHARE IT

Daily coming to God in His Word and prayer will help to cleanse and strengthen my mind.

WEEK 27 WEDNESDAY

TRUTH: EPHESIANS 4:25-32

Here is a list of negative actions that we need to replace with positive actions. We can never get rid of the old ways without replacing them with new ways.

EPHESIANS 4:25

I need to replace lying by speaking the ____________________.

EPHESIANS 4:26

Anger can be holy or unholy. Good anger always helps to stop sin and evil that is offensive to God and hurts people.
Unholy anger turns to wrath and fury against people and against God.

EPHESIANS 4:27

Do not give the devil a ______________ in your life.
Lying and anger open you up to Satanic attack.
Which of these two do I struggle with most? ____________________________

EPHESIANS 4:29

Replace bad language that destroys with good language that

____.

I need to stop saying ____.
I need to start saying ____.

EPHESIANS 4:30

Who is most grieved by my bad language, attitude, and actions?

____

Who has sealed me and marked me as His own until the day of Christ's return?

____

I can never lose my salvation for I am safe and secure by the Holy Spirit who is the seal. ■ **TRUE** ■ **FALSE** ■ **NOT SURE**

EPHESIANS 4:31-32

Replace all the wickedness of **verse 31** with all the righteousness of **verse 32**.
I know that I need to forgive __________________ because Christ has forgiven me.
I will take some time now to journal a prayer to God talking to Him about these sins that are in my life and asking Him by His Spirit in me to replace them. ______________

____

SHARE IT

Remember, when you forgive, you heal.
When you let go, you grow.

THURSDAY WEEK 27

TRUTH: EPHESIANS 5:1-7

EPHESIANS 5:1

God is our faithful Father, and we are to follow, imitate, and pattern ourselves after Him as children who appreciate, respect, and love Him sincerely.
Am I following God with appreciation, respect, and love?

☐ **YES, MOST OF THE TIME** ☐ **NOT AT ALL**

EPHESIANS 5:2

Who is the greatest example of love? ____________
Jesus loves us so much that He gave Himself as an O_ _ _ _ _ _ _ _ and a S_ _ _ _ _ _ _ _ _ to God.
Today I will give of myself to show special love and acts of kindness to __________________ and to __________________.

EPHESIANS 5:3-5

Paul gives a list of vile sins that are not to be part of any Christian's life. Sexual sins are mentioned four times in **verses three** and **five**.

My body is to be set apart and sexually saved for my true love in our marriage relationship. ☐ **AGREE** ☐ **DISAGREE**

Write out **1 Thessalonians 4:3**. ____

____

Speech sins are listed in **verse four**. Filthy talk, filthy stories, and filthy jokes are offensive to God and should be offensive to us.

Do I ever speak, listen to, or laugh at this kind of language?

☐ **YES** ☐ **NO** ☐ **SOMETIMES**

Am I careful with what I watch, listen to, or read?

☐ **YES** ☐ **NO** ☐ **I WILL BE FROM NOW ON.**

EPHESIANS 5:6-7

Do not associate, fellowship, or participate with the children of ____________________!

☐ **I have mostly godly friends.** ☐ **I have mostly ungodly friends.**

SHARE IT

Live like a child of the King.

WEEK 27 FRIDAY

TRUTH: EPHESIANS 5:8-14

EPHESIANS 5:8

We are told to walk in the ____________________ as children of ________________.

God is light and in Him is no darkness at all. (**1 John 1:5b**)

We are not to walk or live in things that are impure, selfish, or worldly.

Write out **1 John 1:7**. ____

____

EPHESIANS 5:9-10

What three fruits of the Spirit are mentioned here? **1.** __________________________

2. ______________________________ **3.** ________________________________

If a vegetable garden is planted in deep shade and surrounded by large trees, it will not grow.

I cannot grow spiritually unless I walk and live in ______________________________.

How are we to act in regard to words, deeds, and attitudes of moral and spiritual darkness? ____

Am I spending too much time hanging out with people who love and live in darkness?

YES **NO**

Do I ever speak out publicly against things that are wrong?

YES **NO** **SOMETIMES**

Today I should say something about ____________________________________.

Romans 16:19 tells us that we are to be educated and wise about good things but simple and innocent about evil things.

I know that I should not listen to ____________________________. I should not watch ____________________. I should not even talk about ______________________________.

I need the light of the Holy Spirit and the light of the Word of God to see what is wrong and avoid those snares.

EPHESIANS 5:14

Christ's resurrection from the dead brought great light to the world. His return to earth will bring even greater light.

People who are spiritually dead in their sins can be raised to new life in Christ by faith in Jesus and walk as children of light!

SHARE IT

Walk in the Light.

SATURDAY WEEK 27

TRUTH: EPHESIANS 5:15-21

List the ways that we are told to walk or to live in **Ephesians**.

4:1 ______________________ **5:2** ______________________

5:8 ______________________ **5:15** ______________________

EPHESIANS 5:15

We are to walk or live very carefully and very wisely.
The world is a minefield; there are many snares and obstacles laid down by our enemies to cause us to fall into sin.
Recently I foolishly fell into the trap of ______________________ .
Today I will be more alert and seek to live wisely. ☐ **AGREE** ☐ **DISAGREE**

EPHESIANS 5:16

My time is very valuable. I don't know how much time is left before Jesus comes, or I go to God.
I need to spend less time ______________________ .
I need to spend more time ______________________ .

EPHESIANS 5:17

What do I need to spend my time understanding and then doing? ______________________

____

One area that I know is God's will for me is: ______________________ .

EPHESIANS 5:18

Some choose to be filled with ______________ and others choose to be filled with the ______________.
I know which one deserves my time and is God's will for me.
I need to be controlled and stimulated by ______________________.

EPHESIANS 5:19

The main purpose of music, singing, and instruments is to glorify God.
The second purpose is to minister to people.
What song will you sing right now to praise the Lord?

____

EPHESIANS 5:20

What kind of an attitude should I have at all times and in all things toward my God?

____

Do I typically have **a thankful heart** or **a complaining heart**?

EPHESIANS 5:21

We are to submit to one another as brothers and sisters in Christ in respect and honor to God.
Who do I find most difficult to submit to? ______________________
Who do I find the easiest to submit to? ______________________
I will keep in mind I should never submit to someone if they ask me to sin.
Read **Acts 5:29.**

SHARE IT

The world is a minefield; live very carefully.

WEEK 28 SUNDAY

TRUTH: EPHESIANS 5:22-33

Paul writes a great description of truth in regard to marriage. The husband and wife relationship is a picture or illustration of the church and Christ's relationship.

EPHESIANS 5:22-24

In the family of God we are to submit one to another (**v. 21**): men submitting to men, women submitting to women, and men and women submitting to each other.

In marriage, the Christian wife is to submit or yield to her husband, just as she would submit to the Lord Jesus Christ.

Does our society understand this? **YES** **NO**
Who is the head or leader of the church? ______________________
Who is the head of leader of the wife? ________________________

This is *not* a plan by which domineering men can run the lives of their wives in an uncaring, cruel way.

Does Christ do that in regard to His church? **YES** **NO**

EPHESIANS 5:25

Husbands are to ________ their wives as Christ loves the ____________.
Husbands are to fully give and sacrifice themselves for their wives.

EPHESIANS 5:26-27

Christ gave Himself on the cross as a sacrifice for sinners. Those who believe in Christ become part of His body the church.

Jesus uses the Word of God like water to ____________and __________ us. Jesus serves and leads His Church to enable us to one day become ____________________, without spots, wrinkles, or blemishes.

Do I know any churches that are perfect yet? **YES** **NO**

EPHESIANS 5:28

Husbands are also to love their wives as they love their own _________.

EPHESIANS 5:31-33

Husbands are to set an example of leadership by leaving their parents and being fully united to their wives in a new family unit, mutually loving and respecting each other.

Will I follow this biblical pattern in my marriage? **YES** **NO**

SHARE IT

Marriage works best God's way!

MONDAY WEEK 28

TRUTH: EPHESIANS 6:1-9

Here are two relationships in which God explains to us the best way to function.

1. The parent-child relationship (**vv. 1-4**)
2. The master-servant relationship (**vv. 5-9**)

EPHESIANS 6:1-3

Children are to ___________ their parents. God says that it is wrong to disobey your parents. (**v. 1**)
Children are to ___________ (*show respect to*) their parents. (**v. 2**)
What does God promise to obedient and respectful children?

____

In what way have I been disrespectful to my mother or father?

____

Today I will respect my parents by _______________________________ .

EPHESIANS 6:4

Fathers are the head of the home and they must show leadership by not ________________________ their children to _______________________________ .
Fathers (and mothers) are to bring up (train) their children in the ____________ and ______________________ of the Lord.

Do I pray for my parents? ☐ **YES** ☐ **NO**
What do I appreciate about my parents? ____________________________

____

☐ I will let my parents know what I appreciate about them today.

EPHESIANS 6:5-6

In Paul's day there were masters and their slaves, and there were employers and their hired servants. These principles applied to both situations.
Servants are to be ____________ to their masters for whose sake? _________________

The person I am truly serving at my job is the Lord Jesus Christ.

I am to be a good worker even when nobody's watching. God will richly reward me even if my employer does not. ☐ **AGREE** ☐ **DISAGREE**

EPHESIANS 6:9

Masters/employers are to be respectful to their servants and treat them well in their work and for their work.
Who have I worked for who treated me very well? ________________
☐ I will take time to send a quick note to say thank you.

SHARE IT

Do a good job; God is always watching.

WEEK 28 TUESDAY

TRUTH: EPHESIANS 6:10-17

EPHESIANS 6:10-11

I can be strong ______________________ and in the power of *His* might. Jesus defeated sin, the flesh, and the devil with *His* death and resurrection. I can put on *His* armor, *His* power, and *His* strength to fight the attacks and temptations I face every day.

EPHESIANS 6:12

TRUE OR FALSE.

T F I am not fighting against physical enemies. I am fighting against satanic and demonic powers who wish to conquer and destroy my life, my testimony, and my service for Jesus Christ.

EPHESIANS 6:13

I am to always stand as a Christian soldier when under spiritual attack and not to run or fall. How many times am I told to stand in these verses? __________

I sometimes feel like giving in or running away when life gets really hard. ☐ **YES** ☐ **NO**

I purpose instead to stand in the strength of Jesus by His Spirit. ☐ **YES** ☐ **NO**

EPHESIANS 6:14-17

Match the pieces of the Armor of God to their description.

a) Sword of the Spirit b) Breastplate of Righteousness c) Belt of Truth

d) Shield of Faith e) Helmet of Salvation f) Shoes of Peace

__ Protects my thoughts
__ Not my good deeds, but Jesus' work for me
__ Holds all of the other pieces together
__ Extinguishes fiery darts of accusation due to God's faithfulness
__ Provides confident footing to share Christ's message
__ The only offensive weapon that Jesus used to defeat Satan when tempted

Evaluate:

How often do I use the offensive weapon of the Sword of the Spirit, the Word of God?
Do I stand strong to share Christ's message?
Do I rest in Christ's righteousness instead of my own "good works"?
Do I compare every lie to the unchanging truth of Scripture?
Do I think of God's faithfulness to extinguish those fiery darts?

SHARE IT

"You are already children of God. What remains is for you to dress like it, to live like it, and to fight like it. The clothes, the fight, do not make you a child of the light. They show that you are a child of the light." ~ John Piper

WEDNESDAY WEEK 28

TRUTH: EPHESIANS 6:18-24

Paul asks for prayer from the Ephesian Church. Prayer is a powerful weapon against the onslaught of the Wicked One, Satan.
Our prayers are to be given in and through the ____________________.
Our prayers are to be carried out with persistence for all ____________________.
Who have I prayed for in the past few days? ____________________

____

Who have I asked to pray for me? ____________________

____

Paul asked for prayer so that he could speak the Gospel to people around him in prison.
Some of the missionaries I pray for are: ____________________

____

☐ I will let them know I have been praying for them today.

We are all ambassadors for Christ (**2 Corinthians 5:20**). We have been sent by God to represent Him before the people of all nations.

Who have I witnessed to recently? ____________________

EPHESIANS 6:21-22

Paul sent Tychicus to the Ephesian Church to inform them of his condition and to bring back word of the health of the church.
Paul warmly describes Tychicus in two ways:

____________________ ____________________

What Christian am I currently helping for Jesus' sake? ____________________

EPHESIANS 6:23-24

Paul desires that the Ephesian believers will experience great ____________________,

____________________, ____________________, and ____________________.

Am I experiencing these four things in my Christian life?

☐ **YES** ☐ **NO** ☐ **SOMEWHAT**

Do I love the Lord Jesus Christ sincerely with a genuine heart?

☐ **YES** ☐ **NO** ☐ **SOMEWHAT**

What will I do today to improve my relationship with Christ?

____

SHARE IT

"Pray also for me, that whenever I speak, words may be given me so that I will fearlessly make known the mystery of the gospel." ~ **Ephesians 6:19** (NIV)

WEEK 28 THURSDAY

TRUTH: JOHN 13:1-11

JOHN 13:1

Jesus loved His own who were in the world. Jesus felt responsible for those whom He loved on the earth.
The people whose spiritual lives I feel the most responsible for are:

____

____

Here is why I feel responsible for those individual's spiritual lives:

____

____

JOHN 13:2

Someone I know who did/does not have my best interest in mind, but I still have to interact with is ________________________.
It is hard for me to have anything other than bad feelings for this person, but it is my job to still love them. Jesus showed the best example as He washed Judas' feet even though He knew what Judas was planning.

One thing that I can do to help myself learn to love this person is to serve them by:

____.

JOHN 13:4-5

Jesus served the disciples by taking the lowest job in the room and doing it. This was an intimate job since He was washing their feet. How comfortable would I be doing what Jesus did, washing the feet of those whom I outrank?

Not Comfortable 1 2 3 4 5 Very comfortable

What act of service have I been able to do for others recently? ____________________

____

JOHN 13:6-10

Peter went from being appalled at the thought of Jesus washing his feet to wanting Jesus to also wash his head and hands. What changed his mind? ____________________

____

Have I been washed by Jesus? ☐ **YES** ☐ **NO**

SHARE IT

"Even if our own troubles are great, we should still serve. Jesus washed His disciples' feet on the way to the cross."
~ Timothy Keller

FRIDAY WEEK 28

TRUTH: JOHN 13:12-20

HN 13:12-14

Jesus asked His disciples if they understood why He did what He just did. I think the disciples were thinking He did it because: ____

____.

HN 13:15

He did this to set an example for the disciples to learn to serve each other. In my life I have observed ____________________ as a person who is excellent at serving others.

Ways I have seen them serve are: ____

____

Ways I have been able to serve lately: ____

____

N 13:18

Jesus said, "He who eats bread with Me has lifted up his heel against Me."
What is He talking about?

- Sharing a meal with anyone is a painful act.
- One of the people at the table will soon betray Him.
- It is disrespectful to eat the bread from another man's plate.
- Jesus also worked as a baker and this was bread that He made.

Who was going to be betraying Jesus?

Peter **Paul** **Mary** **Judas** **Gretchen** **John**

Sometimes I serve people thinking there is a chance I will one day be able to get something out of this; maybe they will serve or honor me for my service. But what is it like to serve a person that you know is about to betray you? ____________________

____

Would I be able to do it?

- **YES, AS LONG AS I KEPT IN MIND THAT I WAS DOING IT FOR JESUS.**
- **NO WAY.**

SHARE IT

"If our hearts resist Jesus taking our place on the floor as a servant, then our hearts also resist Him taking our place on the Cross as our Savior." ~ *Frances Ann Green*

WEEK 28 SATURDAY

TRUTH: JOHN 13:21-30

JOHN 13:26

What symbol did Jesus use to signify it was Judas who would be betraying him?

____

JOHN 13:27

What happened to Judas when Jesus dipped his bread and handed it to Judas?

- ☐ He rejected the bread.
- ☐ Satan entered him.
- ☐ Judas tried to bribe Jesus.
- ☐ The disciples were all angry it was Judas.

JOHN 13:28

True or False.

T F I have shared a meal with someone that I knew would soon be betraying me.

T F After being betrayed by a friend, I have looked back and remembered that we had shared meals together.

T F I have never been betrayed by a friend.

T F I would be able to look my betrayer in the eye before he betrayed me.

JOHN 13:29

Jesus knew that Judas was going out to betray Him, and He just let him go do it. Have I ever been in a situation like that? ____

If I was in a situation like that, how would I handle it? ____

____

In what ways have I been like Judas to Jesus, betraying His trust for simple worldly pleasures? ____

____

____

SHARE IT

"Even people who betray you are part of the plan. Jesus wouldn't get to the cross without Judas." ~ Steven Furtick

SUNDAY WEEK 29

TRUTH: JOHN 13:31-38

JOHN 13:31

Now that Judas was in motion, Jesus said God was now glorified; why does He say this?

____

JOHN 13:33

Jesus was telling the disciples that they couldn't go where He was going.

- They were probably used to His confusing talk and figured that it would make sense eventually.
- They probably understood right away that He was talking about His own death.
- They probably thought that He had an errand to run.
- They probably were planning to just try to follow Him anyway.

JOHN 13:34

"A new ______________ I give to you that you ______________ one another: as I have loved ______________, you also love one ______________."

WORD BANK: **YOU LOVE COMMANDMENT ANOTHER**

This would be a great verse to memorize. I will do my best to try to memorize this verse this week.

- Yes, I will try to memorize this verse.
- I already have this verse memorized.
- No, I will not be trying to memorize this verse.

I like to know what is going on. If I were one of Jesus' disciples, I would have had a hard time with: ____

____.

It is hard for me to trust sometimes when I know I will not like the outcome. Lately, it has been hard for me to trust God with this in my life: ____

____

Spend some time journaling/talking with God about this.

____

____

____

SHARE IT

"Love one another and you will be happy. It's as simple and difficult as that." ~ Michael Leunig

WEEK 29 MONDAY

TRUTH: JOHN 14:1-6

JOHN 14:1

"Let not your hearts be troubled..." Jesus was reminding the disciples not to be anxious over what was about to happen.

When it comes to anxiety and worry:

- I have an everyday battle; sometimes I can trust and other times the anxiety wins.
- I do not relate to those who have a problem with anxiety and worry.
- I do stress about things, but I work hard to continually give things over to Christ.
- This used to be a problem for me, but it is not anymore.

The top 3 things that I do stress about are:

1. ____________________
2. ____________________
3. ____________________

When anxiety and worry are trying to creep in, I have found the best way to deal with them is to ____________________

JOHN 14:6

What 3 things does Jesus identify Himself as?

1. ____________________
2. ____________________
3. ____________________

How does Jesus being those 3 things impact my life? ____________________

"Jesus said to him, 'I am the way, the truth, and the life. No one comes to the Father except through me." Here is what this verse means to me personally: ____________________

SHARE IT

The only thing that can truly satisfy the human heart is the One who made it.

TUESDAY WEEK 29

TRUTH: JOHN 14:7-14

JOHN 14:7

For me, faith in something that I can't see is:

- Really hard, but I am learning to take small steps of faith.
- Easy, but I tend to just throw my faith into anything blindly.
- Something I am learning about by placing my faith in God daily.
- Other ______________________________

Some of the areas where I do have the hardest time with my faith are:

____

____

____

JOHN 14:8

Jesus and the Father are one. Explain this statement.

____

____

TRUE OR FALSE.

T F If I were a disciple, I would have understood what Jesus was saying better than Philip and the other disciples.

JOHN 14:12

Jesus said that whoever believes will do greater works than He did. Did He really mean that?

- Yes, He meant that very literally.
- No, that's not what He meant.
- Kind of, He just meant it in a different way.

I don't find myself doing the same kind of works as Jesus did when He was here on earth, but I do believe that He was telling the truth that I can do greater works than these. An example of the works that I am able to do today are: ______________________________

____

____

JOHN 14:13

What is the last thing that I asked for in Jesus' name? ______________________________

____

SHARE IT

"Jesus Christ is the same yesterday, today, and forever."
~ **Hebrews 13:8**

WEEK 29 WEDNESDAY

TRUTH: JOHN 14:15-24

JOHN 14:15

I certainly do love Jesus, but I often struggle with keeping all of His commandments. Lately my struggle has been with: ______________________________________.

Right now, I will spend a few minutes praying specifically about the struggle to keep His commandments. ■ **YES** ■ **NO**

JOHN 14:16

The Helper that Jesus is talking about is:

- ■ Pastors.
- ■ The Holy Spirit.
- ■ The twelve apostles.
- ■ Other Christians in the local church.

How has the Holy Spirit helped me lately? ______________________________

____

JOHN 14:17

I would say that I know almost everything about my friends; I believe that I know ____________________ inside and out.

In my family, ____________________________ knows me better than anyone alive!

What did Jesus mean when He said that the Holy Spirit is in you and He knows you?

____

____

JOHN 14:18

"I will not leave you as ___________; I will come to you."

- ■ Loners
- ■ Comfortless
- ■ Widows
- ■ Orphans

Do I know anyone that is an orphan? ■ **YES** ■ **NO**

SHARE IT

"Without the Holy Spirit of God we can do nothing. We are as ships without wind, we are useless." ~ C.H. Spurgeon

THURSDAY WEEK 29

TRUTH: JOHN 14:25-31

JOHN 14:26

Who was the best teacher I ever had? ____________________

What are 3 things that made them a great teacher?

1. ____________________
2. ____________________
3. ____________________

Since Jesus calls the Holy Spirit, "Teacher," what are ways that the Holy Spirit teaches me?

____

____

JOHN 14:27

"____________ I leave with you; My peace I __________ to you. Not as the ____________ gives do I give to you. Let not your ___________ be ____________________, neither let it be afraid."

WORD BANK: **WORLD** **PEACE** **GIVE** **TROUBLED** **HEART**

It was really hard for me when ____________________ moved away.

If my best friend were told that their parent was just elected President of the United States and they would have to move to the White House very soon:

- ☐ I would be angry at my friend for moving.
- ☐ I would be happy for them, but be sad to see them go.
- ☐ I would ask my friend to consider staying in town.
- ☐ I would demand a recount!

Explain why Jesus said if the disciples really loved Him, they would be happy He was going away: ____________________

____

JOHN 14:29

Now that I look back, I can see the Holy Spirit was at work when: ____________

____

SHARE IT

"Trying to understand the Bible without the Holy Spirit is like trying to read a sundial by moonlight." ~ Samuel Coleridge

WEEK 29 FRIDAY

TRUTH: JOHN 15:1-11

I like to grow plants. ▢ **AGREE** ▢ **DISAGREE**

When it comes to gardening, I:

- ▢ Know nothing at all.
- ▢ Know a little bit.
- ▢ Know enough to make some plants grow.
- ▢ Am practically a farmer!

JOHN 15:5

Jesus uses the word picture of a vine and branches. What was He talking about?

- ▢ A vine has to have branches to stay alive – the vine is nothing without the branches.
- ▢ A vine and branches together are always destructive and ugly.
- ▢ The branches cannot exist without the vine; the more they embrace the vine the stronger the branches get.
- ▢ Branches and vines will all burn.

Without Jesus, I can do ______________________.

Describe a time when I tried to do something without Jesus' help and how that turned out.

____

____

JOHN 15:7

"...You will ask what you desire, and it shall be done for you." I like the end of that verse: I like that God will do whatever I want, but what does the beginning of the verse say?

____

____

How am I doing with abiding in Jesus and having His words abide in me?

Terrible 1 2 3 4 5 Great

What do I need to do to change that? ______________________________

JOHN 15:11

What would it look like for my "joy to be full"?

____

____

SHARE IT

"Being happy doesn't mean you have it all, it means being thankful to the Lord for all you have." ~ Unknown

SATURDAY WEEK 29

TRUTH: JOHN 15:12-27

JOHN 15:12

I will think about memorizing this fairly easy verse:
"This is My commandment, that you love one another as I have loved you."

- ☐ I will attempt to memorize this verse this week.
- ☐ I will not be trying to memorize this passage this week.
- ☐ I have already memorized this verse.

Right now, I would say that 4 of my closest friends are:

1. ______________________________
2. ______________________________
3. ______________________________
4. ______________________________

How do I know that they love me? ______________________________

____

How do they know that I love them? ______________________________

____

JOHN 15:13

How did Jesus show His love for us? ______________________________

____

JOHN 15:15

What does Jesus call me? ______________________________
What do I think/feel about that? ______________________________

____

JOHN 15:19

Why does "the world hate you"? (Check all that apply.)

- ☐ Because we do not find pleasure in the things that the world finds pleasure in.
- ☐ We do not stand for the things that the world stands for.
- ☐ Our standards are different and we do not allow for things that the world is OK with.
- ☐ Our purpose is different, and a world of people who serve themselves will not relate to a group of people who are following the teachings of Jesus.

SHARE IT

"Our job is to love others without stopping to inquire whether or not they are worthy." ~ Thomas Merton

WEEK 30 SUNDAY

TRUTH: JOHN 16:1-11

JOHN 16:2

Obviously, I don't agree with any terrorist, but when I read this passage, I understand a little more why someone would kill and destroy in the name of their god, because they feel it is a service to their god.

I believe terrorists and extremists are:

- People who should be hunted and destroyed.
- People who should be brought to trial and locked up for life.
- People who are just trying to follow their god, so we should leave them alone and not hold them accountable for any of their actions.
- People who have been taught something false and need our prayers that they can see the Truth.

JOHN 16:5-7

I believe the "Helper" was sent for:

- Just the twelve disciples.
- All people everywhere throughout time.
- Our dead ancestors.
- Those who have a relationship with Jesus Christ.

If I lived in Jesus' day and had the privilege to serve and follow Him in real life, I would have been crushed when He started talking about leaving and sending a "Helper" in His place.

- I agree with this statement.
- I disagree with this statement.

JOHN 16:8-11

The "Helper" would come convicting the world concerning:

- Values, Rules, Regulations
- Oppression, Taxation, Representation
- Sin, Righteousness, Judgment
- Judgment, Punishments, Consequences

How has the Helper convicted me of sin, righteousness, and judgment lately?

____

____

SHARE IT

"Just because the others are doing something, doesn't make it right." ~ Kim Malenke

MONDAY WEEK 30

TRUTH: JOHN 16:12-22

JOHN 16:13

Does the Holy Spirit speak on His own authority? ☐ **YES** ☐ **NO**

What does that mean? ______________________________

JOHN 16:16

Jesus said, "A little while and you will not see Me, and again a little while and you will see Me." Putting myself in the shoes of the ones listening to Him, that had to be so confusing! Now that it's many years later and I know the whole story, I know He means:

____

____

Jesus said so many things that made sense later, but in the moment didn't make much sense. How would I have handled that if I had been His disciple back then?

____

____

How do I handle it today when I am in a situation and it's not going my way and I don't know how it's going to end? ______________________________

____

What is a situation that I am currently in (or have recently been in) where I just don't know how this will end, but I wish I did? ______________________________

____

How should I be praying for this situation?

- ☐ Lord, give me Your answers today!
- ☐ Lord, if you will give me Your answers, I will do two things for You today.
- ☐ Lord, give me the patience I need to wait for Your answer.
- ☐ Lord, I'm tired of waiting; I command You to show me the answer.

In the song called, "The Precipice" by The Classic Crime, the lyrics say "Whatever the cost, whether it works out or not, I'll follow you with my heart."

- ☐ I'm ok with "whatever the cost" if I know it will work out my way.
- ☐ I'm ok with "whatever the cost" even "whether it works out or not!"

SHARE IT

"Patience is the calm accepting that things can happen in a different order than you had in mind." ~ David G. Allen

WEEK 30 TUESDAY

TRUTH: JOHN 16:23-33

JOHN 16:24

I believe that God:

- Honestly wants me to be filled with joy and will do whatever it takes to give me the opportunity for my joy to be full.
- Has things He wants me to do, so He will use my joy as a reward for doing those things.
- Wants me to be filled with joy but wants me to earn it first so He sets up a list of things I need to do to accomplish that.
- Wants me to find pure joy but requires that I seek it out and find it, since He is hiding it from me.

JOHN 16:25

I love the teachings of Jesus but when He uses "figures of speech," it is hard to understand. ☐ **AGREE** ☐ **DISAGREE**

If I were following Jesus and I couldn't understand all of His teachings at this point, what would make me continue to follow Him? ______________________________

____

What is one of the teachings of Jesus that I still don't understand? ______________________________

____

JOHN 16:32

Has anyone ever told you that you would soon be moving to a different location?

☐ **YES**, I can remember moving from one home to another.

☐ **NO**, I have actually never moved.

The disciples were only a couple of years into this adventure of following Jesus and seeing Him slowly change the world. Now He was telling them that they would be breaking up and scattering to different locations. How would I have handled that information? ______________________________

____

JOHN 16:33

Even though I will have tribulation in this world, why can I be of good cheer? ______________________________

____

SHARE IT

"Followers of Jesus don't always know where they are going, but they always know Who they are with." ~ David Platt

WEDNESDAY WEEK 30

TRUTH: JOHN 17:1-13

JOHN 17:1

Jesus asks God to glorify Him, but for what purpose?

____

JOHN 17:4

The last major job I had to do, that I had to pour a lot of effort into but in the end, I got to see it accomplished, was: ______________________________

____

The feeling of accomplishing a major task is:

- Relieving because now I can relax.
- Stressful because now I will be judged on my work.
- Fulfilling because that is what I was working toward.
- Sad because the project is done.

Jesus was at the point where He had accomplished all that the Father set before Him. How do I think He felt about what He had accomplished so far? ______________

____

JOHN 17:5

Where was Jesus before the world existed? ______________________

A recent job I really felt God asked me to do, or that God led me to invest time and energy in was ______________________________________.

Jesus was speaking in this passage about a job well done. However most of the time I feel that I'm just always working on one long job when it comes to my spiritual life. What is the value of setting small goals and seeing them accomplished? ______________

____

Three long-term spiritual goals I have are:

1) ______________ 2) ______________ 3)______________

Three short-term, measurable spiritual goals I have are:

1) ______________ 2) ______________ 3)______________

SHARE IT

"There is no passion to be found in settling for a life that is less than the one you are capable of living." ~ Nelson Mandela

WEEK 30 THURSDAY

TRUTH: JOHN 17:14-26

JOHN 17:15

There are so many opportunities to sin and mess up while we are here on earth, yet God chooses to leave us here on earth even after we become Christ-followers. We recognize this means that there must be a reason for why He left us here, and I believe that reason is:

____

JOHN 17:17

According to this verse, what is "truth"? ______________________________

JOHN 17:18

Have you ever felt like you were being directly sent by God into the world? On a missions trip? To a specific person? To a job that you felt like you had complete leading by God to accomplish?

- **YES**, I felt completely called to ______________________________.
- **NO**, I haven't felt Him leading me that directly.

JOHN 17:20

Jesus said that He was not asking for these that He had interacted with, but He was thinking of the future. He said He was praying also for those who would believe on the word of these disciples. Do I take a future perspective when I am thinking about living my life for God? Have I ever once prayed for those that I will come in contact with in the future?

- **YES**, I am always thinking ahead.
- **NO**, I've never heard such a concept.

I will take some time right now to pray for the people God will put in my path over the next few years.

- **YES**, I took the time to pray for that.
- **NO**, I am not going to do that.

I recognize some of the most influential experiences that people have had for God has been on missions trips. Today I am going to research different missions trips that might be available to me. I will talk with my youth pastor, or google a missions trip opportunity such as Word of Life Student Fusion.

- **YES**, I will look into that.
- **NO**, I will not be doing that.

SHARE IT

Success is knowing that at the end of the day, what you exchanged a day of your life for made a difference in the kingdom.

FRIDAY WEEK 30

TRUTH: JOHN 18:1-14

What is a place that is special to me, one that my friends know about that I like to hang out at? Or a special location my family likes to visit? Or just a special place where I go to sit alone?

____

Have I ever shared this location with someone and then have that come back to hurt me later? They bring more people, they don't treat it the same way that I do? ______________

____

JOHN 18:1-2

How do you think Jesus and the other disciples felt when Judas chose to bring the group of soldiers to that location? ______________________________

____

Judas spent a long time with Jesus and his fellow disciples listening to Him teach on peace, etc., but Judas felt the need to bring a small army of soldiers and officers with him to grab Jesus. Have I ever had someone who I thought was a friend become an accuser?

☐ **YES** ☐ **NO**

What would I think if I were a disciple and I saw that Judas thought he needed to bring an army with him? ______________________________

JOHN 18:6

What did the soldiers do when Jesus said, "I am He"?

- ☐ Drew their swords to fight
- ☐ Set an ambush and jumped out of the darkness
- ☐ Fell back on the ground
- ☐ Rushed Jesus and the disciples to fight

JOHN 18:10-11

Peter was ready to fight, but Jesus told him to back off. What reason did Jesus give?

____

What is something God is asking me to do? ______________________________

____

SHARE IT

Those who don't know the value of loyalty can never appreciate the cost of betrayal.

WEEK 30 SATURDAY

TRUTH: JOHN 18:15-27

JOHN 18:15

What did Peter do after Jesus had been taken into custody?

- Ran and hid with the rest of the disciples
- Hired a lawyer to work for Jesus
- Followed Him to the high priest's house
- Challenged Judas to a duel

JOHN 18:17

Who was the first person to ask Peter if he was a follower of Jesus? ____________________

JOHN 18:20

Jesus answered the high priest by saying, "I have never done anything in secret." He was pointing out that if the Pharisees wanted to accuse Him, they could have done it anyway since He had always been teaching in public.

When my accusers come after me, is it easy to defend myself or do I have to scramble to make people believe what I am saying?

- It is hard for my accusers to find ammunition to use against me.
- My accusers always seem to have something to accuse, and I always seem to be on my toes explaining things.
- I've never been accused of anything.

Jesus said that they could ask anyone what He had said.
The last time someone accused me, it was about ____________________________________
____ and in my defense, I could point them to ____________________________________ to get the whole story.

Do I normally rely on one person to back up my story when I am accused, or am I so above reproach that I can just say, "Ask anyone"? ____________________________________

JOHN 18:25-27

What happened the next two times when Peter was asked if he was a follower of Jesus?

- He boldly accepted the title and didn't worry about the cost.
- He turned and ran.
- He simply denied it.
- He started a fight.

SHARE IT

Do the right thing, even when no one is looking.

SUNDAY WEEK 31

TRUTH: JOHN 18:28-40

JOHN 18:28

Why did the Jewish leaders not go into the governor's quarters?

- ☐ They were not invited.
- ☐ They didn't have any time.
- ☐ They didn't want to be seen.
- ☐ They believed doing so would defile themselves so they would not be able to participate in the Passover meal.

Passover is observed by Jews to remember when God passed over the Jewish homes when killing the Egyptian firstborn during the last of the plagues to set the Israelites free from bondage to Egypt.

Why is it so significant that all of these events with Jesus are happening at Passover?

____

____

JOHN 18:31

Why did the leaders take Him to the Roman government?

- ☐ All rulings had to come down from Roman officials.
- ☐ Jesus had broken Roman law so He had to be tried by Rome.
- ☐ It was illegal for Jews to condemn someone to death.
- ☐ Jesus requested a private audience with Pilate.

JOHN 18:33-40

Read this, paying special attention to Pilate. Does it feel like he was on board with the Jewish leaders?

- ☐ No, it seems that Pilate didn't think of Jesus as a threat.
- ☐ No, he thought Jesus was worse than the Jews thought He was.
- ☐ Yes, Pilate agreed with the Jewish leaders right away.
- ☐ Pilate had been following Jesus for a while and had planned to bring Him into custody.

What kind of answers did Jesus give in this interaction? ______________________

____

How often do I go along with the crowd even when I know they are wrong? __________

____

Do I **search for the truth on my own** or **just believe what anyone tells me**?

SHARE IT

"If it has to choose who is to be crucified, the crowd will always save Barabbas." ~ Jean Cocteau

WEEK 31 MONDAY

TRUTH: JOHN 19:1-11

JOHN 19:2-3

Why did they give Jesus a crown of thorns and why did they choose a purple colored robe?

- ☐ Purple is the color of royalty and the crown is fit for a king.
- ☐ Those were the items that always went with this kind of crime.

The people were mocking Jesus and punching and hitting Him for fun. He could have stopped it at any time. Have I ever been in a situation like that where I had to simply take what was being dished out because it was for a better cause? (Explain) ____________

____

____

How does it make me feel when people make fun of me for being a Jesus follower?

____

JOHN 19:6

Who in the crowd was leading the charge by yelling, "Crucify Him, Crucify Him!"?

- ☐ The disciples
- ☐ The townspeople
- ☐ The chief priests and officers
- ☐ Roman citizens and officials

The Jewish leaders wanted to be innocent of Jesus' blood, but they also wanted Him dead. They needed this to sound like it was coming from the crowd, but what was really happening? ____

Have I ever been in a situation where all of a sudden, a lot of people were against me because of one person stirring them up? (Explain)

- ☐ **YES**: ____
- ☐ **NO**
- ☐ Not me personally, but I have watched it happen to someone else:

____

____

SHARE IT

Remember that voting with the crowd can get you Barabbas instead of Jesus.

TUESDAY WEEK 31

TRUTH: JOHN 19:12-22

Read this passage paying attention to Pilate's actions.

What do I think Pilate's feelings about Jesus were? ____________________

What do I think Pilate's feelings about this situation were? ____________________

What do I think Pilate's thoughts about the Jewish leaders were? ____________________

What do I think Pilate should have done? ____________________

What would I have done in Pilate's place? ____________________

JOHN 19:19

What did Pilate write on the sign to be hung on the cross with Jesus? ____________________

JOHN 19:21

What did the chief priest want Pilate to change the sign to say? ____________________

JOHN 19:22

Pilate decided to keep the sign as it was. What do you think Pilate was trying to say to the Jewish leaders by his actions? ____________________

There are all kinds of stories in the traditions and legends about what went on in Pilate's head throughout this time, conversations with his wife, his advisors, etc. Pretending that I was alive back then, or able to mail a letter back in time to Pilate, write a short letter to Pilate here:

Dear Pontius Pilate,

____

SHARE IT

"It's better to risk saving a guilty man than condemning an innocent one." ~ Voltaire

WEEK 31 WEDNESDAY

TRUTH: JOHN 19:23-30

JOHN 19:23

What did the soldiers do with Jesus's clothing?

- Gave them to the poor
- Put them in a pile with the rest of the clothes from criminals
- Divided His clothing among themselves and cast lots for the last piece
- Put them back on Jesus to give Him some modesty

JOHN 19:24

Which Scripture did it fulfill? ______________________________

How many Scripture prophesies were fulfilled in today's passage? ____________

Think about the events of those days: the disciples were scattered and hiding since the Jewish leaders just killed their leader. If I were one of the disciples, of course I'd like to say that I would be there by Jesus' side the whole time, but the reality is that I would probably be: ______________________________.

JOHN 19:25-27

"The disciple whom He loved" is commonly accepted as John. That is how he refers to himself in this book. We see that John was there at the crucifixion, but apart from that, the people who are listed were all women. Putting myself in the shoes of these women, what would I be thinking right now watching Jesus die? ____________________

____

JOHN 19:28

Do I think Jesus had the presence of mind to know what was prophesied to check each one off the list while He was in the middle of being crucified, or did the noting of the fulfillment come from looking back after the fact? ____________________

____

SHARE IT

"It costs God nothing, so far as we know, to create nice things: but to convert rebellious wills cost Him crucifixion."
~ C.S. Lewis

THURSDAY WEEK 31

TRUTH: JOHN 19:31-42

JOHN 19:31

Why did the Jewish leaders want to speed up the process of crucifixion by breaking their legs?

- Too big of a crowd was forming
- It would break a religious rule of working on the Sabbath to take a man off the cross so they wanted them dead before the Sabbath.
- They were afraid that Jesus would come off the cross and destroy them.
- They were afraid that the disciples would attack.

They were so focused on not breaking the religious rules on the Sabbath, but they are here because they just killed a man. That is the way that they led their religion. I have seen some things done in the name of religion that have really seemed like double standards and really frustrated me.

- **YES**, I have. (Explain)____________________________________
- **NO**, I have never seen anything like that.

When I see hypocrisy done in the name of Christianity, I: ________________________
____.

It is sad that someone would judge Christianity based on some hypocrites that they have met so they never actually start a real relationship with Jesus. What can I say to someone who tells me that they looked into Christianity but they decided against it because of hypocritical Christians that they met? ________________________________
____
____

JOHN 19:37-38

So many different Scriptures are being fulfilled just in this one event. Did the people recognize these things happening at the time or did they realize them later when John mentioned them in his writings? ____________________________________

Do I take the time to look back at my day, week, year, etc. to see all of the things that were actually "God moments" that I just didn't notice at the time?

YES I DO THAT. **I DIDN'T DO IT BEFORE, BUT I WILL START NOW.**

SHARE IT

"Hypocrites get offended by the truth." ~ *Jess C. Scott*

WEEK 31 FRIDAY

TRUTH: JOHN 20:1-10

JOHN 20:1

Who came early to the tomb on Sunday morning?

- Peter
- Mary Magdalene
- Mary the mother of Jesus
- Pontius Pilate

JOHN 20:2

Mary ran to the disciples to tell them that someone had taken Jesus. Remember, they didn't understand that Jesus had told them that He would raise from the dead, so their first instinct was to think that the Jewish leaders took the body of Jesus to do something awful to Him.

If I were one of the followers of Christ then:

- I would have known what the Scripture said and remembered all the times Jesus said things about coming back, and I would have believed that He had raised from the dead.
- I would have been afraid and headed back to my home.
- I would have gone directly to the Jewish leaders and demanded to know where He was.
- I would have sat inside the tomb and waited for an answer.

JOHN 20:5

The disciple whom Jesus loved (most likely John) got to the tomb before Peter, but he hesitated and just looked in; he did not go inside.

What is an area in my spiritual life that I do that same thing: instead of going in to see what Jesus has for me, I hesitate and hang back for a minute and let someone else go first?

____

____

JOHN 20:6

Peter headed right in to where Jesus had been.
What area in my spiritual life have I been able to go headfirst and dive right in?

____

JOHN 20:10

What would I be feeling right now as a disciple? ____________________

____

SHARE IT

"Anyone can claim to be God, but Jesus backed it up with an empty tomb." ~ Lee Strobel

SATURDAY WEEK 31

TRUTH: **JOHN 20:11-18**

JOHN 20:11

The men both went back to their homes. Maybe they were hiding, maybe they felt that they had things to do, but Mary stayed right there. The Bible says she stayed and wept. When is the last time that I wept over something? Not just a cry from pain, or a little emotional cry over something. When is the last time that I wept, and what was it over?

____

____

JOHN 20:12

Mary did not yet believe that Jesus was going to raise from the dead. She told the angels that she wept because they had taken her Lord away. Even though she was not expecting Him to raise from the dead, she still called Him "Lord." Why was that significant?

____

____

At this point would I still be calling Him "Lord"? Or would I be sitting there thinking over the past years wondering if I fell for the tricks of an incredible talker and miracle worker?

____

Do I call Him "Lord" right now in my life? ☐ **YES** ☐ **NO**

JOHN 20:14-16

A man started talking to her: it was Jesus, but she didn't recognize Him. She thought it was:

- ☐ A Roman Guard
- ☐ A Gardener
- ☐ Peter or John
- ☐ Pontius Pilate

Do I recognize Jesus when He is talking to me?

☐ **YES** ☐ **NO** ☐ Sometimes

When she realized it was Jesus, what did she call Him? ______________________________

What has Jesus taught me recently? ______________________________

____

JOHN 20:18

She went to the disciples and told them what she saw. If I am a disciple what would I be thinking and feeling after hearing this? ______________________________

____

SHARE IT

He is risen just as He said He would!

WEEK 32 SUNDAY

TRUTH: JOHN 20:19-31

JOHN 20:19

The disciples were locked in the room out of fear of the Jews who killed Jesus. I probably haven't been in a situation where I needed to physically lock a door and hide for my life, but I do have plenty of locked doors in my life. Some doors I lock so that no one knows what is inside because I am ashamed of the truth. Some doors I lock because I haven't been able to open up and talk with people about it. Other doors I lock because they are things that are special to me, but I'm afraid if others know about it they will tell me I am not good enough or it will never work. So many doors in life are locked out of fear.

What are some of my locked doors? ____________________

____

____

Jesus was standing among them. Notice – no one unlocked the doors! Jesus can get through my locks; I'm not alone in here. How does that make me feel about these locked doors of mine? ____________________

____

JOHN 20:20

They were afraid which makes sense – people don't normally just appear. So Jesus reassured them by showing His nail scarred hands.

When have I seen Jesus' handprints on my life? ____________________

____

____

JOHN 20:27-29

Jesus proved Himself to Thomas in a very physical way. Then He said, "Blessed are those ____________________."

That includes me!

Is it **easy** or **hard** for me to believe in Jesus without being able to see Him? (Circle)

JOHN 20:30-31

Why are some of these miracles that Jesus performed written down for us to read?

____

____

SHARE IT

"Hope is putting faith to work, when doubt would be easier."
~ Thomas S. Monson

MONDAY WEEK 32

TRUTH: JOHN 21:1-14

JOHN 21:1

What was this group of disciples doing when the story picks up?

- Hiding in a locked room
- Out together fishing
- Hunting down the Jewish leaders that killed Jesus
- Scattered throughout the area

They fished because that is what they did. I don't want to over spiritualize my life so that I feel like God only wants me to do things that are seen as "Christian" activities. I need to be going about my regular life because God gave me these desires and skills so that I could glorify Him while I do my regular life.

What are some of the desires that I have or skills that I have that I can be using to let people see Christ's love in my life?

1. ______________________
2. ______________________
3. ______________________

JOHN 21:7

When John said, "It is the Lord," how did Peter respond? ______________________

____

What is a time in my life that I responded directly to Jesus by showing up in a way like Peter responded? ______________________

____

JOHN 21:12

They didn't have to ask if He was Jesus – they just knew it. As I go about my life asking God to show me what He has for me and what He wants me to be doing day in and day out, I get a lot of messages. How do I know which voice is Jesus'?

____

____

JOHN 21:13

They sat and ate breakfast with Jesus. When do you spend your quality time with Jesus?

____

SHARE IT

"There is only one thing more precious than our time and that's who we spend it on." ~ Leo Christopher

WEEK 32 TUESDAY

TRUTH: JOHN 21:15-25

JOHN 21:15-17

Jesus asked Peter the same thing 3 times; what is that question?

____

Why would he have asked Peter 3 times? (Hint: **John 18:17, 25-27**)

____

Each time that Jesus asked and Peter said, "Yes," Jesus gave a different response; write them here:

1. ____
2. ____
3. ____

JOHN 21:22

Jesus told Peter how he would one day die and then Peter asked Jesus about John. How did Jesus respond to him? ___________________________

____

I find myself struggling with comparing myself to others sometimes. My biggest temptation to do that is:_____________________________

____

JOHN 21:24

What would it be like to have the opportunity to follow Jesus and live so closely with Him throughout His ministry, and then have the opportunity to write about it? ___________

____

____

____

JOHN 21:25

John stated that the world could not hold a book that listed all that Jesus had done. If I were to write a book about my life with Jesus so far and I could only write about four things that have happened to me in my life that Jesus was responsible for, those things would be:

1. ____
2. ____
3. ____
4. ____

SHARE IT

"Following Jesus is simple, not easy. Love until it hurts, and then love more." ~ Mother Theresa

WEDNESDAY WEEK 32

TRUTH: EXODUS 12:1-13

EXODUS 12:1-7

God commanded Israel to sacrifice a __________ and to put the ___________ on the doorposts.

The lambs the Israelites were to sacrifice were to be: (Check one)

- Female
- Without blemish
- Several years old

Any household that didn't sacrifice a lamb according to God's instructions would experience death. The lamb's death was a substitute for each household. This truth makes me feel: (Circle one)

CONFUSED UPSET INDIFFERENT CURIOUS UNEASY

Match the passages below with the truths that show how the sacrifice of Jesus Christ was similar to the Passover sacrifice.

1 Corinthians 5:7	**He is our perfect sacrifice (without blemish).**
Hebrews 9:14	**He is our substitute.**
2 Corinthians 5:21	**He is our Passover Lamb.**

The Passover lamb was an important sacrifice, but a greater sacrifice was coming. Why do I think Jesus' death was a greater sacrifice? ______________________________

____

____

How do I think the Israelites should have responded to God's saving grace toward them?

____

Do I believe Jesus is a greater sacrifice than the Passover lamb? **YES** **NO**

If Jesus is the greatest sacrifice, what should my response be to Him?

____

SHARE IT

"But God demonstrates His own love toward us, in that while we were still sinners, Christ died for us." ~ **Romans 5:8**

WEEK 32 THURSDAY

TRUTH: EXODUS 12:14-24

EXODUS 12:14-20

This feast was to be repeated by Israel as a memorial for how many years?

- ☐ One or two years
- ☐ It was not repeated after this.
- ☐ Throughout every generation as a lasting ordinance

Why would it be so important for Israel to celebrate on a regular basis to remember what God was going to do? ____

____

What are some ways I have seen God work in my life? ______________________________

____.

How important is it to me that I remember these works of God in my life?

Not Important 1 2 3 4 5 Very Important

Have I ever praised God's work in my life? ☐ **YES** ☐ **NO**

My favorite way to praise God is:

- ☐ Songs of praise
- ☐ Prayer
- ☐ Writing psalms to Him
- ☐ Something else: ______________________________

EXODUS 12:21-24

The Israelite leaders needed to lead by example.
Have I had opportunities to lead others by example? ☐ **YES** ☐ **NO**

What are some ways I have led others by example?
At School: ______________________________
At Home: ______________________________
At Church: ______________________________
With Friends: ______________________________

Have I ever considered that when I am open about praising God for His work in my life, it will encourage others to praise Him? ☐ **YES** ☐ **NO**

I will lead by example by praising God every day. ☐ **YES** ☐ **NO**

SHARE IT

"I will sing to the LORD, because He has dealt bountifully with me." ~ **Psalm 13:6**

FRIDAY WEEK 32

TRUTH: EXODUS 12:25-36

EXODUS 12:25-28

TRUE OR FALSE.

T F After God told Israel all that they needed to do and all that He would do, they responded by disobeying.

Do I trust that God's promises for the present and future will always come true?

YES **NO**

EXODUS 12:29-36

Match the verses from what happened with the earlier passages when God told Moses these things were going to happen.

12:29 – All the firstborn in Egypt died	**11:2-3**
12:31-32 – Pharaoh told all Israel to go	**12:11**
12:33-34 – Israel left Egypt in haste	**11:1**
12:35-36 – Israel plundered the Egyptians	**11:4-5**

Did God's word to Moses come true in the end? **YES** **NO**

Do you think Moses may have had some doubts about God's promises? **YES** **NO**

How much do I trust God's promises to me that are in the Bible?

Not Very Much 1 2 3 4 5 Complete Trust

What does **Numbers 23:19** say about God and His promises?

What are some of God's promises I struggle to trust in my life?

Because God's word came true for Moses and Israel, His promises to me will also hold true.

I agree with this statement. I disagree with this statement.

I need to think some more.

SHARE IT

"God does not give us everything we want, but He does fulfill His promises, leading us along the best and straightest paths to Himself." ~ Dietrich Bonhoeffer

WEEK 32 SATURDAY

TRUTH: EXODUS 12:37-51

EXODUS 12:37-43

Israel's deliverance by God from Egypt would be remembered every year with what?

- A party
- Passover
- Reading the Bible

Why would it be important for the Israelites to have Passover each year?

____

EXODUS 12:44-51

What was the requirement for the Israelite and foreigner who wanted to partake in the Passover?

- They could not be Egyptian.
- The males had to be circumcised.
- They had to live in Israel at least one year.

If I were an Israelite, each year we celebrated Passover I would feel:

EXCITED BLESSED THANKFUL SAD OBLIGATED NOTHING

As followers of Jesus Christ, what is our special memorial?

- Church service
- Communion/Lord's Supper
- Baptism

What is the point of Communion? (**1 Corinthians 11:23-26**) ____________________

____

Have I ever participated in Communion at church? **YES** **NO**

How do I feel when I celebrate Communion? ____________________

____

Passover was important for Israel to remember God delivered them from Egypt. Communion is important to remember that God through Jesus' death and resurrection delivered me from sin.

- This is my view of Communion.
- I need to think about this more.
- I'm still not convinced Communion is important.

SHARE IT

I will never forget Christ's sacrifice for me!

SUNDAY WEEK 33

TRUTH: EXODUS 13:1-10

EXODUS 13:1-7

God continued to remind Israel how they were to remember what He had done for them.

What are some ways I regularly recognize what God has done in my life?

- ☐ By praising Him in prayer
- ☐ By journaling what He is doing in my life
- ☐ By singing songs of praise to Him
- ☐ By worshiping Him wherever I go

Which of the above could I spend more time doing?

____

EXODUS 13:8-10

Not only was remembering God's works important for each Israelite, but in doing so they would be teaching: (Check one)

- ☐ Each other.
- ☐ Their children.
- ☐ Moses.

Have I ever considered that by outwardly recognizing God's goodness, I could have opportunities to share what He has done with others? ☐ **YES** ☐ **NO**

If someone asked me what God has done in my life, do I know what I would say?
☐ **YES** ☐ **NO**

List some ways that God has blessed me in life. ______________________________

____

____

Have I ever shared these things with others? ☐ **YES** ☐ **NO**

What am I most afraid of when sharing God with those who do not know Him?

____

I am committing to sharing God with others whenever I have the opportunity.
☐ **YES** ☐ **NO**

Spend some time in prayer asking God for opportunities to share Him with others. ☐

SHARE IT

God has blessed me—now I'll bless others by sharing Him!

WEEK 33 MONDAY

TRUTH: EXODUS 13:11-22

EXODUS 13:11-16

In God's continued commands to Israel, He reminds them at the end that they were freed by ______________________________.(**v. 16**)

EXODUS 13:17-18

It would have made sense for Israel to go through the Philistine territory because it was nearby. Why did God lead them through a longer path? ____________________

____

Have I ever felt like God's leading and timing in my life take longer than I would like?

☐ **YES** ☐ **NO**

God had a purpose in taking Israel the long way to the Promised Land, and sometimes He has a purpose taking the long way in my situation.

☐ I agree with this statement. ☐ I disagree with this statement.

☐ I need to think some more.

EXODUS 13:21-22

How did God lead Israel each day so that they knew they were going the right way? (Check one)

☐ The pillar of cloud and pillar of fire
☐ By telling Moses where to go
☐ They just knew where to go

Where can I look to receive God's direction in my life? (Check one)

☐ My pastor
☐ My friends
☐ The Bible

What would some dangers have been for Israel if they went their own way? __________

____

What are dangers I face if I go my own way without God's direction? ______________

____.

What will I do with these truths? (Circle all that apply.)

A. Trust God's timing in my situations
B. Look to God's Word (the Bible) for His direction
C. Stop trying to do things my way, and let Him lead me

SHARE IT

"He makes me to lie down in green pastures; He leads me beside the still waters." ~ **Psalm 23:2**

TUESDAY WEEK 33

TRUTH: EXODUS 14:1-14

EXODUS 14:1-9

God told Moses again what was about to happen.
What was Pharaoh going to do?

____

At this point, Moses had every reason to trust God's Word.
Have I decided to fully trust God's Word also? ☐ **YES** ☐ **NO**

EXODUS 14:10-12

How did the Israelites react to the coming danger?

- ☐ Courage
- ☐ Fear and doubt
- ☐ Trust in God

With all the Israelites had seen God do, how should they have responded? ____________

____

Sometimes when life gets difficult, I doubt God instead of trust Him. ☐ **YES** ☐ **NO**

EXODUS 14:13-14

Moses encouraged the people that they did not need to fear because ______________________ was fighting for them.

What are some things that have caused me to be fearful and doubt God?

____

____

____

God did not promise Israel the road would be easy, but He was with them every step of the way. What does that say about God? (Check all that apply.)

- ☐ He is faithful.
- ☐ He cares for His people.
- ☐ Something else: ______________________________

In the same way, Jesus said His followers would face ______________ in life, but they can "be of good cheer" because He has ______________________________.
(**John 16:33**)

In times of trouble, I will choose to trust God and not doubt. ☐ **YES** ☐ **NO**

SHARE IT

"Never be afraid to trust an unknown future to a known God."
~ Corrie Ten Boom

WEEK 33 WEDNESDAY

TRUTH: EXODUS 14:15-31

EXODUS 14:15-17

What two things was God preparing to do?

- Divide the sea
- Destroy Egypt
- Harden the hearts of the Egyptians
- Nothing

How would you feel knowing God had a specific plan for the situation?

CONFIDENT　SCARED　EXCITED　JOYFUL　UPSET　NERVOUS

EXODUS 14:18-20

After telling Moses this, what did the Angel of the Lord do? ______________________________

____

EXODUS 14:21-31

Was God successful in rescuing His people? **YES** **NO**

The truths this story reveals to me about God are: (Check all that apply.)

- God is more powerful than my circumstances.
- Sometimes God works in ways I do not see.
- God is worthy of my trust.
- Something else: ______________________________

Was it necessary for Israel to fear the Egyptians (**v. 12**) when God was with them? **YES** **NO**

Do I believe God is always with me? **YES** **NO**

What truth does **Hebrews 13:5** reveal to believers about God?

____

If God is always with me, is it necessary for me to fear when troubles and trials arise in my life? **YES** **NO**

Instead of being afraid, how should I respond when trouble surrounds me?

- By trusting God is at work
- Fearing until God proves Himself to me

SHARE IT

"Because God is at work, I'll be at peace." ~ Andrew Krop

THURSDAY WEEK 33

TRUTH: EXODUS 15:1-13

EXODUS 15:1

After God brought about deliverance, who sang praises to Him? ______________________

____

What was the last trouble God delivered me from? ______________________

____

How did I respond to God after He delivered me from that trouble?
- Prayed to God
- Sang praises to God
- Told others about what He had done
- I did not recognize His deliverance in any special way.

EXODUS 15:2-13

What did Israel and Moses sing about? (Check one)
- How scared they had been
- How amazing God is
- About their own greatness

What are my favorite songs to sing to the Lord? ______________________

____

How often do I praise God alongside other believers? (Circle one)

NEVER DAILY WEEKLY MONTHLY RARELY

It is important for believers to worship God together.
- I agree with this statement.
- I disagree with this statement.
- I need to think some more.

TRUE OR FALSE.

T F According to **Romans 15:5-6**, believers should glorify God together.

In light of this truth, I will respond by: (Check one)
- Continuing to worship God with others.
- Not changing how I worship.
- Starting a habit of worshiping God alongside others.

The church where I go to praise God with others is ______________________

____.

SHARE IT

"Oh, magnify the LORD with me, and let us exalt His name together." ~ **Psalm 34:3**

WEEK 33 FRIDAY

TRUTH: EXODUS 15:14-27

EXODUS 15:14-21

Miriam, Moses, and all Israel had immediately responded to God's deliverance with: (Check one)

- ☐ Prayer to God.
- ☐ Setting up a memorial.
- ☐ Singing praises to God.

Have I ever been so excited at God's work in my life that my praise to Him continued for many days? ☐ **YES** ☐ **NO**

EXODUS 15:22-24

Only a few days after praising God, what dilemma did the Israelites face? ____________

____

Have I ever praised God one day to only find myself in a crisis a short time later?
☐ **YES** ☐ **NO**

How did I respond in that crisis? ____________________________

____

EXODUS 15:25-27

The Israelites responded to their crisis by grumbling to Moses; what did Moses do?

- ☐ Grumbled back at them
- ☐ Got angry with God
- ☐ Cried out to God for help

When I face a crisis, who do I go to for help first?

- ☐ My parents
- ☐ My friends
- ☐ God
- ☐ Someone else: ____________________

Sometimes when I focus on my circumstances, I forget the things God has done in my life.
☐ **YES** ☐ **NO**

When I notice that my praise has turned to grumbling, how should I respond?
(**1 Peter 5:6-7**)

____

SHARE IT

"God's plans for your life far exceed the circumstances of your day." ~ Louie Giglio

SATURDAY WEEK 33

TRUTH: EXODUS 16:1-13

EXODUS 16:1-3

After going through hard times in the wilderness, how did Israel begin to describe their time in Egypt? ______________________________

What was Israel's time in Egypt really like? (**Exodus 5:13-14**)

____

Israel's complaint was ultimately not against Moses, but against:
- Aaron.
- Egypt.
- God.

Israel began to forget the pain of Egypt and instead desired their old life. Have I ever found myself desiring sins of my old lifestyle? **YES** **NO**

How do I typically respond when tempted to return to old sins? ______________________________

____

EXODUS 16:4-13

How did God provide for Israel? ______________________________

____

God revealed to Moses and Aaron that this situation was going to:
- End in Israel's destruction.
- Test Israel.
- Challenge Moses and Aaron's leadership abilities.

God had wonderful things planned for Israel's future, but their faith would need to be tested first. Do I believe He has a plan for my life? **YES** **NO**

Do I see ways God tests my faith to strengthen it? **YES** **NO**

What are some situations that have caused me to grow in my faith?

____

According to **James 1:2-4**, what should the testing of my faith produce?

____

SHARE IT

"And not only that, but we also glory in tribulations, knowing that tribulation produces perseverance; and perseverance, character; and character, hope." ~ **Romans 5:3-4**

WEEK 34 SUNDAY

TRUTH: EXODUS 16:14-22

EXODUS 16:14-18

When God provided the bread for the Israelites, they were to gather it according to ______________________________. (**v. 16**)

The Israelites were only to gather what was needed. This would prevent sins such as:

- Gluttony
- Anger
- Greed

EXODUS 16:19-20

Other than only gathering what was needed, what other requirement did Moses command Israel? (**v. 19**) ______________________________

Did Israel obey Moses' instructions exactly? **YES** **NO**

What were the consequences of disobeying? ______________________________

EXODUS 16:21-22

How often did the Israelites go gather this bread?

- Once a week
- Daily
- Three times a day

This test from God was so that Israel would learn to trust God to provide for their daily needs. Do I trust God to do this in my life? **YES** **NO**

Here are some daily needs I see that God provides in my life. ______________________________

____

What is the difference between wants and needs? ______________________________

____

According to **Matthew 6:30-34**, Jesus said that instead of worrying about my daily needs, instead I should do what? (**v. 33**)

____

I commit to trusting God for my daily needs. **YES** **NO**

SHARE IT

"And my God shall supply all your need according to His riches in glory by Christ Jesus." ~ **Philippians 4:19**

MONDAY WEEK 34

TRUTH: EXODUS 16:23-36

EXODUS 16:23

Here God establishes the Sabbath with Israel. What two words are used to describe the weekly Sabbath?

- ☐ Holy
- ☐ Saturday
- ☐ Rest/Observance
- ☐ Manna

The Sabbath was restful because Israel was to do no work; it was holy because it was dedicated to worshiping and focusing on God. Does this mean Israel did not focus on God the rest of the week? ☐ **YES** ☐ **NO**

Is there a particular day of the week that I rest and spend in focused worship on God?
☐ **YES** ☐ **NO**

What day do I intentionally worship God above all other activities?

- ☐ Sunday
- ☐ A different day: ____________________
- ☐ I do not do this at all.

If I do set aside a day of intentionally worshiping God, do I also find time to worship God during the busy days of the week? ☐ **YES** ☐ **NO**

Using the space below, what are some ways that I worship God?

____

____

____

EXODUS 16:24-36

How did God provide so Israel did not have to gather bread on the Sabbath? __________

____

It is important that I spend time each week resting and focusing on God.

- ☐ I agree with this statement.
- ☐ I disagree with this statement.
- ☐ I need to think some more.

Am I willing to commit myself to setting aside one day each week for intentional worship?
☐ **YES** ☐ **NO**

Spend time in prayer and worship now. ☐

SHARE IT

I serve a God so worthy of praise and worship!

WEEK 34 TUESDAY

TRUTH: EXODUS 17:1-16

EXODUS 17:1-7

The next trial the Israelites faced was that they had no ______________________. (**v. 1**)

By complaining about the situation, Israel was actually doubting:
- Moses
- Aaron
- God
- Each other

How did God provide for Israel in this trial? (**v. 6**) ______________________________
____

EXODUS 17:8-14

Now the Israelites faced a battle with ______________________________________.

How did God provide for Israel in this trial?
- By giving them victory
- By turning Amalek away
- He did not provide for them

EXODUS 17:15-16

How did Moses respond when the battle ended?
- Praised Israel's army
- He led Israel to the next place.
- He stopped and built an altar to God.

Israel went through one trial after another, and each time God provided. Do I ever feel like I go through trial after trial? **YES** **NO**

Do I see God providing for me in these trials? **YES** **NO**

Israel's faith was still growing, and so God allowed them to go through the wilderness trials. My faith is still growing, and so God is allowing me to face trials. **YES** **NO**

Sometimes God allows believers to go through trials. I can respond by complaining like the Israelites, or trusting God and praising Him for His provisions like Moses. I choose to respond like: ____________________.

SHARE IT

"Take courage. We walk in the wilderness today and in the Promised Land tomorrow." ~ *Dwight L. Moody*

WEDNESDAY WEEK 34

TRUTH: PSALM 106:1-15

Write out **Psalm 106:1**.

____

____

What are three things I am thankful for right now?

1. ____
2. ____
3. ____

A grateful heart is never a selfish heart. Keep a gratitude journal. Thank God for what He has done, is doing, and will do. Write in it often!

☐ I will do this. ☐ I used to do this, but it's been a while.

PSALM 106:3

Who are blessed according to this verse? ______________________

Is there a person that I have treated unjustly? ☐ **YES** ☐ **NO**
Who?____

I will make amends today. ☐ **YES** ☐ **NO**

Who have I been unkind to that I need to apologize to? ______________

Who is it that needs to be shown kindness today? ________________

PSALM 106:6

When I am in the wrong, I:

BLAME OTHERS. **IGNORE IT.** **AM DEFENSIVE.**

OWN UP TO MY WRONG AND MAKE IT RIGHT.

PSALM 106:7

The Israelites' fathers/ancestors didn't ______________ God's wonders/miracles.
What wonders/miracles has God been doing in my life lately?______________

____

They didn't ______________ the multitude of God's mercies/love/kindnesses.
I will share a memory of God's love with ______________________ .

SHARE IT

When I remember God in thankfulness,
I will not forget Him in the trial.

WEEK 34 THURSDAY

TRUTH: PSALM 106:16-31

Give thanks to the Lord for He is good. Continuing with a heart of gratitude, what are three more things I am thankful for today?

1. ______________________________
2. ______________________________
3. ______________________________

PSALM 106:16-29

Jealousy will bring ruin.
In this passage, what are some things that resulted from jealous hearts?

v. 17 ______________________________
v. 18 ______________________________
v. 19 ______________________________
v. 20 ______________________________
v. 21 ______________________________
v. 24 ______________________________
v. 25 ______________________________
v. 28 ______________________________
v. 29 ______________________________

Have I ever experienced any of these kinds of results from having a jealous heart?

YES **NO** If yes, circle which one(s).

PSALM 106:23, 30

What did God plan to do? ______________________________
Who stood in the gap for the Israelites? ______________________________
Who am I burdened for today that has walked away from God? ______________________________
I will commit to standing in the gap for them in prayer every day. **YES** **NO**
Who also intervened for these people (**v. 30**)? ______________________________

I can show love for others by praying for them.

On a scale of 0-5 how would I rate my prayer life?

Non-existent 0 1 2 3 4 5 Great

Who was the last person I prayed for? ______________________________

I'll make a list of some people who need my prayers today and then let them know I am praying for them.

____

____

SHARE IT

I can show love for others by praying for them.

FRIDAY WEEK 34

TRUTH: PSALM 106:32-48

PSALM 106:34-37

There is a progression of sin. Some may think, "Oh, it's no big deal." As we can see in these verses, one sin led to another. List the sins found in each of these verses and notice the progression.

____

____

____

1 Corinthians 15:33 says, "Do not be deceived: 'Evil company corrupts good habits.'"

As I think about the friendships I have, are there any relationships that are not healthy for my walk with God? ☐ **YES** ☐ **NO**

If yes, list specifically how this relationship has been unhealthy.

____

I am not much different from the people of Israel. Am I guilty of any of these? I'll circle the sin I struggle with most and look up the verse(s) that will help me fight this sin.

SIN	FIGHT SIN WITH TRUTH
Unbelief	**Mark 9:24**
Disobedience	**2 John 1:6**
Grumbling at trials	**Philippians 2:14**
Selfishness	**Philippians 2:3**
Ingratitude	**1 Thessalonians 5:18**
Murder (hate)	**1 John 3:15-16**
Idolatry (what I love more than God)	**Exodus 20:3**
Worldliness	**Romans 12:2**

PSALM 106:44-46

There is hope. There is grace. God remembers me even when I sin. He forgives me even when I do not put Him first. He hears me when I call to Him. Why does God do this? (**v. 45**) Write an acrostic for the word GRACE.

G
R
A
C
E

SHARE IT

When I think seriously about my sin,
I will think seriously about my Savior.

WEEK 34 SATURDAY

TRUTH: PSALM 108:1-13

PSALM 108:1

Write the first sentence/part of **verse 1**.

____

Is my heart steadfast (*faithful, committed, dedicated, devoted, dependable, loyal, solid, and true to God*)? ■ **YES** ■ **NO**

The opposite of steadfast is disloyal. How am I disloyal to God?
Have I lied lately? ■ **YES** ■ **NO**
Have I been disrespectful to a parent or other adult? ■ **YES** ■ **NO**
Have I cheated on my school work? ■ **YES** ■ **NO**
Have I gossiped? ■ **YES** ■ **NO**
Have I looked at inappropriate things? ■ **YES** ■ **NO**
Have I chosen worldly things over obedience to God's Word? ■ **YES** ■ **NO**

I want a heart that is steadfast. ■ **YES** ■ **NO**

PSALM 108:3

A heart that is steadfast will give thanks in all things.
What am I thankful for today? ______________________________

____

A heart that is steadfast will not complain but praise God. I'll praise Him now for what He has done in my life.______________________________

____

PSALM 108:6

A heart that is steadfast will pray to God for help. What circumstance is out of my control where I need help from God today? ______________________________

____

PSALM 108:12-13

A heart that is steadfast does not trust in itself or in another person but in God alone. How am I doing with trusting in God alone? ______________________________

____

SHARE IT

"Our God is abundant in love and steadfast in mercy. He saves us, not because we trust in a symbol, but because we trust in a Savior." ~ Max Lucado

SUNDAY WEEK 35

TRUTH: EXODUS 19:1-13

EXODUS 19:1-6

God told Israel that if they followed Him in obedient faith, they would receive what blessings? (**vv. 5-6**)

____

Because Israel had seen God do amazing things (**v. 4**), should obedience to God have been **easy** or **difficult** for them? (Circle)

Israel was to live as a holy nation in service to a holy God.
What similar command is found for Christians in **1 Peter 1:15-16**?

____

The Bible is clear that Christians will not be perfect in this life, but we are still to strive to live obediently to God. Does this describe me? ☐ **YES** ☐ **NO**

What is most difficult for me about being obedient to God?
- ☐ His commands are too difficult.
- ☐ No one else seems to be obedient to Him.
- ☐ I do not see the point in being obedient.
- ☐ Something else: ____________________________

EXODUS 19:7-13

What was Israel to do next?
- ☐ Consecrate themselves
- ☐ Wash their clothes
- ☐ Pray together
- ☐ Stay away from the mountain

Israel was learning that to serve a holy God takes obedience and reverence. Do I revere (honor/respect) God in my life? ☐ **YES** ☐ **NO**

Do I believe that God is worthy of honor and respect? ☐ **YES** ☐ **NO**

What are practical ways I can show reverence to God in my life? ____________________

____

____

SHARE IT

"As we grow in holiness, we grow in hatred of sin; and God, being infinitely holy, has an infinite hatred of sin."
~ Jerry Bridges

WEEK 35 MONDAY

TRUTH: EXODUS 19:14-25

EXODUS 19:14-20

What were some of the events that took place when God descended on Mount Sinai?

- Thunder and lightning
- Bright light
- The mountain quaked
- A cloud of smoke covered the mountain

These descriptions make me think of God's:

- Power
- Authority
- Greatness

If I had been witnessing these things I would have felt (circle):

SCARED EXCITED ANXIOUS CONFUSED CONFIDENT

EXODUS 19:21

Because of God's great glory and holiness, sinful mankind cannot look at Him and live. What does this say about sin?

- It cannot come into God's presence.
- We have to stop all our sins to be with God.
- It does not say anything about sin.

Romans 3:23 tells us that "_______ have sinned and _________ _____________ of the glory of God."

Sin cannot enter God's presence, but the good news in **Romans 5:1-2** is that those who believe in Jesus as their Savior will one day enter God's glory because they have been "____________________ by faith."

EXODUS 19:22-25

Moses thought the people did not need another warning, but he needed to understand that God knows what is best. Do I believe God knows what's best for me also?

YES **NO**

Jesus commanded all believers to share the Gospel (**Matthew 28:18-20**) so that others will be able to one day enter God's glory. Because God knows what's best for me, how will I respond to this command? ____

____

SHARE IT

"The God who knows you best knows the best for you."
~ Woodrow Kroll

TUESDAY WEEK 35

TRUTH: EXODUS 20:1-17

EXODUS 20:1-2

When giving the Ten Commandments, God first reminds Israel who He is to them (their Lord). Who is God to me? ______________________________

____

EXODUS 20:3-11

The first four commandments are focused on:
- ☐ Treating others right.
- ☐ Worshiping God properly.
- ☐ Attending church.

What are things that keep me from worshiping God throughout the week? __________

____

When something in my life becomes my primary focus instead of God, that thing or person is becoming an idol in my life.

Are there any idols in my life right now? ☐ **YES** ☐ **NO**

EXODUS 20:12-17

The final six commandments are focused on:
- ☐ Minor sins.
- ☐ Treating other people right.
- ☐ More idols.
- ☐ Repeating the first four commandments.

Which of these final commandments is most difficult to obey in my life?

____

How did Jesus summarize the Ten Commandments in **Matthew 22:36-39**?

____

____

Do I see how putting anything above God in my life keeps me from loving Him with all my heart, soul, and mind? ☐ **YES** ☐ **NO**

Do I see how breaking any of the last six commandments keeps me from loving others as myself? ☐ **YES** ☐ **NO**

Spend time in prayer now, asking God for forgiveness if necessary, and for His help to love Him and love others the way He wants you to. ☐

SHARE IT

"We love others best when we love God most."
~ Kyle Idleman

WEEK 35 WEDNESDAY

TRUTH: EXODUS 24:3-12

Have you been practicing loving God and loving others based on yesterday's lesson?
☐ **YES** ☐ **NO**

EXODUS 24:3-8

After receiving all the Lord's instructions, how did Israel respond?
- ☐ By agreeing to be obedient
- ☐ By questioning some of God's commandments
- ☐ By refusing to obey

Israel was excited about the new words they had received from God. Do I get excited when God teaches me something new in His Word? ☐ **YES** ☐ **NO**

What is something exciting God has been teaching me recently?

____

EXODUS 24:9-12

Moses and a select number of individuals were blessed to get a glimpse of God's glory. Why could they not see God completely? (Look back at **Exodus 19:21** for help.)

____

If you had been among these individuals, what would you have done after coming down from the mountain?
- ☐ Told everyone about it
- ☐ Kept it to myself
- ☐ Only told my friends or family about it

This experience with God for these individuals would have been a great witness (or testimony) for them in sharing about God with others.

Have I ever shared my testimony with others? ☐ **YES** ☐ **NO**

When was the last time I shared my testimony of God's work in my life with someone?

____

Who will I share my testimony with this week:
At School? ______________________________
Among my friends? ______________________________
Anywhere else? ______________________________

SHARE IT

God has been such a big part of my story, and now I want to share that story with others!

THURSDAY WEEK 35

TRUTH: EXODUS 24:15-25:9

EXODUS 24:15-25:2

The Israelites were to bring an offering to God:

- Out of obligation
- Willingly
- Abundantly

According to **2 Corinthians 9:7**, why is it important in God's sight that the one who gives does so willingly and not grudgingly? ______________________________

____

EXODUS 25:3-9

What were some of the different types of things that the Israelites could offer to God?

____

Have I ever made an offering to God of my resources? **YES** **NO**

What are some things I have given to God as an offering?

- Money
- Time (serving Him)
- Resources (donating items to churches/others)
- Something else: ______________________________

When I think of giving an offering to God it makes me feel: (circle one)

FRUSTRATED **ANNOYED** **JOYFUL** **EXCITED** **CONFUSED**

According to **1 Timothy 6:17-19**, what are two reasons I should give to God joyfully?

- All I have comes from God.
- Because I'm obligated to give
- By giving, I'm storing up eternal treasures.
- Because God will be mad if I do not give

What are some things God has blessed me with that I can now offer back to Him cheerfully? ______________________________

I will commit to giving to God on a regular basis because He has blessed me in so many ways!

YES **NO**

SHARE IT

"A lack of generosity refuses to acknowledge that your assets are not really yours, but God's." ~ Tim Keller

WEEK 35 FRIDAY

TRUTH: EXODUS 25:10-22

EXODUS 25:10

What did God command Israel to build?

- A kingdom
- An ark of acacia wood
- Tablets with the 10 Commandments on them

EXODUS 25:11-21

What are some words that are repeated that describe the ark that was to be built?

____

With all the precise details and measurements God was giving Israel, how important do you think it was that they followed His instructions?

Not Very Important 1 2 3 4 5 Very Important

Have I ever considered the fact that God is specific in His commands toward me in the Bible? **YES** **NO**

Because God's commands in the Bible are precise, they should be important to me.

- I agree with this statement.
- I disagree with this statement.
- I need to think some more.

EXODUS 25:22

The ark was so important because it was there that God would __________ with Israel.

How do you think Moses felt whenever he came into God's presence at the mercy seat of the ark? ____

When I enter into God's presence in prayer, reading Scripture, or worshiping in church, how do I feel? ____.

Why should I take God's presence so seriously?

- Because He is holy
- Because He is worthy of reverence
- Another reason: _______________________________

I will honor God when I come into His presence to worship. **YES** **NO**

SHARE IT

"It is in the process of being worshiped that God communicates His presence to men." ~ *C.S. Lewis*

SATURDAY WEEK 35

TRUTH: EXODUS 31:12-32:6

EXODUS 31:12-18

The last instructions Moses received from God on the mountain were about:
- ☐ Honoring parents
- ☐ The Sabbath
- ☐ The ark

The Sabbath was about a holy day of rest for the purpose of:
- ☐ Worshiping God
- ☐ Sleeping
- ☐ Doing nothing

Have I been working on spending intentional time worshiping God?
☐ **YES** ☐ **NO**

EXODUS 32:1

While God was establishing the importance of Sabbath worship with Moses on the mountain, what was Israel doing? ______________________________

____

EXODUS 32:2-6

Have I ever become impatient with God (the way Aaron and Israel became impatient) and chosen sin over Him? ☐ **YES** ☐ **NO**

Have I ever felt like I was the only one among my friends, family, or group that was being obedient to God? ☐ **YES** ☐ **NO**

When that moment came, did I give in and follow everyone else or continue to act in a way that pleased God? ______________________________

Aaron had a chance to lead Israel the right way, and he failed to do so. Have I ever used similar situations in my life to lead others the right way? If so, how did I lead them?

____

Moses was not tempted to go along with Israel because he was with God. What does that mean for my life? ______________________________

____

SHARE IT

"My son, if sinners entice you, do not consent."
~ **Proverbs 1:10**

WEEK 36 SUNDAY

TRUTH: EXODUS 32:7-20

EXODUS 32:7-10

God's anger and judgments toward sin are justified.

- ☐ I agree with this statement.
- ☐ I disagree with this statement.
- ☐ I need to think some more.

EXODUS 32:11-14

Although he knew God's judgments are just, Moses responded to the coming consequences for Israel by: (Check one)

- ☐ Remaining silent.
- ☐ Pleading to God on Israel's behalf.
- ☐ Forgiving Israel in his own heart.

When was the last time I prayed for a believer who was not walking with God the way they should? ______________________________

How often do I pray for others? (Circle one)

NEVER **RARELY** **ONCE A MONTH** **ONCE A WEEK** **DAILY**

EXODUS 32:15-20

Moses saw their sin and responded with:

- ☐ Patience
- ☐ Anger
- ☐ Kindness

According to **Ephesians 4:26**, is all anger sinful? ☐ **YES** ☐ **NO**

God's wrath (**v. 10**) and Moses' anger (**v. 19**) were not sinful and a result of impatience, but came from a righteous rejection of sin.
Have I ever been angry over sin? ☐ **YES** ☐ **NO**
How did I respond in that anger?

____

Using the space below, what are practical ways I can be angry over sin and respond without sinning? ______________________________

____

____

SHARE IT

"He who is slow to anger is better than the mighty, and he who rules his spirit than he who takes a city." ~ **Proverbs 16:32**

MONDAY WEEK 36

TRUTH: EXODUS 33:12-23

EXODUS 33:12-16

What made Israel so different from all the other nations? (**v. 16**)

- They were a bigger nation.
- God was with them.
- Nothing made them different.
- They were more righteous.

Do I believe God is present with me also? (see **Matthew 28:20**) ☐ **YES** ☐ **NO**

EXODUS 33:17

When I think about the fact that God knows me by name and knows everything about me, it makes me feel: (Circle)

SPECIAL LOVED SAFE UNIQUE CARED FOR CONFIDENT

Knowing that God is always with me and knows everything about me reminds me of God's:

- Omniscience (infinite knowledge)
- Love
- Protection
- Something else: ______________________________

EXODUS 33:18-23

Have I ever had a great desire to know God more? ☐ **YES** ☐ **NO**

Moses wanted to see God, but was reminded that to see God in all His glory would result in ____________________.(**v. 20**)

In this moment, Moses was recognizing that God is great, and that He loves His people dearly. Have I come to recognize these truths in my own life?

☐ **YES** ☐ **NO** ☐ **STILL WORKING ON THIS**

Who will I share with this week about God's greatness and His love for them?

____

SHARE IT

"God loves each of us as if there were only one of us."
~ Augustine

WEEK 36 TUESDAY

TRUTH: EXODUS 34:1-17

EXODUS 34:1-5

Why did Moses need to replace the first tablets God gave him? ____________________

____

EXODUS 34:6-7

Which of these attributes of God have I never thought of or known before? ____________

____

Do I believe all these attributes are true of God? ☐ **YES** ☐ **NO**

EXODUS 34:8-9

When I read about who God is, it makes me want to:

- ☐ Worship Him.
- ☐ Meditate on who He is.
- ☐ It does not make me want to do anything different.
- ☐ Something else: ____

What was Moses' response when hearing the attributes of God? ____________________

____.

Moses was passionate about God. ☐ **YES** ☐ **NO**

Am I passionate about God in my life? ☐ **YES** ☐ **NO**

EXODUS 34:10-17

Although Moses was passionate about God, God knew that worshiping _________ (**v. 15**) would cause Israel to lose their passion.

The biggest thing that causes me to lose my passion for God is:

☐ My friends ☐ Music/Movies/Gaming ☐ A particular sin
☐ Wifi ☐ Other: ____

Do I desire to be passionate about God in my life? ☐ **YES** ☐ **NO**
In light of this, I will trust God to help me regain my passion for Him by giving me the strength to stop, ignore, flee from listening, watching, reading, associating with

__________________________.

My greatest passion in life will be my God. ☐ **YES** ☐ **NO**

SHARE IT

"I am passionate about God, about Jesus, and what His influences do to me." ~ *TobyMac*

WEDNESDAY WEEK 36

TRUTH: EXODUS 34:18-35

EXODUS 34:18-28

God said that the firstborn (**v. 19**) and the firstfruits of harvest (**v. 26**) were to be dedicated to Him. Do I dedicate the firstfruits (best) of all I have (money, time, resources, etc.) to God? ☐ **YES** ☐ **NO**

What are some practical ways I can offer the best of what I have to God?

____

EXODUS 34:29-35

What was so spectacular about Moses' appearance when he came down from meeting with God? (**v. 30**)

____

If I saw Moses' face shining like that, I would have been: (Circle)

SCARED CONFUSED EXCITED JEALOUS ANXIOUS HAPPY

To keep the people from being scared, Moses would wear a __________ over his face.

Whether they saw Moses with a shining face or with a veil on, these were reminders to the people that Moses had been with God.

What are ways people know that I have spent time with God?

- ☐ My actions
- ☐ My words
- ☐ My overall attitude
- ☐ People never know when I have spent time with God.
- ☐ Something else: ______________________________

Does spending time with God make an impact in my life? ☐ **YES** ☐ **NO**

If spending time with God impacts me, I should be willing to let that impact be a testimony and witness to others.

- ☐ I agree with this statement.
- ☐ I disagree with this statement.
- ☐ I need to think some more.

Who are some specific people in my life that could benefit from knowing that I have been with God? ______________________________

SHARE IT

"Let your light so shine before men, that they may see your good works and glorify your Father in heaven." ~ **Matthew 5:16**

WEEK 36 THURSDAY

TRUTH: EXODUS 40:1-16

EXODUS 40:1-11

God's instructions to Moses for when and how to set up the tabernacle were: (Check one)
- Vague
- Specific

When I receive clear instructions, it is easier to follow them. ☐ **YES** ☐ **NO**

Do I believe God has given me clear instructions in the Bible for how to live for Him?
☐ **YES** ☐ **NO**

EXODUS 40:12-15

After the tabernacle, Moses would then focus on those who would serve in the tabernacle. God's specific instructions to Moses show that He is a God of…
- Confusion
- Difficulty
- Order

Do I believe that God is a God of order? ☐ **YES** ☐ **NO**

What excuses do I normally give for not following God's commands?
- They are too difficult.
- I do not know His commands.
- They do not make sense.
- Something else: ______________________________

If God gives specific and orderly instructions to His people, can I continue making excuses when I do not obey Him? ☐ **YES** ☐ **NO**

In light of this truth, how should I respond to God's commands? ____________________

____

EXODUS 40:16

How did Moses respond to God's commands? ____________________

____

How will I respond to serving a God of order? ____________________

____

SHARE IT

"For God is not the author of confusion but of peace, as in all the churches of the saints." ~ **1 Corinthians 14:33**

FRIDAY WEEK 36

TRUTH: EXODUS 40:17-27

EXODUS 40:17

Did Moses follow God's command to set up the tabernacle on the correct day? (**Exodus 40:2**) ☐ **YES** ☐ **NO**

Have I ever let something get in the way of following through on instructions I had been given from a parent/teacher/leader? ☐ **YES** ☐ **NO**

Have I ever let something get in the way of following through in obedience to God's commands? ☐ **YES** ☐ **NO**

EXODUS 40:18-27

If Moses had only done some of the things God had commanded, would he still have been considered obedient? Why or why not? ______________________________

____

When I obey God, is it in full obedience, or do I tend to leave out some minor details or commands? ______________________________

A reoccurring phrase throughout this passage is, "as the LORD had ______________ ______________________________ ______________."

Because this phrase is repeated it must be: **important / unimportant**.
(Circle one)

The phrase "as the Lord commanded" means that Moses obeyed all the details, no matter how time-consuming or difficult they may have been. Could this phrase be used to describe me? ☐ **YES** ☐ **NO**

What are some of God's commands I need to start following completely?

____

Where can I go to receive all the details of God's instructions?
- ☐ My friends
- ☐ The Bible
- ☐ TV and movies

I commit to begin obeying all the details of God's commands. ☐ **YES** ☐ **NO**

SHARE IT

"If you know that God loves you, you should never question a directive from Him." ~ *Henry Blackaby*

WEEK 36 SATURDAY

TRUTH: EXODUS 40:28-38

EXODUS 40:28-35

What happened after Moses finished setting up the tabernacle?

____

EXODUS 40:36-38

God's glory was present with Israel and was made visible as a ____________ during the day and ________________________ during the night.

How might God's visible presence have given the Israelites comfort and courage during their journeys? ____

____

Would God's presence give me comfort and courage? ☐ **YES** ☐ **NO**

Do I believe that God is with me always? ☐ **YES** ☐ **NO**

When did Israel know it was the right time to go somewhere else? (**v. 36**)

____

Israel was sensitive to follow God's leading.
When I see God leading me, do I respond by following Him? ☐ **YES** ☐ **NO**

Although God no longer dwells in the tabernacle Moses built, where does His Spirit dwell now? (**1 Corinthians 6:19**)

- ☐ Far away
- ☐ In a temple in Israel
- ☐ In believers

Do I believe that as a Christian God's Spirit dwells within me? ☐ **YES** ☐ **NO**

Because the Holy Spirit is within me, God is always here for me. ☐ **YES** ☐ **NO**

I am going to follow God's Spirit wherever He leads me in life. ☐ **YES** ☐ **NO**

Spend some time in prayer asking God to guide you where He wants you to be. ☐

SHARE IT

"The Christian life is a life that consists of following Jesus."
~ A.W. Pink

SUNDAY WEEK 37

TRUTH: ROMANS 1:1-7

Paul was called to be an apostle (*sent one*) separated for the preaching of the Gospel of God.

ROMANS 1:1

Paul knew what his calling was; do I know mine according to God's instructions?

☐ **YES** ☐ **NO** ☐ **STILL FIGURING THIS OUT**

I believe that my calling . . .
Among my friends is ______________________________ .
At school is ______________________________ .
At home is ______________________________ .
At church is ______________________________ .

I believe that sharing the Gospel of Jesus to others is one sure purpose for my life as far as God's calling is concerned. ☐ **YES** ☐ **NO**

Just the thought of sharing the Gospel with someone makes me feel: (circle)

NERVOUS CONFUSED AFRAID CONFIDENT EXCITED

The reason I feel this way is because ______________________________ .

Matthew 28:19 reminds me that I am called by Jesus Himself to
" ___________ therefore and make disciples of all men . . ."

The one person I feel God is placing on my heart to GO to and share the Gospel with this week is ____________________.
My plan is to do this by ______________________________
(text, message, call, face to face, etc.).

ROMANS 1:5-7

To enable me to fulfill this goal, I am going to take time to pray to God right now about:

☐ Using His grace to do what He has placed on my heart to do. (**vv. 5,7**)
☐ Being confident in knowing that it is God who has given me this responsibility. (**v. 5**)
☐ Giving me peace of heart as I go and do this. (**v. 7**)

SHARE IT

I believe that sharing the Gospel of Jesus with others is one sure purpose for my life.

WEEK 37 MONDAY

TRUTH: ROMANS 1:8-17

ROMANS 1:8

I am thankful to God for (*person's name*) ____________________.
My reason for being thankful for this person is ______________________________
____.

Talking about my personal testimony or character, one word that people use to describe me:
At Home ______________________
At Church ______________________
At School ______________________
Among Peers ______________________

ROMANS 1:9-10

Who is God laying on my heart right now to pray for?
____

What am I to pray about for this person? ______________________________
____

ROMANS 1:11-17

Who is God placing on my heart that may need to be established/strengthened by me right now? ______________________

I am going to be a support to the following people in this way:
By prayer ______________________________
Sending a message of comfort ______________________________
Sending a note of encouragement ______________________________

I know I can do with some support/encouragement right now, and the one person I can trust to help me with this is: ____________________.

The reason I have chosen the person above is because of their:

- Reputation of living a godly life characterized by faith. (**vv. 8,17**)
- Continued ministry of encouragement to me. (**vv. 11-12**)
- Way of making me feel comfortable to share with them.

My prayer: ***Lord, help me today to be an encouragement to those I meet and to be thankful in all I go through.***

SHARE IT

Be an encourager! The world has enough critics already.

TUESDAY WEEK 37

TRUTH: ROMANS 1:18-32

ROMANS 1:20

Today I will purpose to take some time to pause and praise God as I acknowledge His greatness in Creation when I observe the: (circle one)

SUN MOON STARS MOUNTAINS LAKES OCEAN RIVERS

ROMANS 1:21-25

I do have a relationship with God, but I sure do need help with:

- ☐ Glorifying Him as God.
- ☐ Being more thankful to God no matter the circumstance.
- ☐ Seeing God's gracious hand in all that happens in life.

Could I really be a fool before God and yet not know it? If any of the following is a characteristic of my life, then I need help from God to be wise and forsake the following foolish ways in my life:

- ☐ There is something or someone else that's more important to me right now than God. (**v. 23**)
- ☐ I have strong cravings for something and will do almost anything to get it. (**v. 24**)
- ☐ I am not taking good care of my body as I am allowing it to be used in shameful things. (**v. 24**)
- ☐ There is some other source that I listen to more than I listen to God's Word. (**v. 25**)

ROMANS 1:26-28

For some time now I have been suppressing God's truth regarding the following areas: (circle any that apply)

WHAT I WATCH WHAT I LISTEN TO MY RELATIONSHIPS MY SPIRITUAL GROWTH SEXUAL IMMORALITY HOMOSEXUALITY LESBIANISM WICKED DEEDS ENVY MALICE GOSSIP HATRED OF GOD VIOLENCE PRIDE QUARRELING EVIL THOUGHTS DECEPTION DISOBEDIENCE TO AUTHORITY UNTRUSTWORTHY UNLOVING UNFORGIVING SHOWING NO MERCY AT ALL

I pray (and will write down my prayer in a journal or notebook) asking God to help me to be sensitive to His voice regarding any area(s) I have circled above and that He will help me bring about change by His Spirit and the power of the Gospel (**v. 16**). I'll write what I would like to see that area replaced with that is God honoring. ☐

SHARE IT

"There is no fool so great a fool as a knowing fool."
~ Charles Spurgeon

WEEK 37 WEDNESDAY

TRUTH: ROMANS 2:1-16

Before beginning today's Quiet Time, take the next few minutes and pray for sensitivity (*a heart that will respond*) to God's Word.

Am I expecting Him to speak to me through it? ☐ **YES** ☐ **NO**

ROMANS 2:1

Whatever I do that's not pleasing to God is without excuse, especially when I judge others. Maybe it's because I need to remove the log out of my eye before I condemn others. (**Matthew 7:1-5**)

☐ I agree with this statement. ☐ I disagree with this statement.
☐ I need to think about this some more.

ROMANS 2:3-4

I realize that I am a candidate for God's judgment if the following is true of me: (check any that apply.)

- ☐ I criticize others for the same things I am dealing with. (**v. 3**)
- ☐ I am despising and taking for granted God's goodness and patience while living in habitual sin. (**v. 4**)
- ☐ I am knowingly resisting God's guidance in my life due to a hardened heart.

ROMANS 2:13

As far as listening to God's Word and doing what it says, I can say that I:

- ☐ Desperately need help with this.
- ☐ Am growing in this area.
- ☐ Am good enough.
- ☐ Am definitely thriving and enjoying it!

ROMANS 2:15

Thinking about my conscience (*the sense of right or wrong*) and the inner "small voice," I am:

- ☐ Consistently ignoring it.
- ☐ Damaging it or reprogramming it with wrong standards.
- ☐ Consistently paying attention to it.

The biggest culprit for me in setting wrong standards and making me insensitive to the wrong things is:

☐ Music ☐ Video Games ☐ Movies ☐ Friends ☐ Books ☐ Other

In light of the above, I am now trusting God to help me listen to His small voice and choose to (stop, destroy, ignore, flee from) ______________________________

____.

I now choose to have God's Word guide my heart. ☐ **YES** ☐ **NO**

SHARE IT

Lord, may Your still small voice not be drowned out by the distractions I place in my life, and may I be led by YOU.

THURSDAY WEEK 37

TRUTH: ROMANS 2:17-29

ROMANS 2:17-20

As a Christian this is true of me:

- ☐ My faith and hope are based on God's Word. (**v. 17**)
- ☐ My confidence is based on God and God alone. (**v. 17**)
- ☐ I know and desire to live by His will. (**v. 18**)
- ☐ I rejoice when good prevails. (**v. 18**)
- ☐ I have a heart for reaching out to others with the love of Christ. (**v. 19**)

I may be doing all the above and believe all the above, but a close scrutiny of my life reveals that the following issues are standing in the way of me being a good witness of God to others:

☐ Pride ☐ Shyness ☐ Attitude ☐ Fear of what people will say/think
☐ Other: ______________________________

ROMANS 2:25-29

The reason I am usually involved in church activities and why I believe what I believe is based on the fact that:

- ☐ That's what my family has always believed and done.
- ☐ It's the only way I can fit in.
- ☐ I just have to make myself appear that way to create and protect my image.
- ☐ It is my heart's conviction and direction.

I will take some time to pray that all I do for God will be guided through heart convictions driven by a genuine love for God. ☐ Done

Today I will purpose:

- ☐ To be myself and not try to pretend to be someone else.
- ☐ To ask a mature believer how they learned to live by convictions.
  I'll ask:____ .

SHARE IT

"The basic trouble with the church today is her unworthy concept of God." ~ A.W Tozer

WEEK 37 FRIDAY

TRUTH: ROMANS 3:1-8

Considering yesterday's challenge, how did it feel for me to be myself and not pretend?

- Normal
- Strange
- Freeing
- Didn't do it yet
- I don't have a problem with this.

As a child of God, I tend to view the Bible as: (circle all that apply)

A BLESSING **A REQUIREMENT** **A PRIVILEGE TO HAVE**

OUTDATED **IRRELEVANT** **AN ANTIQUE**

As a result of my view of the Bible, I therefore tend to:

- Try to put into practice what I read from the Bible.
- Take having a Bible for granted.
- Find it hard to relate it to what I am going through.
- Enjoy my Bible reading and studying opportunities.
- Read my Bible daily.
- Generally let other activities get in the way of reading my Bible (homework, chores, friends, technology, etc.).

ROMANS 3:3-4

I've got the Word of God to learn from each day. Would I say God's Word hasn't proven faithful on the days that I don't read it?

- **YES**
- **NO**
- **NOT SURE**

This is what I can depend on: from Genesis to the book of Revelation, every word is true, and GOD is faithful to His Word. So now, I've just got to get in gear! Not so God can love me more, but so I can love HIM more!

Do I want to dig deeper? I'll write out **Psalm 119:10** below and make it part of my prayer for the next 3 days:

____

____

____

____

SHARE IT

"The very practice of reading (the Bible) will have a purifying effect upon your mind and heart. Let nothing take the place of this daily exercise." ~ Billy Graham

SATURDAY WEEK 37

TRUTH: ROMANS 3:9-20

ROMANS 3:10-17

When I look at others and myself, I:

■ **AGREE** ■ **DISAGREE**: that there is no one righteous before God. (**v. 10**)

■ **AGREE** ■ **DISAGREE**: that we would rather follow our own desires rather than seek after God. (**v. 11**)

■ **AGREE** ■ **DISAGREE**: that we have used our words to curse and hurt others. (**vv. 13-14**)

■ **AGREE** ■ **DISAGREE**: that we have done sinful things before God. (**vv. 15-17**)

ROMANS 3:19

In light of the above and looking at this specific verse, it therefore makes all of us "________________________ before God."

I also ■ **AGREE** ■ **DISAGREE**: that there is nothing we as human beings can do by our own power to please God in order to escape the GUILTY charge.

All this makes me feel:

■ **HOPELESS** ■ **SAD** ■ **STUCK** ■ **INDIFFERENT** ■ **REPENTANT** ■ **CONFUSED**

I'll read **Romans 5:6-8** and write down how these verses make me feel:

____

____

____

How am I going to remember what I learned today from God's Word?
If I could boil it down to one word, that might make it easier.

What is the one word I'll remember? ____________________

Who will I share it with? ____

SHARE IT

There is nothing we as human beings can do by our own power to please God in order to escape the "guilty" charge.

WEEK 38 SUNDAY

TRUTH: ROMANS 3:21-31

ROMANS 3:23

This verse shoots straight with me. It is God's Word and says that "__________ have sinned."

ROMANS 3:24

The only way to get through this is being "________________ freely" by God. Speaking of justification, I know that this is something I cannot gain through anything I can do for myself. (**v. 20**)

☐ **AGREED** ☐ **STILL NOT CONVINCED ABOUT THIS**

Time to define some terms as I shall be seeing more of these later:
(Match the right word with its definition.)

SIN	*The legal act of being declared righteous* (**v. 24**)
JUSTIFICATION	*Satisfaction of God's anger at sin* (**v. 25**)
REDEMPTION	*To miss the mark of God's holiness* (**v. 23**)
PROPITIATION	*Purchased, loosed, and set free* (**v. 24**)

I think it's awesome to know that I cannot earn justification from God because it is something:

☐ **HE FREELY GIVES ME BY HIS GRACE.** ☐ **I SHALL NEVER ATTAIN.**

I therefore am in agreement with the Bible's conclusion that I can only be justified by grace through faith alone. ☐ **AGREE** ☐ **DISAGREE**

How many times was the word faith mentioned in the verses I read today? ___________
So what do I do with all this information then?

A. Admit that I am a sinner and need a Savior (**v. 23**).
B. Agree that only by faith can I be justified by God (**v. 28**).
C. Believe on Jesus Christ as the only way to gain righteousness before God (**v. 26**).

Evaluate:

☐ I believe A-C fully.
☐ I am not sure if I believe it fully.
☐ I'm going to keep reading the Word to answer questions I might have regarding this.
☐ It's time. God's placing someone else on my heart to share the Gospel with.
It's ____, and I'll do it. ☐ **YES** ☐ **NO**

SHARE IT

"God does not justify us because we are worthy, but by justifying us makes us worthy." ~ *Thomas Watson*

TRUTH: ROMANS 4:1-12

ROMANS 4:2

Sometimes I catch myself doing ______________________________ with the idea that it could earn me some form of favor before God.

However, looking at Abraham's example I realize that even this is:

- ☐ Something I can boast of before God.
- ☐ Nothing worth boasting of before God.

Galatians 6:14

Therefore, before God, as far as my salvation is concerned, the only thing I can boast of or glory in is the ____ of our Lord Jesus Christ.

ROMANS 4:6-8

Knowing that my sins are forgiven and God is the One Who makes me righteous makes me feel ______________________________________.

As a kid, did I ever hear the song, "Father Abraham, had many sons . . . and I am one of them . . ."? Pretty cool, really.

According to **verse 3**, Faith = ____.

ROMANS 4:9

During Paul's time, obviously some people thought that ceremonies such as circumcision would earn them favor before God, just like I believe that the following ceremonies can do the same for me: (circle any that apply)

Going to church on Easter **Helping little old ladies across the street**

Celebrating Christmas **Singing on the worship team**

Having my quiet time **Other:** ____

None of these, because Jesus did it all for me!

ROMANS 4:11-12

He is "the father of all those that ___________________" and a father to the Jews (of circumcision) and non-Jews (not of circumcision) who also "walk in the steps of the _______________ which our father Abraham had."

SHARE IT

"For by grace you have been saved through faith; and that not of yourselves, it is the gift of God; not of works, lest anyone should boast." ~ **Ephesians 2:8-9**

WEEK 38 TUESDAY

TRUTH: ROMANS 4:13-25

Just like Abraham, I believe that God does have promises for me from His Word.

☐ **TRUE** ☐ **I DON'T THINK SO.**

1 John 2:25

As a child of God, I know I can rejoice over the following promise for me from God:

Promise of __________________ ______________.

ROMANS 4:16

For me to get the above promise, this is what is required of me:

- ☐ Regular church attendance.
- ☐ Giving my money to a good cause.
- ☐ Regular praying and reminding God of His promise to me.
- ☐ Having faith in the gracious act of God through the death and resurrection of Jesus.

Okay, I have to be honest and admit that the following things sometimes make me doubt God's promises for me:

____

____

I sometimes feel like some of God's promises can never come true in my life.

☐ **I AGREE.** ☐ **I SOMEWHAT AGREE.** ☐ **I TOTALLY AGREE.**

ROMANS 4:18-19

The one person in my life that is kind of like Abraham and believes God even in nearly impossible situations is _________________________.

Send them a note or message this week saying: "Looking at the way you have ______________________________________, I am encouraged by your faith in God, and I am praying for you!"

Write down **verse 21** as a personal prayer. Begin with – "Lord, help me this week to be fully . . ."

____

____

SHARE IT

"The stars may fall, but God's promises will stand and be fulfilled." ~ *J.I. Packer*

WEDNESDAY WEEK 38

TRUTH: ROMANS 5:1-11

ROMANS 5:1-10

Looking at my unsaved friends, sometimes it seems like life is so easy and fun for them.
☐ **YES, AND I WANT TO JOIN THEM.** ☐ **YES, BUT I DON'T ENVY THEM AT ALL.**

I feel as a Christian I get the short end of the stick and no benefits at all in being saved.
- ☐ That's exactly how I feel.
- ☐ Sometimes it feels that way.
- ☐ I have thought about it that way, but it's not an issue for me.
- ☐ Definitely not how I feel because I am happy to be a Christian.

Please, Lord, help me to be "fully persuaded" of the following privileges I have as a Christian:

____________________ with God (**v. 1**)
_________________ by faith into God's grace (**v. 2**)
God's ________________ shed (poured) abundantly in my heart (**v. 5**)
The __________ ___________ given to me (**v. 5**)
Being ________________________________ to God by the death of His Son. (**v. 10**)

Of the privileges outlined above, I am most excited about the one that talks about

____ .

ROMANS 5:1

Knowing that I "have peace with God" and that I am not a target of His wrath/anger (**v. 9**) makes me feel: ____________________________.

I am glad to have peace with God, but I sure could use some peace:
☐ With my parents. ☐ With my sibling(s). ☐ With my friend(s).
☐ With my schoolmates. ☐ With ______________________________________ .

I need to seek to be at peace with: (Write name of the person.)

____.

ROMANS 5:10

It took God to sacrifice His Son for me to have peace with Him.

I may need to make the following sacrifices for peace to exist with the person named above: ☐ My pride ☐ My comfort ☐ My rights

SHARE IT

"While you are proclaiming peace with your lips, be careful to have it even more fully in your heart." ~ *Francis of Assisi*

WEEK 38 THURSDAY

TRUTH: ROMANS 5:12-21

The whole issue of death makes me feel:

☐ **SO SCARED.** ☐ **UNMOVED.** ☐ **SORROWFUL.** ☐ **CONFUSED.**
☐ **I DON'T WANT TO THINK ABOUT IT.**

Probably the reason why death is such a scary thing to me is:

- ☐ It's just a mystery.
- ☐ The uncertainty of what happens after death.
- ☐ Because it's the end of everything.
- ☐ Because it reminds me of God's judgment afterwards.

ROMANS 5:12-14

I do understand, though, that death is a result of ____________. (**v. 12**) that affects all mankind as descendants of ____________. (**v. 14**)

TRUE OR FALSE.

T F The real sting or problem according to **1 Corinthians 15:56** is for me to die with my sinfulness not having been forgiven by God.

Reading **1 Corinthians 15:57**, however, reminds me that as a Christian, I have been given ____________________ over death through Jesus Christ who forgave me of my sins.

- ☐ I believe that.
- ☐ I am not sure that this victory over death is a free gift upon all men through Jesus Christ leading to eternal life. (**vv. 18, 21**)

Talking about death reminds me of ______________________________ who lost someone recently. One way I will be an encouragement to them in dealing with the pain of their loss is by:

____.

Today's passage has been helpful to me because:

____

____

____

____

SHARE IT

"When the time comes for you to die, you need not be afraid, because death cannot separate you from God's love."
~ Charles Spurgeon

FRIDAY WEEK 38

TRUTH: ROMANS 6:1-12

ROMANS 6:1

Even as a child of God, I find myself doing certain things that I know are sinful, but I think it's not an issue because: (check what applies)

☐ I know God will forgive me anyway.
☐ It's usually a small sin that God wouldn't punish me for.
☐ God isn't as harsh today as He was in the Old Testament.
☐ No, that's not me; sin really is an issue to me.

ROMANS 6:2

I also realize that my sinfulness can never exhaust God's grace and His willingness to forgive me. However, this doesn't mean I should continue to live in sin.

☐ I agree. ☐ I don't agree because grace covers all this sin anyway.

ROMANS 6:4

For me to abandon a life of intentional sinfulness and take on one of newness of life in Christ will mean I need to: ______________________________ .

____

ROMANS 6:6-7

When I look back at the old self that I was before salvation and the new man/woman that is being changed to be more like Christ:

☐ I feel like I have changed and grown tremendously.
☐ I feel like I have been stagnant in my growth with very little difference.
☐ I feel like things took a turn for the worse, and the "old man" was a saint compared to me now.
☐ I really haven't paid much attention to this, but I will now.

A sin or habit I have struggled with for some time is: ____________________ .

Instead of living in the sin or habit above, I believe God is calling me to live a life of freedom from it and that means now I will have to: ____________________

______________________________ .

ROMANS 6:10-11

Even though I have struggled with this issue in my life, I will consider God's Word to be true that I am dead to this sin.

☐ **YES** ☐ **NO** ☐ **MAYBE**

SHARE IT

I shouldn't continue to live in sin just because I can't ever exhaust God's grace.

WEEK 38 SATURDAY

TRUTH: ROMANS 6:13-23

ROMANS 6:13

According to this verse, what is one sure way of overcoming the constant yielding to sin in my life?

- Work hard at following some secret steps that I haven't found yet to help me overcome the sin.
- Just give up and accept that, after all, I live under grace.
- Prayerfully give my body, heart, and mind daily to Christ and trust Him to change me by His power.

ROMANS 6:16-18

The following statement is true of me:

- It certainly feels like I am a slave to sin in my life since I feel like I am hooked on it.
- I rejoice that generally I can say I am God's slave since I regularly experience victory over sin and temptation by His grace.
- I kind of feel it's 50-50 for me as I move between being a slave to God in obedience and a slave to sin.

As part of not despairing and giving up on pursuing righteousness, I need to remember: (check all that apply)

- To be thankful to God for He did, and still does, deliver me from sins. (**v. 17**)
- That I have been set free from sin's stronghold and thus it is possible to overcome sin in my life. (**v. 18**)

ROMANS 6:22

Only God can set me free from sin and grant me victory over temptation. Knowing this will cause me to: (check all that apply)

- Genuinely confess my sin and resolve to turn away from it by God's grace.
- Pray to God every time I am under pressure to sin so He can help me overcome it.
- Find someone to regularly check on how I am doing in the area I struggle with. That person will be: ______________________________.
- Read the Bible more to help build my faith in God and reliance on Him to change me.
- Intentionally take note of the victories God grants me over sin and humbly thank Him for it.

SHARE IT

Only God can set me free from sin and grant me victory over temptation.

SUNDAY WEEK 39

TRUTH: ROMANS 7:1-13

Before I was saved, the one thing or practice that I really placed my hope and confidence in to help me get close to God and be a better person was ____________________________ (e.g., being born into a Christian family, going to church, doing good deeds, etc.)

I actually thought, or was taught to believe, that the above practice would get me to Heaven if I diligently kept up with it.

- True of my past experience
- Not true of my experience
- That's still me.

It's possible to get stuck in what is called legalism, ***an attitude which conforms to a code or rules, in order to put oneself above others.***

Sometimes I think I'm better than ________________________________ because I ____.

ROMANS 7:5-6

This is really about releasing me from a system of rules which would only focus on the external and move me to focus on what's happening inside.

Follow the path of thinking:

- In the past I tried to measure up by doing certain things, proving I was a good person, promoting myself.
- When I failed, it just magnified how terrible I felt. (**v. 5**)
- But that's the issue, I have to realize I'm released from an old way of thinking (legalism) to follow a new way, led by the Holy Spirit. (**v. 6**)

ROMANS 7:7

One word is repeated three times in this verse. What is it? __________
In the Old Testament that was the rule of conduct. The problem was, no one could keep it. There were 613 rules!!

ROMANS 7:8

Because they had to follow that law or code, it was very obvious when they sinned. Bottom line is, I know when I sin too; it's just easier at times to:

- Ignore it.
- Blame someone else.

The choice to sin kills me internally! It magnifies my pride. That's what needs to be dealt with. Thankfully, Jesus Christ came to be the Savior to rescue me from myself!

SHARE IT

"If you feel that you can follow a few little rules or some clever gimmicks to make you a mature Christian, then you have fallen into a subtle trap of legalism." ~ J. Vernon McGee

WEEK 39 MONDAY

TRUTH: ROMANS 7:14-25

ROMANS 7:15

It's almost like Paul is reading my mind when he states in relation to the battle within that:

- ■ I do not understand why I am not practicing what I *would* like to *do*.
- ■ I do not understand why I do the very thing I hate.

Here's a perfect example: I hate that I keep ______________________________.
The conflict within me as a child of God makes me feel:

CONFUSED **FRUSTRATED** **ASHAMED** **HELPLESS**

Probably the reason this issue is so frustrating to me is because:

- ■ I have tried everything I can to get rid of sin in my life, but it's still a struggle.
- ■ I have been a Christian for a long time, and I feel I should be over certain sinful struggles.
- ■ I always thought when I became a Christian I should not be able to sin.
- ■ I know I shouldn't be sinning and I don't want to, but I just can't resist falling into sin.

ROMANS 7:18

When it comes to what I want to do or not do, and what I end up doing or not doing, it sometimes feels like I have two different personalities.

■ I totally agree. ■ I somewhat agree. ■ I don't agree.

The place I normally face this struggle within me is mainly ____________________ (at home, at school, during sports, at the mall, etc.), and it's usually when (person's name) ____________________ is involved.

ROMANS 7:24

Wow, I'm really getting called out here! I admit that this verse pretty much describes who I truly am. ■ **YES** ■ **I HATE TO ADMIT IT AND WON'T.**

ROMANS 7:25

Don't miss this. I can be victorious because of Whom? ____________.

God, let me stop and thank You right now, that You set me free.
I'm no longer held captive to: ____________________.

I may need my youth pastor or a mentor to place some accountability around me to live in this freedom. ■ **YES** ■ **NO** I'll talk to ________________.

SHARE IT

God, let me stop and thank You right now, that You set me free.

TUESDAY WEEK 39

TRUTH: ROMANS 8:1-11

So, yesterday's passage that brought out the inner struggle with sin that constantly exists within me, left me feeling:

- **GUILTY.**
- **A FAILURE.**
- **UNFORGIVABLE BY GOD.**
- **NOTHING AT ALL.**
- **FREE.**

ROMANS 8:1-2

I am **confident** / **somewhat confident** of this one thing:
that as a child of God, in spite of my inner struggle, God:

- Wants nothing to do with me.
- Does not condemn me but desires for me to walk in the life-giving Spirit in Christ Jesus.
- Condemns me since I am guilty anyway.
- Doesn't care at all how I live my life.

ROMANS 8:2-3

I believe that:
Only Christ can truly set me free from my sin struggle. **YES** **NO**
Any attempt at trying to use my strength to overcome the sin issue is futile (pointless).
YES **NO**

ROMANS 8:3-4

In my struggle with my flesh (sin), I realize that all MY methods and techniques have proven to be: **HELPFUL** **INEFFECTIVE** **FRUSTRATING**

ROMANS 8:8

I realize that if there is anything I am doing with the hope of pleasing God so that He can accept me as His child, then this is:

- Pleasing to Him.
- Something He is NOT impressed with at all.
- Something I need to do more and more until I get His attention.

ROMANS 8:10-11

The solution then remains for me to: **quit** / **continue** trying to realize that my victory over sin is only possible through a continuous and daily dependence on Christ.

Complete the following personalized prayer:
Dear LORD, ***since Your Spirit who raised Jesus from the dead dwells in me, I pray that:***

____.

SHARE IT

I realize that my victory over sin is only possible through a continuous and daily dependence on Christ.

WEEK 39 WEDNESDAY

TRUTH: ROMANS 8:12-25

ROMANS 8:12-15

The following statement best describes how I live my life and make decisions:

- "If it feels good, then I do it."
- "I have to do everything to control every bodily desire."
- "I put my faith in God's Spirit and Word to direct me as I joyfully seek to obey."

ROMANS 8:16

As far as being a child of God is concerned,

- That is something I am constantly aware of, thanks to God's Spirit who regularly reminds me.
- That is something I occasionally doubt since I don't feel like it.
- That is something I cannot claim to be since I don't even know how that is possible.

Choose and fill in one of the two:

- I am having issues believing that I am a child of God, and I think talking to (name) ______________________ this week will help me better understand this.

OR

- I am pretty confident about my status as a child of God, but I know ______________________ who has challenges with this so I will help explain this to them this week.

ROMANS 8:17

I have always known that:

- Being a child of God would guarantee a life of no suffering.
- Suffering is part and parcel of being a Christian.

ROMANS 8:18

"For I consider that the sufferings of this present time are not worthy to be compared with the glory which shall be revealed in us."

- I strongly believe this.
- I have difficulties believing this.
- Lord, I really need Your help to believe this.

SHARE IT

"If I had not felt certain that every additional trial was ordered by infinite love and mercy, I could not have survived my accumulated sufferings." ~ Adoniram Judson

THURSDAY WEEK 39

TRUTH: ROMANS 8:26-39

ROMANS 8:26

I **Somewhat / Totally / Do not** identify with this verse, in the sense that I sometimes get overwhelmed by situations in life when I don't even know how or what to pray about.

ROMANS 8:26-27

Knowing that I am not alone and that the Holy Spirit prays on my behalf in times of my weaknesses makes me feel:

- ENCOURAGED
- NOTHING
- ECSTATIC
- SPECIAL

ROMANS 8:28

God says that all things work out for my good if I love Him. Yet, when I am in the midst of a hard time:

- I find it hard to believe because ______________________________.
- I feel so ______________________________.
- I choose to ______________________________.

ROMANS 8:31

When I mess up (I should call it what it is: sin!) or when faced by hard times, I've got to be honest and ...

- Admit that sometimes I find it hard to believe that God is on my side.
- Admit that I sometimes feel other things, people, or situations are bigger than God.
- Admit that sometimes even if I know God is for me, He still feels distant from me.
- Admit that I have grown to believe that God is with me no matter what.

ROMANS 8:33-39

I believe the following can bring distance between me and God and can make Him stop loving me: (circle any that apply)

GUILT SIN TRIALS HARD TIMES DEATH

POWERFUL ANGELS EVIL FORCES NOTHING

From today's passage, I choose verse(s) ▢ **32** ▢ **37** ▢ **38-39** as my verse(s) for the week because it reminds me that:

____.

SHARE IT

There is no power, person, or ruler in or out of this world that can separate me from God's love.

WEEK 39 FRIDAY

TRUTH: 2 KINGS 1:1-18

2 KINGS 1:2-3

Ahaziah (son of Ahab and Jezebel) was the new king of Israel.
What kind of king was he?

- Faithful to God like King David, governed by God's will & power
- Unfaithful to God like his dad, served false gods

2 KINGS 1:4

God used His prophet Elijah to get Ahaziah's attention. Because Ahaziah rejected God's power and authority, God's message was, "You shall surely __________."

2 KINGS 1:10-12

How did God protect Elijah when Ahaziah sent soldiers to capture him? ____________

____

2 KINGS 1:13-15

What was different about the third captain who came to Elijah?

- He was smart and brought water to put out the fire before he burned.
- He recognized God's power and authority and asked for mercy.
- He joined Elijah and fought against the king.

The captain recognized who God is, asked for mercy, and received mercy while the king ignored God, served a false god, and received judgment.

Who do I recognize as God in my life? ___________________________

Do I let anything keep me from worshiping God? If so, what is it?

____

Do I recognize God's power and reign in my life? **YES** **NO** **SOMETIMES**

In what area of my life do I need to surrender to God's reign?

____

SHARE IT

When we recognize who God is and who we are, the only option is to ask for mercy. The good news is that God loves giving out mercy.

SATURDAY WEEK 39

TRUTH: 2 KINGS 2:1-11

2 KINGS 2:1-6

Elijah had known for some time that when God was done using him, Elisha would be taking over. (**1 Kings 19**) Elijah had spent the last several years training Elisha and was now ready to pass the torch.

How many times did Elijah give Elisha a chance to leave him? ______
Why do I think Elijah kept giving Elisha a chance to back out? ________________

____

By not backing out, Elisha proved that he was a loyal and committed person. What kind of things am I loyal and committed to? ______________________________

____

2 KINGS 2:8

What word is defined this way?
- Literally: *a loose, sleeveless outer garment similar to a cloak*
- Figuratively: *a person's role or area of responsibility*

Circle One: **MANTLE HERITAGE COLLAR**

What did Elijah's "mantle" represent?
- The supernatural power of God to perform miracles
- The responsibility to represent God to Israel
- The role of delivering God's messages to Israel's people and leaders
- All of the above

Would I want to receive Elijah's mantle? Why or why not? ________________

____

After receiving Elijah's blessing, Elisha got to watch as God supernaturally pulled Elijah away and up into Heaven.
How would I feel if I got to watch that happen? ________________________

Do I have responsibilities to represent God like Elisha? **YES** **NO**
Do I have the same kind of commitment Elisha had? **YES** **NO**

Who is someone I can represent God and His message to today? ______________

____

SHARE IT

I am a representative of the one true King.

WEEK 40 SUNDAY

TRUTH: 2 KINGS 2:12-22

Yesterday I wrote down the name of someone I could represent God to. Did I actually represent God yesterday? ☐ **YES** ☐ **NO**
How? Or Why Not? ____

2 KINGS 2:13-14, 21

Elisha literally picked up Elijah's mantle and began to perform miracles for God and His people.
What is his first miracle? ____
What is his second miracle? ______________________________________

In **Acts 1:8** Jesus was about to go up into Heaven, and He left instructions for His followers. He said, "But you shall receive ___________ when the Holy Spirit has come upon you; and you shall be ______________ to me…"

How is **Acts 1:8** similar to what happened to Elisha? ______________________
____

Now God does not seem to use miracles today the way He did with Elisha and the Apostles, but I can still be a witness for Him like Elisha and the Apostles were.

On the following scale, how good am I at being a witness for God?

0 1 2 3 4 5 6 7 8 9 10
TERRIBLE **OK** **AWESOME**

What is one thing I can change in my life today to make me a better witness? _______
____

Am I willing to do it? ☐ **YES** ☐ **NO**

Someone that I admire for being a great witness for God is:
____

I will reach out to this person and ask them to teach me how to be a better witness for God.
☐ **YES**, I will do this. ☐ **NO**, I don't have time for this.

SHARE IT

"Now then, we are ambassadors for Christ, as though God were pleading through us: we implore you on Christ's behalf, be reconciled to God." ~ **2 Corinthians 5:20**

MONDAY WEEK 40

TRUTH: 2 KINGS 4:1-17

Something about this passage feels so familiar, probably because it's almost a duplicate of **1 Kings 17:8-24**. Let me see if I can separate the two stories.

Which prophet did what?

Helped a widow in Sidon	**Elijah**	**Elisha**
Helped the widow of another godly prophet	**Elijah**	**Elisha**
Produced enough oil to pay back a debt	**Elijah**	**Elisha**
Produced enough flour and oil to make food	**Elijah**	**Elisha**
Raised a widow's dead son back to life	**Elijah**	**Elisha**
Miraculously caused a couple to give birth to a son	**Elijah**	**Elisha**

The prophets have changed, but really awesome stuff keeps happening. That is because their God has stayed the same. What are at least three things I can learn about God through the miracles His prophets performed?

God is ____________________.

God is ____________________.

God is ____________________.

Elijah and Elisha did not perform miracles for every widow and older couple in Israel, but we see God's character in the ones they did. I have to remember that I serve the same God, and I can go to the same God that worked through Elijah and Elisha. I am going to do that right now.

I'm going to journal my prayer here, talking to God about how awesome He is and how desperately I need His power in my life today.

____

____

____

____

____

____

____

____

____

SHARE IT

"You cannot do God's work without God's power."
~ John C. Rice

WEEK 40 TUESDAY

TRUTH: 2 KINGS 4:18-37

Resurrection from the dead is the signature move of God. Only by the power of God can someone return from death to life. There is not a single verifiable record in human history of a resurrection outside of the Biblical narrative. Without looking it up online, how many instances of resurrection do I think there are in the Bible? ____________

Now, using Google, how many people were raised from the dead in the Bible? ________

2 KINGS 4:29-35

Do I think this resurrection was an easy or hard process? **Easy / Hard**

Why do I think the writer included all these details about what happened?

- ☐ As proof it really happened; the more details you include in a testimony, the harder it is to make it up
- ☐ Because the writer really likes details
- ☐ I have no idea.

The fact that God has the power over death is one of the foundational truths of Scripture. When Jesus rose from the dead, He proved not only that He had the power of God, but that resurrection is in store for all who believe in Him.
(**John 11:25; 1 Thessalonians 4:16**)

Do I personally know any Christians that have died? If so, who? ____________

____

Who do I miss? Who do I really want to see alive again? ____________

____

Do I really believe God will raise the dead back to life when He comes back?

☐ **YES** ☐ **NO**

Do I think I will be resurrected? Why or why not? ____________

____

I should be comforted and encouraged to know what will happen to me when I die if I have trusted in Jesus' death and resurrection to save me from my sins. I will to pray to God right now thanking Him and talking to Him about the day I will get to meet Him face to face. ☐

SHARE IT

"In Your name I come alive to declare your victory. The resurrected King is resurrecting me!"
~ Elevation Worship (Lyrics from "Resurrecting")

WEDNESDAY WEEK 40

TRUTH: 2 KINGS 4:38-44

What is the longest I have ever gone between meals? ______________________

Israel had chosen to turn away from God and serve many false gods but especially the god known as Baal. Baal was supposedly the god of thunderstorms, bringer of rain, and fertility. Baal was supposed to make the land and the people prosperous.

So why was Israel experiencing famine, and why do we keep meeting widows with dying or dead children? ____

____

2 KINGS 4:38-41

Elisha had an interesting opportunity to teach a lesson at dinnertime. There was a famine, but they had to eat, so Elisha's followers went out to the field, found items that looked good, and put it all in the pot.

What happened next?
- They had a feast!
- They all started getting sick.

The men realized they accidentally poisoned themselves, and they cried out to Elisha for help. What did Elisha do next?
- He prayed over the men, and they were all healed.
- He added flour to the soup to neutralize the poison.

The men had to eat, but they had to eat the right food, or they would die.

Israel had made the same mistake the men had made. Instead of following God's direction, they headed out into the world and grabbed things and brought them back home to make a part of their lives.

What happened next?
- The things they brought back made their lives wonderful.
- The things they brought back started killing them.

As Israel realized things were not going well, what did they do?
- The majority cried out to God for salvation.
- The majority turned to false gods for salvation.

Israel needed the right thing to worship or they would die.

I need to be careful about the things I bring into my life. Is there anything that I've brought into my life that is slowly poisoning me? If so, what? ______________________

____

What am I going to do about it today? ______________________________

SHARE IT

"The recognition of sin is the beginning of salvation."
~ Martin Luther

WEEK 40 THURSDAY

TRUTH: 2 KINGS 5:1-16

There are a lot of people and places mentioned in the verses today, let me see if I can get them all straight. (Match the columns)

Naaman	Leader of the Syrian army
Syria	The largest river in Israel
Naaman's slave	A young girl taken captive from Israel
Samaria	Rivers in Syria
Elisha	The part of Israel where Elisha lived
Abanah & Pharpar	The prophet from Samaria
Jordan	Country on Israel's northern border with Israel

2 KINGS 5:1

What was Naaman's problem? ______________________________

This disease was incredibly painful, deadly, and incurable.

2 KINGS 5:3-4

How did Naaman learn that God could heal him? ______________________________

____

2 KINGS 5:10

What did Elisha tell Naaman he had to do in order to be cured? ____________________

____

2 KINGS 5:14

In order to be cured, Naaman needed to humble himself and wash in what he considered a dirty or insignificant river, but when he did, he came up with skin that had been made new: "…his flesh was restored like the flesh of a ____________ ____________ ..."

Naaman's story is just like our own. He had to come to God in humility, willing to do things God's way, and trusting Him to do the cleansing.

Do I have that kind of faith? **YES** **NO** **SOMETIMES**

Do I need to come to God for cleansing? **YES** **NO** **SOMETIMES**

Do I need to right now? **YES** **NO**

SHARE IT

"If we confess our sins, He is faithful and just to forgive us our sins and to cleanse us from all unrighteousness." ~ **1 John 1:9**

FRIDAY WEEK 40

TRUTH: 2 KINGS 5:17-27

2 KINGS 5:17-19

Naaman was overjoyed at the miraculous healing he received from God. It led him to truly believe in God, and he said in **verse 17** that he would "no longer offer either burnt offering or sacrifice to _______ ______, but to the ________."

2 KINGS 5:20

Naaman wanted to pay Elisha for his healing, but Elisha refused the payment knowing that God did not want people to buy or earn their healing but receive it through faith. However, there was someone there who did not understand all this.
Who was it? ____________________

TRUE OR FALSE.

T F Gehazi was greedy for Naaman's wealth.
T F Gehazi celebrated that Naaman had become a believer.
T F Gehazi tricked Naaman.
T F Gehazi delivered a false message from Elisha.
T F Gehazi stole money and clothes from Naaman.
T F Gehazi lied to Elisha.

Unfortunately, this is far too common. People lie and steal by misrepresenting God, His work, and His Word in order to get ahead in life. Elisha swiftly caught Gehazi in his lies, and Gehazi was severely punished by God.

Do I know anyone who misrepresents God for personal gain? ■ **YES** ■ **NO**
Do I let them trick me? ■ **YES** ■ **NO**
Do I ever try to use God for my personal benefit? ■ **YES** ■ **NO**

Who is someone I can ask to hold me accountable in my efforts to represent God? Who will help me be the best representative I can be? _________________________

I will talk to them today. ■ **YES** ■ **NO**

SHARE IT

"If a sinner comes into your assembly or you otherwise come into contact with him, remember that he is a human being for whom Christ died. He stands at the foot of the cross, just as you stand at the foot of the cross." ~ J. Vernon McGee

WEEK 40 SATURDAY

TRUTH: 2 KINGS 6:1-7

2 KINGS 6:1

The "Sons of the Prophets" were a group of men who began training as prophets under Elijah (they are first mentioned in **1 Kings 20:35**) and continued their training under Elisha. These men were part of the few faithful members of Israel who worshiped God and wanted to help point their fellow citizens to God.

What was the problem they had in **verse 1**?

- They were running out of food.
- Their numbers were growing, and they were running out of room.
- There had been a fight, and they needed a mediator.

2 KINGS 6:2-5

In this passage I can learn a lot about the character of these men who were training to serve God and represent Him to their country.

Match the characteristic with the action:

ACTION	CHARACTER TRAIT
They wanted to build a simple wooden building.	**They were hardworking and willing to work with their hands.**
They collected their own materials.	**They were respectful.**
They asked for Elisha's permission.	**They were honest and cared for others.**
They asked for Elisha to come with them.	**They sought godly leadership and companionship.**
They did all the work themselves.	**They were modest, not worried about being fancy.**
They were upset they accidentally lost something that did not belong to them.	**They were financially conservative and not materialistic.**

Which of those characteristics do I also have? ______________________

Which of those characteristics do I struggle with? ______________________

Which of those characteristics do I think is most important in a spiritual leader like a pastor? And why? ______________________

____

Who could I go to in order to help me become more like the "Sons of the Prophets"?

____

SHARE IT

"A true and safe leader is likely to be one who has no desire to lead, but is forced into a position of leadership by the inward pressure of the Holy Spirit and the press of the external situation." ~ A.W. Tozer

SUNDAY WEEK 41

TRUTH: 2 KINGS 6:8-23

It is really easy to forget that there is a whole world out there that I do not understand and powers at work that I can never compete with or control. That is the lesson learned in these verses first by the king of Syria, then by Elisha's servant, and finally by the king of Israel.

2 KINGS 6:8-12

Why did the king of Syria think there was a spy in his army? ____________________

____

2 KINGS 6:13-14

What did the king of Syria do when he learned of Elisha? ____________________

____

2 KINGS 6:15-17

With the Syrian army all around them, what did Elisha ask God to do for his servant?

____

2 KINGS 6:18

What did Elisha ask God to do to the Syrian army? ____________________

2 KINGS 6:19-20

Where did Elisha take them? ____________________

2 KINGS 6:20-23

When God removed their blindness, the Syrian army realized that they had been captured. How about me?

Is it possible that I am spiritually blind to things in my life?	YES	NO	SOMETIMES
Do I always see God at work around me?	YES	NO	SOMETIMES
Is it possible that God is there but I do not see Him?	YES	NO	SOMETIMES
Are there people in my life that I blindly follow?	YES	NO	SOMETIMES
Are there things that trick me and lead me captive?	YES	NO	SOMETIMES
Do I need God to open my eyes?	YES	NO	SOMETIMES

PRAY: *Dear God, I ask today that You would open my eyes to see You in my life and all the things You are doing in, and through, and around me. I also ask that You keep me from being blinded by sin and led into captivity. In Jesus' Name, Amen.*

SHARE IT

"If the Lord's people will humble themselves by admitting that deception is quite possible to them, they will be the less deceived." ~ Watchman Nee

WEEK 41 MONDAY

TRUTH: 2 KINGS 6:24-33

How do I usually react when I realize that I am in a mess or when things start to go wrong in my life?

- I blame myself.
- I blame others.
- I blame God.

2 KINGS 6:24-30

What had to happen for Joram (the king of Israel) to realize just how bad things had become in Samaria?

- He met an angel that warned him.
- He saw two men fighting over a bucket of water.
- He found out two women had eaten one of their own children.

2 KINGS 6:33

Who did Joram blame for the desolation of his people?

- He blamed himself.
- He blamed the Israelites.
- He blamed God.

Why do I think God had let the situation get so bad in Israel? ______________________

____

God was in control, and He had sent the famine and the Syrians, but who do I think was really to blame for everything? ______________________

Am I facing any tough situations in life right now? If so, what is it? ______________________

____

Why do I think God lets tough situations come at me? ______________________

____

Sometimes difficult life situations are God's way of getting my attention, sometimes they're a natural consequence for my actions, and sometimes they just happen because I live in a messed-up world.

How do I think I should respond to difficult life situations? ______________________

____

Do I know anyone going through a tough situation that I can pray for right now? If so, who? ______________________

SHARE IT

"The Lord is not slow to fulfill his promise as some count slowness, but is patient toward you, not wishing that any should perish, but that all should reach repentance."
~ **2 Peter 3:9** (ESV)

TUESDAY WEEK 41

TRUTH: 2 KINGS 7:1-11

When would the Israelites learn that God could truly handle all their problems? God kept proving His might and power over and over, and they just kept rejecting Him.
Do I do that? ☐ **YES** ☐ **NO** ☐ **SOMETIMES**

2 KINGS 7:1-2

Did the officer believe Elisha when he said everything would be better by the next day?
☐ **YES** ☐ **NO** ☐ **I DON'T KNOW.**

2 KINGS 7:3-8

Why did the lepers go out to the camp of the Syrians? ____________________

What did the lepers do when they found the camp empty? ____________________

2 KINGS 7:9-11

The word was spreading now that God had saved the day again. How would I react if I had been living in Samaria at the time? ____________________

It is so easy to forget that God really is in control and that He can handle any situation that I face. Yesterday I was asked if I am facing any difficult situations in life right now. I need to talk to God about the hardest thing I am facing and ask Him to step in to help me. I am going to journal my prayer here so that I can process through it:

SHARE IT

"The name of the LORD is a strong tower; the righteous run to it and are safe." ~ **Proverbs 18:10**

WEEK 41 WEDNESDAY

TRUTH: 2 KINGS 7:12-20

Yesterday I prayed that God would help me.
Has He helped me yet? If so, how? ______________________________

____

2 KINGS 7:12-17

Initially the king of Israel did not believe that the Syrians were really gone. He was convinced that the Syrians were playing some kind of trick. Have I ever had something happen that was so good I did not think it could be true? What happened? __________

____

When it became clear that something miraculous had happened, what do I think the king should have done?

- Declare a full day of worshiping God
- Hold a feast in God's honor
- Go honor Elisha as God's prophet
- Just let the people plunder the empty camp

How do I react when God does amazing things in my life?

- I give God the glory and tell everybody how wonderful He is.
- I thank God for His mercy and care.
- I take advantage of what He has done without ever thanking Him or giving Him the credit for it.

When was the last time I noticed God do something incredible for me? __________

____

How did I respond to His work? ______________________________

____

Who will I tell today about what God has done for me?

____

SHARE IT

"What are you really living for? It's crucial to realize that you either glorify God, or you glorify something or someone else. You're always making something look big." ~ Ken Sande

THURSDAY WEEK 41

TRUTH: 2 KINGS 9:1-10, 30-37

What did God say He would do to King Ahab in **1 Kings 21:20-22**?

____

What did God say He would do to Jezebel in **1 Kings 21:23**?

____

2 KINGS 9:1-3

God is ready to follow through on His word to Ahab. Who does God tell Elisha to go anoint as the new king of Israel? ______________________

2 KINGS 9:7-10

What is God's message to Jehu in **verse 7**?
"You shall ___________________ the house of _________ your master, that I may ____________ the blood of My servants the __________, and the blood of all the servants of the __________, at the hand of Jezebel."

2 KINGS 9:30-37

While being pretty graphic, what do these verses teach me about God?

- He keeps His word.
- His judgment of the wicked is brutal and decisive.
- He avenges His martyrs.

Do I want God to keep His word? **YES** **NO** **SOMETIMES**
Do I want God to judge the wicked? **YES** **NO** **SOMETIMES**
Do I want God to avenge His martyrs? **YES** **NO** **SOMETIMES**

I have seen throughout 1st and 2nd Kings that God loves to give mercy, but He is also just. Which do I think is more important?

- Justice is more important than mercy.
- Mercy is more important than justice.
- Both are equally important.

Do I try to be just/fair with people in my life? **YES** **NO** **SOMETIMES**
Do I try to be merciful with people in my life? **YES** **NO** **SOMETIMES**
What is something I can do differently today to do both better? ____________________

____

SHARE IT

Mercy, detached from justice, grows unmerciful. ~ C.S. Lewis

WEEK 41 FRIDAY

TRUTH: 2 KINGS 13:14-21

Elisha's ministry on earth was coming to a close, but I get one more glimpse into God's power at work in him. I get to see a prophecy and a resurrection.

2 KINGS 13:14-19

Elisha's final living miracle was to reassure the king of Israel that God would grant him victory over the Syrians.
What does this tell me about God's feelings toward Israel? ______________________

____

2 KINGS 13:20-21

Elisha was dead now but still had one more miracle to perform. What happened when a dead corpse accidentally touched Elisha's corpse in his tomb? ______________________

____

After both of these miracles and all the other miracles in his life, what would I think of Elisha if I had lived in those days? ______________________

____

Would I have listened to Elisha or would I have ignored him? ______________________

____

Almost a thousand years later, when Jesus was on the earth, during a parable He said this, "If they do not hear Moses and the prophets, neither will they be persuaded though one rise from the dead." (**Luke 16:31**) How does this relate to the life of Elijah and Elisha?

____

People think that if they could just see miracles, then they would believe in God and follow Him. Do I think this way? ☐ **YES** ☐ **NO**

Did the people of Israel follow God after watching His prophets perform incredible miracles for decades? ☐ **YES** ☐ **NO**

Do I believe and follow God or am I waiting for a miracle to happen before I will?

____

SHARE IT

"A faith built on seeing miracles is no faith at all. Such a faith is merely entertainment fascination, and it goes away as soon as the performer does." ~ Unknown

SATURDAY WEEK 41

TRUTH: 2 KINGS 17:6-23

God keeps His word. For Israel (the northern kingdom), this meant their time had finally come to an end.

2 KINGS 17:6, 23

What did the king of Assyria do to Israel? ______________________________

____

2 KINGS 17:7-17

The author took the time to list out all of the sins that had led Israel to their judgment and destruction; let me see if I can catch the highlights:

"Israel ____________ against the LORD their God." (**v. 7**)
"They had _________ other gods." (**v. 7**)
"They did __________ things to provoke the LORD to anger." (**v. 11**)
"They _________ His statutes and His covenant." (**v. 15**)
"They left all the ________________ of the LORD their God." (**v. 16**)
"They worshiped all the host of heaven, and served ______." (**v. 16**)

2 KINGS 17:13-14

God sent His prophets to warn the people and call them back to God, but how did the people respond? (Choose One)

- They listened and returned to God.
- They were stubborn and ignored God.

2 KINGS 17:22-23

This is the legacy of the northern kingdom of Israel, and I need to put it in my own words:
Because Israel did this ____
God did this ____.

Is there a sin in my life that I know God has been trying to get my attention about? Is there a sin that I have been holding onto that I do not want to give up? If so, what is it?

____

Has God sent people to talk to me about it? **YES** **NO**
Am I ready to do something about it? Or am I going to be like Israel? ____________

____

SHARE IT

"Truly, these times of ignorance God overlooked, but now commands all men everywhere to repent." ~ **Acts 17:30**

WEEK 42 SUNDAY

TRUTH: 2 KINGS 17:24-41

2 KINGS 17:24-29

As was their custom, after taking all the people of Israel out of the northern kingdom, Assyria moved some of its own people to go live in the land of Israel.

TRUE OR FALSE.

T F The foreigners brought their own false gods to the land.
T F The foreigners were God's people.
T F God was ignored by the people in the Promised Land.
T F God sent bears into the land to eat people.
T F The foreigners realized they needed to honor God.
T F The foreigners built altars to God and feared Him.
T F The foreigners continued to serve their own gods.

2 KINGS 17:41

The new residents of Israel figured out that as long as they recognized God and gave Him some honor, they could still serve their other gods and pretty much do whatever they wanted.

Did this make them true followers of God? **YES** **NO**
Did they ultimately become God's new people? **YES** **NO**

What do I think about today?

TRUE OR FALSE.

T F People today act like those foreigners.
T F Many people today admit that there is probably a God.
T F Many people today serve their own will and their own "gods."
T F Some people think living like this makes them followers of God.
T F Many people think as long as they give God some honor they can do their own thing, and it will all be ok.

Do I ever live like that? If so, how? ______________________________

____

Do I fear God but serve other "gods"? If so, how? ______________________

____

What are some "gods" I can remove from my life as I try to fully follow God? ______

____

SHARE IT

"If we exalt money, status, or sex above the Word of God, we are living in idolatry. Every time we inwardly submit to the strongholds of fear, bitterness, and pride, we are bowing to the rulers of darkness. Each of these idols must be smashed, splintered, and obliterated from the landscape of our hearts." ~ Francis Frangipane

MONDAY WEEK 42

TRUTH: 2 KINGS 19:5-20

Let me make sure I got the details right: (Match)

Judah	**King of Assyria**
King Hezekiah	**King of Judah**
Isaiah	**Capitol city of Judah**
Jerusalem	**Prophet of God living in Judah**
Sennacherib	**Southern Kingdom of Israel**

2 KINGS 19:5-7

Sennacherib was threatening to conquer Jerusalem, and trying to intimidate Hezekiah and the people. What was Isaiah's message from God to Hezekiah? ____________________

____

2 KINGS 19:8-13

When Sennacherib heard that Isaiah told Hezekiah not to fear or surrender, what was his response?

- Do not trust your God.
- I will destroy you like I destroy everyone.
- No god has ever been able to stop me and neither will yours.
- All of the above.

2 KINGS 19:14-19

What did Hezekiah do when he got the response from Sennacherib?

____

Why did Hezekiah want God to get involved? (**v. 19**)

____

How was Hezekiah's response different from the behavior of the kings of the Northern Kingdom when they were in trouble? ____

____

2 KINGS 19:20

God reassured Hezekiah that He was going to fight for Judah and His own glory because Hezekiah had prayed to Him. All Hezekiah had to do was ask. What do I need to ask God to do in my life today? I'm going to write it down and then pray about it. ____________

____

____

SHARE IT

"Our God is the Lion, the Lion of Judah, He's roaring with power and fighting our battles and every knee will bow before Him!"
~ Big Daddy Weave (Lyrics from "The Lion & The Lamb")

WEEK 42 TUESDAY

TRUTH: 2 KINGS 19:35-20:11

2 KINGS 19:35-37

Sennacherib had boldly declared that he could defeat God and destroy Jerusalem. How did God handle the Assyrian army? ______________________________

____

How did God handle Sennacherib? ______________________________

2 KINGS 20:1-6

Hezekiah had a terminal illness and called out to God to heal him.
What was Hezekiah's claim in **verse 3**? "…I have ______________ before You in ______________ and with a ______________________, and have done what was __________ in Your sight."

Because of Hezekiah's humility, devotion to God, and his godly leadership of Israel, God healed him and gifted him more years of life.
How many more years did God promise Hezekiah? ______________

What is the sign God performed through Isaiah in order to prove His promise to Hezekiah?

- ☐ He made writing appear on the bedroom wall.
- ☐ He moved the sun to turn back time on the sun dial.
- ☐ He killed 15 sheep with lightning.

The king who raised his fist toward God in proud defiance had his life ended early by his own sons.

The king who got on his knees before God and asked for help had his life supernaturally extended.

What can I learn from these two men? ______________________________

____

Do I know anybody living today who is like Sennacherib? If so, who? ______________

Do I know anybody living today who is like Hezekiah? If so, who? ______________

Which one am I like? ______________________

SHARE IT

"They that know God will be humble, and they that know themselves, cannot be proud." ~ John Flavel

WEDNESDAY WEEK 42

TRUTH: 2 KINGS 20:12-21

What are the things I am most proud of in my life? What are my greatest achievements or possessions? ____________________

____

If the leader of my country came to my house and asked for a tour, what would I show him and why? ____________________

____

2 KINGS 20:13

What do I think was the most powerful and valuable thing or presence in Israel?

____

If Hezekiah wanted to show off the splendor and glory of Israel, what (or who) should he have introduced to the visiting diplomats? ____________

Instead of introducing the diplomats to God or His prophet Isaiah, Hezekiah decided to show off all of his ____________________.

When I meet someone for the first time, what do I want people to know about me?

____

When people want to learn about me, **do I talk about my God** or **do I talk about myself and my abilities, experiences, or possessions**?

I wonder what it would look like if I used opportunities to talk about myself to actually talk about God. I am going to write a list right here to help me be ready:

I am ____________________, but my God is ____________________.

I used to ____________________, but my God always ____________________.

I have ____________________, but my God has ____________________.

Isaiah warned Hezekiah that one day his valuables would be stolen. I need to ask God to help me value the right things in my life.

PRAY: *Dear God, please help me to value You and my relationship with You above all else. Help me remember that You are the only thing that can never been stolen from me, and You are the only thing worth boasting about. Help me to make much of You with my life. In Jesus' Name, Amen.*

SHARE IT

"My soul shall make its boast in the LORD; the humble shall hear of it and be glad." ~ **Psalm 34:2**

WEEK 42 THURSDAY

TRUTH: 2 KINGS 22:3-10; 23:1-3

Four important words to define in this text: (Match the word with its definition)

Commandment	**An account, witness, or record**
Testimony	**An alliance, pledge, or agreement**
Statute	**An ordinance, custom, or something prescribed**
Covenant	**A divine rule, precept, or law**

2 KINGS 22:3-7

Josiah was the last godly king of Judah. He wrote a blank check to do repair work on the Temple which had fallen into disrepair. During the construction work, the high priest found the Book of the Law.

Why was this such a big deal? (Choose One)

- ☐ The Book of the Law was the earliest version of the Bible, and it was probably the only copy in Jerusalem at this time.
- ☐ It held secrets that had been written down by the early kings of Israel.

Why do I think that something so valuable had been lost? ______________________________

____

2 KINGS 23:1-3

How did King Josiah respond when he heard what was written in the Book? (Choose one)

- ☐ He told the priests to lock it back up in the Temple so that no one else would hear it.
- ☐ He got the whole city together and read it out loud.

Verse 3 says that after reading the Book of the Law, Josiah made a covenant with God to, "______________ the Lord, and ______________ His commandments…"

Verse 3 also says, "all the people ______________________________ the covenant."

Am I committed to the Bible the way Josiah was?	☐ **YES**	☐ **NO**	☐ **MAYBE**
Will I be more committed?	☐ **YES**	☐ **NO**	☐ **MAYBE**
Am I willing to take a stand for the Bible?	☐ **YES**	☐ **NO**	☐ **MAYBE**

SHARE IT

"I believe the Bible is the best gift God has ever given to man. All the good from the Savior of the world is communicated to us through this Book." ~ *Abraham Lincoln*

FRIDAY WEEK 42

TRUTH: 2 TIMOTHY 1:1-7

2 TIMOTHY 1:1-2

Notice the "to" and "from" in these verses? Paul is writing to Timothy because Timothy needs to be reminded why life is worth living for Jesus. During this period in history, Christians were being horribly persecuted for their faith.

How about me? Have I ever felt under attack because of my faith?

- At school because I stood up for what the Bible said rather than what the teacher taught
- By my friends/peers because I wouldn't back down from doing what was right when it wasn't popular
- By my family because I believe in Jesus, but they don't
- Some other way? ______________________________

Just like me, Timothy was scared about what would happen if he lived his life out loud for Jesus! Often Timothy is called Timid Timothy.
Have I ever felt timid about something I know I should do? **YES** **NO**
If yes, then why?

- Fear of the unknown (worry), not knowing what to do
- Lacking confidence
- Shy - I don't like to be the center of attention

2 TIMOTHY 1:3-5

Paul and Timothy obviously had some history. Paul knew about what kind of home Timothy grew up in and had watched how God had worked in Timothy and his family.
What is in my history? What have I or my family gone through?
Sickness (maybe cancer?), divorce, losing a loved one, getting dumped, feeling left out, something else? ______________________________

____

2 TIMOTHY 1:6-7

If I saw God work in the situation above, I know He can work in and through my life right now. He has given me tools to face whatever scary/hard thing is happening right now.
Today, with God's strength, I will choose to face this fear:

____

____

SHARE IT

"For God has not given us a spirit of fear, but of power and of love and of a sound mind." ~ **2 Timothy 1:7**

WEEK 42 SATURDAY

TRUTH: 2 TIMOTHY 1:8-12

2 TIMOTHY 1:10-12

Was Paul ashamed of the Gospel? ■ **YES** ■ **NO**

Have I known anyone who did something that wasn't popular? ■ **YES** ■ **NO**

The truth is that the Gospel isn't always popular either. There are times when the Bible says one thing, while culture, friends, and family say the other.

How does someone act when they are ashamed of Jesus? ______________________

____

Have I ever acted ashamed of Jesus? ■ **YES** ■ **NO**

Being ashamed of Jesus implies that what He did on the cross doesn't matter or that it was pointless. Could it be that I don't totally understand the Gospel accurately?

Read **1 Corinthians 15:3-4**. This is the Gospel!
Has there been a time when I realized that Jesus took the punishment for my sins by dying on the cross? ■ **YES** ■ **NO**
Does it make any sense for me to be embarrassed by this? ■ **YES** ■ **NO**

Am I aware of verses that speak about salvation? ■ **YES** ■ **NO**
Answer these questions and read the verses if unfamiliar with them:

Do I consider myself to be a "good person" and is that enough to have a relationship with God and get to Heaven? ■ **YES** ■ **NO** Read **Romans 3:23**

On a scale of 1-5, I think sin is a "big deal."
No, it's not. 1 2 3 4 5 Yes, it is. Read **Romans 6:23**

I sometimes struggle believing that God would be willing to die in my place.
■ **YES** ■ **NO** Read **Romans 5:8**

How can I trust Christ as my Savior? Read **Romans 10:9-10**

Do I ever wonder if God really forgives me? ■ **YES** ■ **NO** Read **Romans 10:13**

These verses are called the "Romans Road."
Do I believe it to be truth? ■ **YES** ■ **NO**
Would I consider memorizing it so I'll be able to share it? ■ **YES** ■ **NO**

SHARE IT

Jesus died for you in public so don't only live for Him in private.

SUNDAY WEEK 43

TRUTH: 2 TIMOTHY 1:13-18

2 TIMOTHY 1:13-14

Paul is asking Timothy to be loyal to the pattern of faith that he showed him. More importantly, Paul asks Timothy to guard/keep what? ______________________________

____

Paul is telling Timothy to stick to what is true, first and foremost. Not everyone has the same values. But the bottom line is, what Jesus did for me on the cross is always the most valuable thing. Stick with that. Stick with the Gospel!

Do I treat it that way, as a highly valued gift? ☐ **YES** ☐ **NO**

Heroes are a fun part of life. Sometimes it's good to see someone with skin on them who is doing it right. Who are some people I know that stick to the principles found in God's Word? (Circle all that apply.)

PASTOR MISSIONARY YOUTHLEADER MENTOR PARENT FRIEND

Have I ever stopped to thank them for their example? ☐ **YES** ☐ **NO**

☐ I will let them know of my gratitude today.

2 TIMOTHY 1:15-16

Which group was loyal to Paul?

Phygelus & Hermogenes **The household of Onesiphorus**

Paul considered a loyal friend a great gift from God! Onesiphorus refreshed Paul, wasn't ashamed of him, and sought out Paul even when he was hard to find.

Do I have friends like this? ☐ **YES** ☐ **NO**

Am I this kind of friend? ☐ **YES** ☐ **NO**

BRAINSTORM: How can I be a better friend to ______________________________ ?

PRAY: *I am thankful for my friend______________________ because they are loyal to You, God. Today I pray for creativity as I seek to refresh them by serving them as You would have me to do. Maybe this is what I could do:* ________________________

____.

SHARE IT

"A true friend holds you up when you stumble and holds you down when you stray." ~ James MacDonald

WEEK 43 MONDAY

TRUTH: 2 TIMOTHY 2:1-7

2 TIMOTHY 2:1

Paul lays out a spiritual workout plan. What does Paul say gives strength? ___________

Grace from Jesus gives me a different perspective about my circumstance and empowers me to live out my faith! Let's check out the illustrations Paul gives to get a better grasp on the topic of grace.

2 TIMOTHY 2:4

Example of a S__________: he doesn't complain about things that most people do. He has a mission to complete!

Am I a complainer? ☐ **YES** ☐ **NO**
What have I complained about recently? ____________________________________

So where's the grace in this example? God gives me purpose and aim. The goal dictates my present choices so that what others see as pain, I can see as opportunity.

2 TIMOTHY 2:5

Example of an __________: competes according to the rules.

Is there a sin in my life that I am having a hard time getting rid of because I'm making my own rules? ☐ **YES** ☐ **NO**
If yes, name it: ____.

Where's the grace in this example? God gives us guidelines and counsel. It is so nice to know what is expected and how best to succeed! The discipline will pay off in the end!

2 TIMOTHY 2:6

Example of a F___________: Benefits from his/her hard work.
How's my work ethic? ____
If it's bad, in what area am I slacking off? __________________________________

Where's the grace? God rewards hard work!

Looking at my answers above, am I spiritually **fit** or **unfit**? (Circle)

SHARE IT

"Nothing whatever pertaining to godliness and real holiness can be accomplished without grace." ~ St. Augustine

TUESDAY WEEK 43

TRUTH: 2 TIMOTHY 2:8-14

2 TIMOTHY 2:8-10

Who does Paul say we need to remember as we serve? ________________

When I do things for the wrong reasons, it's easy to quit when the going gets rough.

In what ways have I served Jesus in the past? (Circle all that apply.)

Did community service **Helped at church** **Witnessed to someone**

Gone on a missions trip **Gave/Raised money for a good cause**

Encouraged someone **Other:** ________________

Have I ever found myself serving for the wrong reason? ☐ **YES** ☐ **NO**

If yes, for what reasons did I do "good"? Be honest.

- ☐ So I didn't get in trouble
- ☐ To make myself look/feel good
- ☐ So a girl/guy would notice me
- ☐ Something else: ________________

Is there some "good thing" I am involved in currently that I have had the wrong motives about? ☐ **YES** ☐ **NO** ________________

2 TIMOTHY 2:11-13

Which of these do I identify with today? (Check all that apply.)

- ☐ I am dead to my sin. (**Romans 6:1-2**) This means when I see sin in my life, I am actively dealing with it and seeking to live for Jesus.
- ☐ I am enduring in the faith. I am facing something right now that is difficult but am seeking to bring glory to God through this hard thing.
- ☐ I have serious doubts about who God is and if He even exists.
- ☐ Who cares what God says? I know better for my life.
- ☐ I am an unfaithful follower of Jesus. I know that I am saved, but I am mostly doing my thing, not God's thing.

Considering my answers above, which application(s) below is for me:

- ☐ I am feeling driven to let go of this sin/distraction ________________ because I know when I turn from it, Christ will be able to use my life in amazing ways to impact the world around me.
- ☐ I need to begin a serious search for truth. Right now, I will contact someone whom I know loves Jesus and ask them to help me.

That person will be: ________________

- ☐ Today my prayer is that I can endure outside pressures and live brightly for Jesus. God, I need your strength to endure this thing and be found faithful.

SHARE IT

"I know of nothing which I would choose to have as the subject of my ambition for life than to be kept faithful to my God till death." ~ Charles Spurgeon

WEEK 43 WEDNESDAY

TRUTH: 2 TIMOTHY 2:15-19

2 TIMOTHY 2:16

My words affect others. In fact, this passage says that not caring what comes out of my mouth will lead others to act against God! This is serious business!

How would I rate what comes out of my mouth?

Not caring 0 1 2 3 4 5 Caring

2 TIMOTHY 2:18

Hymenaeus and Philetus were telling people that Jesus had already come back, when it was not true!

This is a lot like people I know. There are rumors and drama all the time!
What do I do when I hear rumors? ______________________________

Proverbs 4:24 - Where should I put crooked speech and devious talk? __________

____

Proverbs 17:9 - What happens to someone who repeats an offense/transgression?

____

Have I ever had a friendship end because of gossip? ☐ **YES** ☐ **NO**

Have I ever considered trying to make that right? ☐ **YES** ☐ **NO**

If no, will I consider making it right? ☐ **YES** ☐ **NO**

Proverbs 26:4 - If I find myself being the target of someone's gossip, what should I do?

____

Here's the secret: A person who gossips twists things to work the way they want. Giving the simple truth will make the situation clear.

Today I will write one of these Proverbs on an index card and will meditate on it as I go about my day. ☐ Done

SHARE IT

Not caring what comes out of my mouth will lead others to act against God!

THURSDAY WEEK 43

TRUTH: 2 TIMOTHY 2:20-26

2 TIMOTHY 2:20

Which kind of vessel is most useful?

GOLD AND SILVER **WOOD AND CLAY**

2 TIMOTHY 2:21

Christians are compared to containers in a large house. I get to choose which kind of "container" I will be! What does a Christian need to do in order to be like an honorable vessel? ______________ his/her self from what is ________________________

2 TIMOTHY 2:22

Having zeal and passion for God is a good thing, but that isn't what Paul is talking about here. He's referring to the kind of passions mentioned in **Ephesians 2:3**. These *youthful passions* are desires that are selfish. They distract me from being a witness for Christ.

What selfish desires (sin) do I struggle with?

- ☐ My reputation or popularity above all else
- ☐ Lust after another person sexually
- ☐ Anger built up toward __________________
- ☐ Other ____

What does Paul say needs to happen when these things come into my mind?
________ them! (**v. 22**)

Notice that the largest portion of this verse handles things that I am to pursue such as righteousness, faith, love, peace, and I'm not supposed to do this alone! I need accountability from other people who are also honestly looking to serve God.

Looking around me, who is a Christian friend(s) who is also growing in their walk with God? __________________________

☐ I've got to get closer to this person!

Hard to find a name? I commit right now to daily pray for a friend to team up with to grow my faith! ☐

2 TIMOTHY 2:23-25

Look through these verses and do an examination.
Yesterday, was I quarrelsome or kind? __________________________________

When was the last time someone sinned against me? ______________
My reaction? (Circle) **I defended my rights** or **I was patient with them.**

SHARE IT

God doesn't want me to do the Christian life alone.

WEEK 43 FRIDAY

TRUTH: 2 TIMOTHY 3:1-7

2 TIMOTHY 3:1

Paul says that there will be what kind of times in the last days (*the time from Jesus' first coming until His second coming*)? ______________

Matthew Henry's Commentary has this to say about this chapter: "Perilous times shall come, for men shall be wicked. Note, sin makes the times perilous. When there is a general corruption of manners, and of the tempers of men, this makes the times dangerous to live in; for it is hard to keep our integrity in the midst of general corruption."

What did Matthew Henry say would make the times perilous? ________

2 TIMOTHY 3:2-7

If I want unbelievers to see Christ in me, I can't live like an unbeliever. Below, I will circle which of these sins I have seen in myself the past few days. I will look up the verses for the sin I have been struggling with and circle them, or better yet, memorize them!

Sin Problem	Biblical Truth about this sin
Lover of Self	Philippians 2:3
Lover of money/pleasure	Proverbs 11:4; Hebrews 11:25
Proud/arrogant/abusive	Proverbs 11:2
Abusive	Proverbs 11:17
Disobedient to parents	Proverbs 1:8-9
Ungrateful, unappeasable	1 Thessalonians 5:18
Heartless, Treacherous	Proverbs 11:20-21
Reckless	1 Peter 5:8; Psalm 101:2
Appearing godly but denying power	2 Peter 1:3
Always learning but never finding truth	Proverbs 14:6

In **Psalm 51:1-13** we see King David's prayer after committing murder and adultery. God was faithful to forgive him, and He will do the same for me.

I have gotten on my knees and prayed about this. ☐ **YES** ☐ **NO**

SHARE IT

"I do not know when I am more perfectly happy than when I am weeping for sin at the foot of the cross."
~ Charles Spurgeon

SATURDAY WEEK 43

TRUTH: 2 TIMOTHY 3:8-12

Have I ever had to write a paper on an historical figure or personal hero who has had an influence on my life? Two opposite kinds of influences are given in this passage: a good influence and a bad influence.

2 TIMOTHY 3:8

Who were the examples of a bad influence? ______________ and ______________

What did these type of men oppose/resist? ______________________________ :
Therefore, they were corrupt in mind and were not saved.

Who have I sought counsel from in the past? (Check all that apply.)

Friend **TV/Online** **Parent** **Grandparent** **Teacher** **Pastor/Youth Leader**

If this person is not using truth from God's Word and/or not in a relationship with Jesus, this passage explains that I may be getting some bad or twisted life advice.

2 TIMOTHY 3:9

"Their folly will be manifest to all." Interesting: Jewish tradition says that Jannes and Jambres may be the names of Pharaoh's magicians who tried to copy the miracles God was doing through Moses. (**Exodus 7:11**) In the end they were stumped and unable to explain away what was genuine.

Am I currently being satisfied with advice that makes me feel good, but I'm realizing isn't true? **YES** **NO** If yes, what is it? ______________________________

I am realizing that I need to be careful where I get advice from.

2 TIMOTHY 3:10

Paul commends Timothy for living a life modeled after a good influence.

Do I know a person like Paul? While no one is perfect, is there someone around me whom I have seen walk faithfully with Jesus through some deep waters? (It could be a peer, upper classman, a parent, an older woman/man in church, a relative, or perhaps a neighbor.)
Name: ______________________

In the next week I will purposefully spend quality time with ______________________ so that I can pick up some of their good habits and learn how they live out their faith.

SHARE IT

"Influence never dies; every act, emotion, look, and word makes influence tell for good or evil…" ~ Thomas A. Kempis

WEEK 44 SUNDAY

TRUTH: 2 TIMOTHY 3:13-17

Paul explains the impact of studying the Bible.

Ever hear the saying, "You reap what you sow"? Where do I spend most of my leisure time? (Circle)

Watching TV/YouTube **Hanging out with friends** **Sports/Exercise** **Art/Music** **Video Games** **In my Bible** **Reading books** **On FB/Pinterest/Instagram/Snapchat** **Other** ______________________________

2 TIMOTHY 3:13

I can say I believe something, but until I live it out, there is no evidence that I really believe what I say. Think about it. Look back at Friday's devotion. Which sins did I say I was struggling with? ______________________________

Have my actions & thoughts changed since seeing what God's Word says about this issue? **YES** **NO**

2 TIMOTHY 3:16

The Bible isn't just a good book. It is God's clear communication to me. It has authority and power.
The Bible is profitable/useful ______________________________
______________________________.

No matter how young I am, I can be taught and be a teacher. There are younger people who are watching me.
Who am I am influencing? ______________________________

Am I **teaching them about how to live like the world**, or
am I **showing them my relationship with Jesus**? (Circle)

2 TIMOTHY 3:17

What is the benefit of studying God's Word? So I can be
______________________ for every ____________ ____________.

Am I memorizing Scripture? **YES** **NO**
Am I regularly spending time reading God's Word? **YES** **NO**
When little trials come up, am I using what I know from the Bible to walk through it? **YES** **NO**
Am I telling others about how to follow Jesus? **YES** **NO**
Am I surrounding myself with influences that seek to live for Jesus? **YES** **NO**

SHARE IT

The Bible isn't just a good book. It is God's clear communication to me. It has authority and power.

MONDAY WEEK 44

TRUTH: 2 TIMOTHY 4:1-4

2 TIMOTHY 4:2

While actions are important, clear communication always involves discussion. If I am going to be an effective witness, I need to both live how God wants me to and use words to explain the Gospel. Timothy is told to always be ready to share truth. I need to share truth with the unsaved and also with other believers.

Have I ever choked on my words when I tried to share the Gospel with an unsaved person? ☐ **YES** ☐ **NO**

In my own words, what does a person need to know to be saved and what Scripture would I give them? ____

____

____

____

I talk about what I am thinking about. If I am continually thinking about Scripture, then it will be easy to share what is already on my mind.

Today will I share what stuck out to me during Quiet Time with someone? ☐ **YES** ☐ **NO**

2 TIMOTHY 4:3

Have I ever been confronted by someone and didn't like what they told me? ☐ **YES** ☐ **NO**
What was my reaction? (Circle those that apply.)

I got an attitude. **I got depressed.** **I used it to get better.**

I got to a quiet spot with God to listen and see if it was true about me.

I made fun of the person. **I ignored them.** **I got angry.**

When things don't make sense when I'm reading the Bible, what do I do?

- ☐ I ask someone for an explanation.
- ☐ I ignore the problem.
- ☐ I do my own research using Bible commentaries.
- ☐ I look for an answer from somewhere else.

2 TIMOTHY 4:4

While myths make great fireside fun, making decisions based on myths will handicap me.

What source should I use to bust myths? **B**__________

SHARE IT

"If you have a Bible that's falling apart, you'll have a life that's not." ~ Adrian Rogers

WEEK 44 TUESDAY

TRUTH: 2 TIMOTHY 4:5-8

2 TIMOTHY 4:5

The word "watchful" (*sober-minded or keeping one's head in all situations*) sounds similar to another passage in **1 Peter 5:8**.

Why am I supposed to be alert and sober-minded in that verse?

____

"Endure afflictions" - **Have I ever had enough of being made fun of? Tired of feeling awkward? Tired of being different?** (Circle if it's true of you.)

Paul, like a coach, encourages Timothy to keep going.
How can I encourage other Christians around me to keep going strong for Jesus? Today I will seek out ____________________ and encourage them.

"Do the work of an evangelist" - Today I will look for an opportunity to share the Gospel with ____________________.

"Fulfill your ministry" - Starting something is the first step, but faithfulness takes endurance, strength, and determination!

Is there something that I've started, but I don't want to finish? ☐ **YES** ☐ **NO**

If so, what is it? ____

Why did I start this in the first place? ______________________________
I will pray that God will give me the strength to finish what He has led me to do.
☐ **YES** ☐ **NO**

2 TIMOTHY 4:6-7

Paul had done his job and done it well. It was time for Timothy to step up into the role Paul once had. Have I ever thought about the day when I will have to be the responsible adult?
☐ **YES** ☐ **NO**

I commit to try to see things from my parents'/adult authority's perspective because I know that one day I will be an adult too! ☐ **YES** ☐ **NO**

2 TIMOTHY 4:8

Paul was thinking of the end goal. Because he was faithful, he would be rewarded by the Lord Himself.

It's said that only two things are forever: the Word of God and the souls of men. In light of eternity (*forever in Heaven with my Savior*) will it make a difference if
____ happens/doesn't happen?

What will make a difference? ____

SHARE IT

It's said that only two things are forever: the Word of God and the souls of men.

WEDNESDAY WEEK 44

TRUTH: 2 TIMOTHY 4:9-15

It is important to encourage other believers, especially when they are in a time of trial.

2 TIMOTHY 4:10

Paul probably felt abandoned by Demas.
Have I ever felt rejected in the following ways? (Circle all that apply.)

Left out of a group **Dumped by a girlfriend/boyfriend**

Forgotten or left by parents **Made fun of** **Other:** ____________________

2 TIMOTHY 4:10

The other men listed probably left in order to do ministry, but still Paul felt alone.
Have I ever felt alone because someone was busy or moved away? ☐ **YES** ☐ **NO**

Like Paul, when I am alone for too long, I can easily get discouraged.
☐ Totally me ☐ I'm kind of a loner.

LONER: Check out **Proverbs 18:1**. While there is nothing wrong with needing alone time, there is such a thing as too much time away.

Am I currently isolating myself from other believers? ☐ **YES** ☐ **NO**

EXAMINE: Could I be running away from a problem? Afraid to get hurt? Wanting to do things my own way? Avoiding saying something wrong?

What are my thoughts? ____

____

Paul knew that he needed to have Christian fellowship and asked for some of his good influencers to visit him.

Maybe my good Christian friends can't visit me right now, but could we

SKYPE/FACETIME/VIDEO CHAT? **FACEBOOK?** **TEXT?** (Circle)

Whom can I contact when I begin to feel discouraged? ____________________ (Make sure that this person is truly a good influencer - Mom and Dad's approval says a lot!)
I often feel discouraged, so I know how others may feel at times. Sometimes, even the happiest people are lonely. Who could I reach out to and encourage today?

____

2 TIMOTHY 4:13

A great way to encourage someone is through giving a gift so the discouraged friend knows they are valuable.
☐ I will do this for ______________________________ this week.

SHARE IT

It is important to encourage other believers, especially when they are in a time of trial.

WEEK 44 THURSDAY

TRUTH: 2 TIMOTHY 4:16-22

2 TIMOTHY 4:16-17

Remember how Paul was in prison because of his faith? He was called into court for his trial, but no one came to be a witness for him.

Was there ever a time when I felt really lonely and there was no one around to encourage me?
☐ **YES** ☐ **NO**

Paul's situation was life and death. It was scary, and he wasn't sure if he would be able to live through it.

Have I ever felt so weak that I thought that I would fall over? A heavy emotional or spiritual burden can bring a person to their knees! What was my experience? ________

____

____

____

☐ I haven't experienced a huge burden like this yet, but I know that I will someday. It is one reason why training in righteousness (**2 Timothy 3:16**) is so important.

Evaluation on my training:
How many days of Quiet Time have I spent with God this week? ______
Have I memorized any verses? ☐ **YES** ☐ **NO**
Have I faced any small trials this week? ☐ **YES** ☐ **NO**
Did I respond **my way** or **God's way**? (Circle)
Who am I allowing to influence me? ☐ **Bad influences** ☐ **Good influences**

Paul was one who trained for trials and when the time came, he was able to stand. Who did Paul say stood by him at his trial? (**v. 17**)__________

Wow! While Paul was weak, he felt the presence of God so vividly that it felt like God was by his side supporting his weight. God's presence kept Paul from choking on his words! God can and will do the same for me!

☐ In the moments I feel weakest I will cry to God for strength!

I don't have to wait to experience deep weakness to feel God's presence. Today I will seek a quiet place alone with just me and God and have a time of worship on my knees in prayer.

☐ I've just finished my time with God.

SHARE IT

In the moments I feel weakest, I will cry to God for strength!

FRIDAY WEEK 44

TRUTH: REVELATION 6:1-17

The Tribulation will be a crazy time. God will be punishing/judging the world for rejecting Him and refusing to believe in His Son, Jesus. People who follow Jesus now will not be here during this time because Jesus will take them to Heaven before these events happen. There will be people who decide to follow Jesus during this time, and will be persecuted and killed by those who do not.

WHICH OF THESE AM I? (Check all that apply)

- I am glad that I know Christ. I believe that Jesus died on the cross for my sins. I believe that I cannot know God the Father unless I place my faith in Jesus Christ and believe that He died for my sins.
- I am not sure where I will be when the end times happen. I feel like this because I am not sure if I even know Jesus as my Savior. I would like to know Him for sure.
- I know that I do not have Christ in my life. I should talk to someone about what it might be like to be here for the Tribulation. This is who I can talk to: ________________________.
- I know that I am safe in the arms of Christ, but I know some of my friends and relatives who are not. Their names are: ________________________ ________________________________.

REVELATION 6:1-14

This chapter introduces the first of the judgments from God on the people that have rejected Him. These judgments are called the seven Seal Judgments. Match the judgment to where it is found:

v. 2	Great Earthquake (sun turns black, moon turns red)
v. 4	People saved during Tribulation killed by Antichrist
vv. 5-6	Famine (Black Horse)
vv. 7-8	Death (Pale Horse)
v. 9	Conquering Antichrist begins to rule (White Horse)
vv. 12-14	War (Red Horse)

REVELATION 6:15-17

Is anyone going to be able to hide from God's great wrath? ☐ **YES** ☐ **NO**

PRAY: *God, please give me opportunities and boldness to share the truth of this time and the truth of the Gospel with the people You have placed in my life so they don't have to go through this time.*

SHARE IT

The wrath of God is serious business.

WEEK 44 SATURDAY

TRUTH: REVELATION 7:1-17

The author, John, is noting some of the special things (attributes) that make God Who He is. An attribute is like a characteristic, but doesn't only describe someone, it is who they are. An example of this is, "God is Love."

REVELATION 7:10

It is very clear that although there is crazy confusion and bad things happening in the text, I can know that salvation belongs to ________.

PRAY: ***Lord, thank You for saving me. I know that my life belongs to You. No matter what dangerous situation comes my way, the big question has been answered. I will be with You forever based on the fact that Jesus died on the cross for my sin and then came out of the grave and is alive!***

REVELATION 7:12

I noticed the following characteristics and attributes of God:

- [ ] **Wise**
- [ ] **Glorious**
- [ ] **Powerful**
- [ ] **Eternal**
- [ ] **Forever**
- [ ] **Honorable**

I will list some other words that make me think about God and His love for me. ________

____

REVELATION 7:14-16

By these verses I can know that Heaven is a wonderful place and that God takes care of His children.

What is my eternal destination?

- [ ] I know that I have an eternal home in Heaven.
- [ ] I am not certain. This is who I can talk to about it ________________.

REVELATION 7:17

What will God wipe away? ________________________________

Tears are very important to God. According to **Psalm 56:8**, what does He do with them?

____

How does this make me feel to know that God not only keeps my tears but also will one day wipe them away? ________________________________

Who in my life right now needs to know that God cares for them in such a personal and intimate way? ________________

I will talk with them about this truth today. [ ] **YES** [ ] **NO**

SHARE IT

"As the blood of His saints and their deaths are precious in the sight of the Lord, so are their tears, not one of them shall fall to the ground." ~ *Matthew Henry*

SUNDAY WEEK 45

TRUTH: REVELATION 8:1-13

REVELATION 8:1

As the last of the seven Seal Judgments were opened, what is the reaction in Heaven?

______________________________ For how long? ______________________

Have I ever seen something so powerful that my first response was silence? This silence in Heaven most likely is due to the sobering, shocking reality of the judgments to come. Heaven looks on in silence as the people on earth are being punished for their sins.

I know that I should be more in awe of God and His power. I realize that He has done so much for me, yet I still:

- ☐ Struggle to get excited about what God has done for me.
- ☐ Forget to start my day thanking God for Who He is.

REVELATION 8:3-4

What went up before God? ___________________

How often do I pray?

☐ A lot. I think about Him and talk with Him throughout my day.

☐ Once in a while if I think about it. ☐ I just don't have the time.

REVELATION 8:6-12

The next set of God's judgments on the people that continue to reject Him are called the Seven Trumpet Judgments. Today's passage covers the first four. Match the verses with the corresponding Trumpet Judgments.

v. 7	1/3 of the sea turned to blood, 1/3 sea creatures died.
vv. 8-9	1/3 of fresh water became bitter. Many people died.
vv. 10-11	1/3 of vegetation burnt up from hail, fire mixed with blood.
v. 12	1/3 of sun, moon, and stars were darkened.

These first four Trumpet Judgments show that God is serious about sin. He will take away what people have come to depend on for life.

On whom do I depend each day of my life?

☐ **Friends** ☐ **Family** ☐ **God**

God is still showing mercy during these judgments as they are only destroying one-third of each item. He wants to lead rebellious people to repentance before it is eternally too late.

The Holy Spirit brought this person to mind just now that I need to show mercy to in order to help them turn to Jesus before it's too late: ______________________________.

SHARE IT

Am I as serious about my sin as God is?

WEEK 45 MONDAY

TRUTH: REVELATION 9:1-21

Yesterday we looked at four of the seven Trumpet Judgments on the people that continue to reject God and His offer of salvation. In **Revelation 8:13**, why did the loud voice cry out, "Woe, woe, woe to those who dwell on the earth"? ______________________

____

REVELATION 9:1-11

The fifth angel blew the trumpet. What was the fifth judgment that came up out of the Abyss? (**v. 3**) ______________________

In **verse 4**, they were commanded not to harm grass, trees, or green plants. They were only allowed to torment the people that did not have what? ______________________

____

Read **Ephesians 1:13**. After I believe in the truth of the Gospel of salvation, I am sealed with Whom? ______________________

In Eastern culture, seals were so important that documents were not considered to be authentic without one. A seal served as being the personal signature of the owner. If I have chosen to become a follower of Jesus, I have God's personal seal on me through His Holy Spirit to not only show that I belong to Him, but to also protect me from Satan.

How do I feel about that? ______________________

REVELATION 9:13-15

The sixth Trumpet Judgment released four angels to kill whom? ______________________

____

REVELATION 9:20-21

Did the two-thirds of the remaining people repent of their sins? ☐ **YES** ☐ **NO**

Check any of these sins I need to repent (turn away) from.

- ☐ Slander and gossip
- ☐ Pornography
- ☐ Bullying
- ☐ Sexual impurity
- ☐ Drugs/Drinking
- ☐ Worrying
- ☐ Cutting
- ☐ Overeating/Anorexia
- ☐ Lying

The Lord has made me aware of my sin of ______________________.

PRAY: ***God, I pray that through Your Spirit I will make better choices and overcome sin. I also pray that my friends would be sorry for their sin and be "awestruck" by Christ's work in their life.***

SHARE IT

If I have chosen to become a follower of Jesus, I have God's personal seal on me through His Holy Spirit to not only show that I belong to Him, but to also protect me from Satan.

TUESDAY WEEK 45

TRUTH: REVELATION 11:1-14

Persecution is real and happens all over the world every day. Webster's Dictionary defines persecution as ***the infliction of loss, pain, or death for adherence to a particular creed or mode of worship***. However, the Bible is clear that these men in the verses I read are hated because Jesus was hated first (**John 15:18**).

I know I may not have the kind of persecution that happened to the witnesses, but I see from these verses that:

- Being friends with Jesus will bring some kind of persecution in my life.
- If I am not experiencing some kind of persecution (even teasing), maybe I do not follow Jesus as well as I think.

REVELATION 11:3-12

God is going to send how many witnesses to prophesy (speak God's message) for 1,260 days? (**v. 3**) ______

What happens to anyone that tries to harm them during these days? (**v.5**)

____

What do they have the power to do? (**v. 6**) ______________________________

____

When does the beast come against them and kill them? (**v. 7**)

____

Will God take me home before He is finished with my testimony for Him? ☐ **YES** ☐ **NO**

The witnesses are killed in Jerusalem, the same city that Jesus was crucified. How do the people react to their death? (**v. 10**) ______________________________

How do I react when someone that has hurt me has something bad happen to them?
☐ Hey, what goes around comes around. ☐ I feel bad & pray for them.

What happens to the two witnesses after three and a half days? (**v. 11**)

____

REVELATION 11:13

After they went up to Heaven, there was a severe earthquake where 7,000 people were killed. The survivors were terrified and gave what? ______________________________

____

I will stand up for what is right no matter what. ☐ **YES** ☐ **NO**

SHARE IT

"Courage is being scared to death but saddling up anyway."
~ John Wayne

WEEK 45 WEDNESDAY

TRUTH: REVELATION 12:1-17

Notice all of the different things happening in these verses! There is quite a fight going on between good and evil. The Bible is clear in **Ephesians 6:12-13** that the battle is really not with my parents, my friends, or my enemies. This means I don't fight a physical fight, but a spiritual one.

When something bad happens to me or I struggle with something:

- ☐ I forget that my struggle might be spiritual.
- ☐ I forget to remember that God has control over my enemies.
- ☐ I get mad and want to get revenge.

In **Matthew 4:1-11** I see how Jesus won a battle against Satan. What was His weapon of choice found in **verses 4, 7**, and **10**? "It is ____________________."
This is one of my go-to verses when I am in the middle of a spiritual battle:

____.

REVELATION 12:9-10

The enemy has many names in this verse. It is important that I know who my true enemy is. I see the following names for the enemy: ______________________________

____

In **verse 10**, Satan is called "the accuser of our brethren." How often does it say that Satan accuses (*to charge with a fault, offense, or crime*) followers of Jesus?

____

While Satan may accuse me of sin, **1 John 1:7** says that Jesus' blood has cleansed me from how much of my sin? ____________

Satan's accusations have no power over me because Jesus already paid the penalty that my sins deserved. Jesus' blood has made me righteous.

REVELATION 12:11

List the three ways that the tribulation saints overcame Satan, the Accuser:

1) ____

2) ____

3) ____

Knowing and remembering what God has done in my life, protects me from believing Satan's lies. This is a memory that I have of what God did in my life: ______________

____.

I will share it with this friend, ________________, and ask them to share a memory of something that God has done in their life.

SHARE IT

Knowing and remembering what God has done in my life protects me from believing Satan's lies.

THURSDAY WEEK 45

TRUTH: REVELATION 13:1-18

REVELATION 13:1-4

REAL OR FAKE? Today's passage introduces us to the beast. Another name for the beast is the Antichrist. The prefix, "anti" usually makes me think of the word "opposite," and I might picture the Antichrist as being the opposite of Jesus: ugly, evil, and repulsive. However, he will appear as charming, wonderful, and powerful - an imitation of the true Jesus.

REVELATION 13:2

Where does the Antichrist get his power from? ____________

Looking back at yesterday's Quiet Time, who is the dragon (**Revelation 12:9**)?

____

REVELATION 13:5-6

What did the beast (Antichrist) do with his mouth? ______________________________

____

To blaspheme means to speak evil against or to be abusive with your speech.

SPEECH CHECK: What words have I been using lately?

- Swearing (*including using God's name other than for worship*)
- Mean
- Encouraging
- Hateful
- Kind
- Thankful
- Slandering (*ruining someone's reputation by telling lies about them*)

According to **Colossians 4:6**, what should my speech always contain?

____

Today, I will choose to use words that are full of grace. **YES** **NO**

REVELATION 13:8

According to this verse, who will worship the beast? ______________________________

____

REVELATION 13:15

What happens to those who refuse to worship the beast? ________________________

____

Yesterday, I learned about the persecution (*the infliction of loss, pain, or death*) of Jesus-followers.

Do I really love Jesus, the One Who died for me, that I would be willing to die for Him?

YES **NO** **I HOPE SO**

SHARE IT

Lord Jesus, today I pray that I will bring honor to You in life and in death.

WEEK 45 FRIDAY

TRUTH: 1 PETER 1:1-8

The people that Peter was writing to were going through some intense stuff: there was persecution from the government and sometimes even from their friends and family.

A difficulty in my life right now is:

____

____

When I think about my problems, I often find myself:

- Upset or depressed.
- Unsure about how I should handle the stress.
- Filled with worry.
- Confused about why God allows them into my life.

1 PETER 1:3

Peter says that through salvation in Jesus Christ, I can have a living hope. If I'm honest with myself:

- I feel like I never have hope.
- My hope comes and goes.
- I often put my hope in things besides Christ.
- I consistently experience that living hope.

The hope of salvation doesn't mean that the pain I experience disappears or doesn't hurt anymore, but it allows me to view the pain in light of how God is using it in my life.

Read **James 1:2-4**. God wants to use my pain to improve my faith, but am I OK with that? **YES** **NO**

The question I need to ask myself is, which is more important to me?

Having an easy and comfortable life / Having a deep relationship with God

My relationship with God really is the most important thing to me, but sometimes I forget that and focus only on wishing that my life could be easier. I'm going to take a few minutes to refocus my thoughts and desires toward Him. Done

SHARE IT

Through salvation in Jesus Christ, I can have a living hope.

SATURDAY WEEK 45

TRUTH: 1 PETER 1:9-16

The one question that I would love to have answered is:

____.

1 PETER 1:10-12

Peter explains that the prophets in the Old Testament and even angels in Heaven had a burning question: “How will God save people from their sins?”

God’s offer of free salvation by grace through faith is something absolutely no one saw coming! Have I ever truly accepted God’s gift of salvation and trusted Jesus alone as my Savior? ☐ **YES** ☐ **NO**

1 PETER 1:13

This points out that if I want to grow spiritually, I need to discipline and focus my mind.

Right now, my thoughts are:

- ☐ Mostly focused on myself.
- ☐ Filled with things besides God and His Word.
- ☐ Sometimes focused on God, but not usually.
- ☐ I don’t really know.
- ☐ Other: ____

1 PETER 1:14-16

Did you know that the word ***holy*** means ***separated from sin and devoted to God***? As a follower of Christ, I need to have a totally different way of thinking (a holy way) than the world around me if I’m going to deal with hard times the way God wants me to.

In light of my salvation, I am able to see my circumstances differently because I know that God is working through them. ☐ **YES** ☐ **NO**

Knowledge can change how I react to pain: feeling a sharp prick in the arm is different with the knowledge that it’s a doctor administering medicine to make someone healthy. Seeing what Christ did for me on the cross proves that God loves me and always uses hard times to make me more like Christ.

Here is my prayer telling God that I trust Him even when He allows painful things into my life: ____

____

____

SHARE IT

I want to live separated from sin and devoted to God.

WEEK 46 SUNDAY

TRUTH: 1 PETER 1:17-25

1 PETER 1:17

If God is my Father, my actions should change accordingly. If someone was watching my actions, would they conclude that I was a child of God? ☐ **YES** ☐ **NO**

What is one negative trait that they would observe? ______________________________

____

I am repenting of (*turning away from*) this now and am seeking God's forgiveness in this area. ☐ **AGREE** ☐ **DISAGREE**

1 PETER 1:18-23

Today's passage shows just how much it cost God to buy back my freedom. It didn't cost Him money or riches (**v. 18**), it cost Him the life of His perfect, holy Son (**v. 19**). This points out that being saved from sin should lead me to have love for others. In general, I find:

☐ It's hard for me to think about someone else's needs before mine.
☐ I can love most people, but there are a few I really struggle with.
☐ I'm usually a loving person, but sometimes I can be very selfish.

However, knowing how much God paid for my freedom makes it possible for me to love those around me.

☐ I agree with this statement. ☐ I disagree with this statement.
☐ I need to think about this some more.

Here is my prayer of thankfulness to God for saving me: ___________________________

____

____

Today, I will:

☐ Put the prayer above on a sticky note somewhere I'll see it every day.
☐ Go out of my way to show love to someone who is hard for me to love.
☐ Ask a parent, leader, or spiritual mentor to help me live in a way that points others to God, my Father.

1 PETER 1:25

How long does God's Word last? ______________________________

Since God's Word endures forever, can I trust it? ☐ **YES** ☐ **NO**

SHARE IT

"But the word of the Lord endures forever. Now this is the word which by the gospel was preached to you."
~ **1 Peter 1:25**

MONDAY WEEK 46

TRUTH: 1 PETER 2:1-10

The last few days have been talking about how God wants us to deal with hard times in life. Peter moves from that discussion into a section about learning and obeying God's Word. Without exposing myself to God's truth, I won't be able to respond to pain and hardship the way He wants me to.

1 PETER 2:2

This says that I should come to God's Word like newborn babies come to their milk. Here are some words and phrases that come to mind when I think about a baby about to get their milk: ____

____.

A baby is also submissive when it comes to his food. He is totally trusting whatever his parents give him without knowing what it is or if it has all of the nutrients he needs. God wants me to come to His Word in submission as well. I need to be ready to believe and act on whatever God shows me from His Word.

Up until now, what has my response to God's Word been?

- ☐ I usually avoid it.
- ☐ I know some of what it says, but I don't really care.
- ☐ I obey and believe some of what it says, but not everything.
- ☐ I do my best to submit to everything in God's Word.

God, I know that I need to be in Your Word consistently to know it and apply it. I'm committing to be like a newborn baby and seek hard after Your Word.

One way I'm going to do this is to do at least **3 4 5** (circle one) days of Quiet Time between now and Sunday.

1 PETER 2:4, 7-8

Peter closes out this section with a reminder of when the Israelites weren't willing to submit to God's Word (**v. 8**). Instead they chose to believe what made sense to them and ended up rejecting the Savior they were waiting for! (**vv. 4, 7**)

How often do I just do what makes sense to me instead of submitting to God's Word?

Too often to count / Once in a while

SHARE IT

The Word of God is not only inspired and without error but was written to equip me for life.

WEEK 46 TUESDAY

TRUTH: 1 PETER 2:11-17

1 PETER 2:13, 17

My definition of the word *freedom* would be: ______________________________

____.

Western society likes to pump up the idea of freedom, but most of the time little attention is given to what that word even means. It was once said, "Freedom consists not in doing what we like, but in having the right to do what we ought." God has placed authorities in my life to guide me in what I ought to do.

Submission means *to rank under* such as in the military. Peter stresses two kinds of submission in this passage. The first is found in **verses 13** and **17**. According to these verses, I am to submit to my human or earthly authorities.

Here are some people that have direct authority in my life:

- Parents
- Siblings
- Police and public officials
- God and His Word
- Teachers/principals
- Coaches
- Pastors and leaders at church
- Holy Spirit
- Jesus

After thinking through my earthly authorities (parents, teachers, coaches, government officials), here's how well I've been doing with submitting to them:

Not Submissive 1 2 3 4 5 Very Submissive

1 PETER 2:16-17

The second kind of authority mentioned in the passage is spiritual authority. Peter tells the readers to live as servants of God and to fear God. Fearing God is what I need to put on, but I also need to put off the sinful things in my life that I sometimes submit to that prevent me from submitting to God.

Something I will work to submit to more today: ______________________________

____

Something I will work to submit to less today: ______________________________

____

SHARE IT

When I don't submit to my earthly authorities, I'm not submitting to God, my Spiritual Authority.

WEDNESDAY WEEK 46

TRUTH: 1 PETER 2:18-25

Yesterday, Peter gave a command from God that sounds pretty crazy: show proper respect and honor to *everyone*.

1 PETER 2:18

Today it gets even more insane. He gives an example of the kind of person that God wants me to honor and respect: people that are good to me as well as people who are unfair and mistreat me.

It's easy to respect and honor someone who is nice to me and treats me fairly, but honoring someone who is mean or unfair to me can seem impossible! Here are a few people that I find it hard to honor and respect: ***(list first names or initials)***

____

1 PETER 2:21-24

There's someone else who chose to honor those who mistreated Him: His name is Jesus.

Peter reminds us that Christ left us a path to follow when it comes to honoring those who cause pain and suffering. He died for the very people who killed Him and did not insult them or threaten them.

Here's my prayer thanking Jesus for the way He loved me even through His suffering:

____

____

The only way I will be able to honor and respect those who hurt and mistreat me is by following the path that Jesus laid out for me. When I see how Jesus loved me through His pain, I can show that love to others.

I'm going to look/think back through some of the people who are difficult for me to honor and pick one to show the love of Christ to today.

Here are their initials: __________

Here is one really specific way that I will honor them and show them Christ's love:

____

SHARE IT

You can't enjoy the glory of Christ without also being willing to identify with His suffering.

WEEK 46 THURSDAY

TRUTH: 1 PETER 3:1-7

I followed through on my commitment yesterday to show honor to someone in a specific way.
YES **NO**

Often, the hardest people to honor and submit to are in our family. In today's passage, Peter shows that every member of a family has a God-given role to fill.

1 PETER 3:1

According to this verse, wives are to ______________________________ to their husbands.

I may not be a wife, but I still need to be submissive to my parents/guardians and show them the love of Christ.

Thinking back over the last week, here's how I'm doing with that:

Not Very Well 1 2 3 4 5 Very Well

Look up **Ephesians 5:21** and check the group of people I am to submit to according to that verse:

- Those who are older
- Those who have authority over me
- One another (i.e. any Christian)

I realize that I need to ask forgiveness from one of my family members for not submitting to them. **YES** **NO**

That person's name is: ____

I will ask their forgiveness today. **YES** **NO**

1 PETER 3:7

According to **verse 7**, husbands are supposed to:

- Love their wives.
- Show honor to their wives.
- Protect their wives.
- Live with their wives according to knowledge and understanding.

I may not be a husband, but I still need to honor and have understanding toward my family. Since I know my family so well, I can show them love better than almost anyone else in the world. Here is one way I will show love to someone in my family today:

____

____

SHARE IT

The place to begin to find my perfect mate is in the mirror of God's Word.

FRIDAY WEEK 46

TRUTH: 1 PETER 3:8-12

I learned that the book of **1 Peter** was written to a group of people who were going through:

- Good times.
- Hard times and trials.
- Persecution.
- Confusion about God's truth.

1 PETER 3:8-9

It would be very easy for someone who was struggling to be totally focused on their own problems and needs. Peter totally flips that idea upside down in this passage! These verses are all about focusing on those around us and having love, humility, and tenderness toward them.

On a scale of 1-5, my life right now is:

Hard 1 2 3 4 5 Pretty Easy

1 PETER 3:9

I can receive a blessing by: ____ .

1 PETER 3:10

Even with the difficulties in my life, I can receive joy, fulfillment, and blessing as I work to love others and prioritize pursuing peace and righteousness.

Here are 2 people in my life and their needs or struggles I know they have:

Name: ____________________ **Need/Struggle:** ______________________________

Name: ____________________ **Need/Struggle:** ______________________________

I'm going to take a moment right now to pray for those people and their needs. ☐ Done

I will commit to showing love toward these two people this week and doing whatever I can to help them with their need or struggle. ☐ **YES** ☐ **NO**

Here are a few things I'm going to do this week to be a blessing to those people:

____

____

SHARE IT

As a Christian, I am to actively seek ways to do good things for all people.

WEEK 46 SATURDAY

TRUTH: 1 PETER 3:13-22

Peter is addressing a specific issue that the believers to which he is writing were going through. Around this time period, the local laws were pretty much left up to the local judges. It didn't matter whether or not something was true; it only mattered if the judge could be convinced of it. Christians became easy targets for people who wanted to tell lies about them in order to make their lives harder.

1 PETER 3:14-15

Peter says that I should not fear those who might bring attacks or accusations against me. Instead, I need to be concerned about my heart being right with Christ and also be ready to explain my hope in Christ to others who might ask.

Do I sometimes forget to focus on my own personal relationship with Christ and get distracted by people and situations around me? ☐ **YES** ☐ **NO**

If someone asked me, am I ready to explain my relationship with Christ and why it gives me hope? ☐ **YES** ☐ **NO**

If not, I will ask this person to help me get ready to do this: ______________________

Am I living in such a way that no false accusations will stick, no matter what people are saying about me? ☐ **YES** ☐ **NO**

1 PETER 3:16

Peter says that I am to have a good conscience. What are the specific things in my life that prevent me from living with a clean conscience before God and others? ________

____

After taking some time to think through my life, here are some reasons those things are still a part of my life:

- ☐ I'm just not ready to get rid of some of those sinful things.
- ☐ I feel pressured by people/circumstances to do those things.
- ☐ I want to get rid of those things but I'm not sure how; I feel stuck!
- ☐ I know there are issues in my life, but I don't really know why.

A godly person that I will share these areas with and ask them for help:______________

(It's often easiest to go to someone who will agree with us, rather than hold us to view things Biblically. Really think through who might HELP!)

SHARE IT

I need to always be ready to explain the hope that I have as a believer.

SUNDAY WEEK 47

TRUTH: 1 PETER 4:1-6

1 PETER 4:1

Peter makes a bold statement in the first verse here: he says that I am to have the same way of thinking that Jesus did when He suffered and died on the cross.

To get a better idea of what that mindset was, look up and read **Matthew 26:39**. Here are some things that I think Jesus was feeling in that verse:

____ .

Jesus was not looking forward to suffering on the cross, but He trusted His Father and was willing to accept anything from God's hand, no matter how painful it was.

Am I willing to adopt that way of thinking in my life even it means accepting painful things from Him? ☐ **YES** ☐ **NO**

☐ I commit to praying that I will do God's will, and not my own.

1 PETER 4:3-4

Peter says that there was a "flood" of sinfulness and evil all around them. The same is true in my culture and country today.

The only way for me to live victoriously in spite of such an overwhelming flood is to get on board with what God has provided to grow me spiritually. If I fail to give myself to God and His plan, I run the risk of drowning spiritually.

In what ways am I allowing myself to be influenced by the evil around me?

____

How can I more fully align myself with the things that God has provided for my growth?
☐ Be faithful to my local church
☐ Build close friendships with others who love Jesus
☐ Ask my parents and/or another spiritual adult in my life for accountability in key areas

SHARE IT

To avoid drowning spiritually in the flood of sinfulness, I must get on board God's lifeboat and grow.

WEEK 47 MONDAY

TRUTH: 1 PETER 4:7-11

Today's passage is stuffed with practical insight and challenging ideas.

1 PETER 4:7

Peter says that the end of all things is ______________________.

Do I sometimes find myself valuing (***focusing on, getting upset over, seeking hard after***) material and temporary things even though I know they won't last forever? ■ **YES** ■ **NO**

The Bible is clear that Christ could return at any moment. With that in mind, I don't have time to be living my life on accident. Instead, I need to be sober minded (***living life purposefully and making choices carefully***) to make the most of my time on earth and my relationship with God.

If I am the kind of person that lives my life on purpose, I will: (circle)

make wise decisions

make quick decisions without thinking them through

I will ask ____________________________ to help me grow in this area.

1 PETER 4:8-9

Peter knows that people will hurt and mistreat each other. His solution is not to try to "fix" them but to grow in love toward others and allow that love to cover many sins.

Are there people in my life whom I get picky with, getting angry over every little thing, and never cutting them a break? ■ **YES** ■ **NO**

Here are some of them: (initials) __________________________________

The solution is to show hospitality (kindness, generosity) to these people without complaining about it. Here are two specific ways I will be kind or generous to someone from the list I made above:

1) ____

2) ____

SHARE IT

Live life on purpose.

TUESDAY WEEK 47

TRUTH: 1 PETER 4:12-19

1 PETER 4:12-13

Peter has already made it clear that God allows hard times into our lives in order to help us grow in our relationship with Christ. Here he takes it even further and says to expect difficulties in life and even rejoice when they come.

The end of **verse 13** explains in more detail why to rejoice and how all of this is possible. The logic goes like this:

1 – I will rejoice when Christ comes back and His glory is revealed.
2 – This is because I want to know Him and be close to Him.
3 – If I know that hard times also help me know Him and be close to Him...
4 – Then I should rejoice in the hard times of my life too.

Of course, all of this only makes sense if I truly am someone who values having a close relationship with Jesus. How often do I find myself wanting an easy life more than wanting to be close to Jesus?

Almost Always 1 2 3 4 5 Only Once In A While

1 PETER 4:19

A huge question for those in hard times is, "Who do I believe God is?" Since God allows and controls everything that comes into my life, and because I believe God is good and faithful, then I have no need to worry about difficult things that happen to me. I can, as Peter says, trust my soul to my Faithful Creator.

How well am I doing at trusting my soul to God's hands?

Not Very Well at All 1 2 3 4 5 Pretty Well

Based on the numbers I circled in the questions above, I have realized that I have some growing to do in these areas. Here is my prayer to God asking Him for grace and wisdom as I work to change my thinking:

____

____

____

SHARE IT

I will trust my life to my God
Who created me and will never fail me.

WEEK 47 WEDNESDAY

TRUTH: **1 PETER 5:1-7**

1 PETER 5:5

God hates pride but gives grace to the humble. Peter gives me two basic ways to begin humbling myself.

First, I am to be subject to the elders. In this verse, "elders" refers to pastors and leaders of local churches. But the principle is that I need to submit to those who have spiritual authority over me. Here are the names of some people in my life I need to submit to:

____.

Second, I need to act with humility toward others. This one sounds way harder! I need to be humble toward people no matter who they are: my siblings, my family, my friends… everyone!

Here is what I think it might mean to act with humility toward others:

- ☐ Making sure I get my fair share.
- ☐ Focusing on how I can help people around me.
- ☐ Being careful to act with kindness.
- ☐ Giving up what I want so someone can get what they want.

1 PETER 5:6

Even more importantly, I need to humble myself under God's hand! He is the Creator of the universe, my Rescuer, and completely above anyone or anything else.

Here are the things I'm willing to receive from God's hand.

- ☐ Surprises that don't line up with my plans.
- ☐ Challenges that I might need to work through.
- ☐ Painful or hurtful circumstances.
- ☐ Something difficult I am experiencing right now: ______________________________

____

1 PETER 5:7

When the hard times do come, I will cast my ________________ on Him because I know how much He loves me!

SHARE IT

"Humility is nothing but the disappearance of self in the vision that God is all." ~ *Andrew Murray*

THURSDAY WEEK 47

TRUTH: 1 PETER 5:8-14

1 PETER 5:8-9

It makes sense that Peter ends his discussion about dealing with hard times in life by talking about Satan. Many difficulties on earth are brought about because of Satan's influence in the world. Even knowing that, I can be confident that God will always make the hard times work for my good.

After reading **verses 8** and **9**, and finding that Satan is on the prowl, like a lion, searching for prey, I have recognized that he is attempting to destroy me in the following areas of my life:

- Purity
- Speech
- Attitude
- Other: ____________________

I will resist him by looking up and memorizing this verse about what I am struggling with: ______________________________.

1 PETER 5:12

After a brief discussion of Satan and the danger he can pose to believers, Peter begins wrapping up the discussion of what the Christian's response to hard times should be.

THE SUMMARY IS: Stand firm in the true __________ of God.

After exploring the book of **1 Peter**, I have picked up some key ideas that I want to make sure I carry with me the next time I have difficult circumstances in my life, so I will take a minute to review the Quiet Time days in **1 Peter**. I am writing down the top three things (quotes, ideas, verses) that I want to remember to help me to be steadfast in my faith (**1 Peter 5:9**).

1) ____________________
2) ____________________
3) ____________________

SHARE IT

If I don't stand firm in my faith, I won't stand at all.

WEEK 47 FRIDAY

TRUTH: REVELATION 14:1-13

REVELATION 14:1-5

Revelation is full of pictures and images that can be pretty confusing, but this one seems really clear. There will be 144,000 people set aside for a very specific purpose. They will be identified with God clearly (with His name on their foreheads), and they will be drastically different from the people with the beast's number on their heads or their hands.

Being identified as a Christian can be hard sometimes, especially when my friends or family are doing things I know they shouldn't do.

- Totally agree.
- Sometimes it's easier to just go with the flow and not stand up for what I believe in.
- I don't really struggle with this.

These 144,000 will be up against a lot of people who have decided to be on the side of the beast. I think I would feel ____________________.

The last time I felt like this was ____________________.

One area that I know I am weak in standing up for Jesus is ____________________ ____________________.

One person I can ask to help me get stronger in this is ____________________.

REVELATION 14:6-13

God uses angels to announce what is happening and what is going to happen to the people who decide to worship the beast instead of believing in God and His salvation. But the first angel starts out by inviting people to repent and believe in God. God is the Creator, and worthy of being worshiped, and He is offering people a way to be saved from all of the bad things that are coming for those who don't turn to Him.

I have friends who need to hear the first angel's message. **YES** **NO**

I am determined to share God's message with this friend ____________________ in this way ____________________ at this time ____________________.

This culture tries to tell me that there is not a God who created the earth, but I can see His fingerprints all over creation. Something God created that amazes me is ____________________ ____________________.

SHARE IT

Stand up for what you believe in even if it means standing alone.

SATURDAY WEEK 47

TRUTH: REVELATION 14:14-20

This is such a vivid picture of things that are going to happen in the future! The authority of Heaven is clearly displayed here. Angels are given assignments, each for a specific reason. They interact with those who are on the earth, and have a very real presence and job that will definitely affect people when this happens. These aren't just stories, these are real!

REVELATION 14:14

The "One like a Son of Man" has a golden crown and is obviously set apart on a white cloud. He is Jesus, as seen in **Daniel 7:13-14**. This Scripture was written centuries before Revelation will come true!

- ☐ I read the Daniel portion.

Believing the Bible, from the Old Testament to the New Testament, can be really challenging. I find myself: (check any that apply)

- ☐ Asking a lot of questions.
- ☐ Just accepting things I read, even if I don't understand it.
- ☐ Asking God to help me understand what was written.
- ☐ Studying the Bible to try to get more out of it.

REVELATION 14:15-20

The picture of the harvest of grapes from the earth is not so good. Blood is pressed out of the grapes that are harvested by the second angel with a sickle, and it says it rises as high as a horse's bridle for 1,600 stadia.

Look up how big 1,600 stadia is. ____________________ yards

When I think about that much blood, I feel ______________________________.

Am I living as if the things that I read in Revelation are really going to take place someday? ☐ **YES** ☐ **NO**

I need to pray for my friends who don't know what the Bible says about the future. Three friends I will pray for today are:

____

I'll send a text/message and let these friends know that I prayed for them today. With the future of their hearts at stake, who cares what they think of me? There are more important things coming. I should care about them more than I care about being "cool"!

SHARE IT

Nothing proves that you love someone more than mentioning them in your prayers.

WEEK 48 SUNDAY

TRUTH: REVELATION 15:1-8

REVELATION 15:1

The fact that John, the author, is calling this next stage of signs as "great" and "marvelous" is a big deal! He had already seen so much, how could anything still be big enough to make him write this way? But it was! Even though so much had happened already, there was more to come, and it was big enough to make John say, "Whoa! Look at this!" Finally, he says that he sees a light at the end of the tunnel, "With them the wrath of God is finished."

Sometimes, the bad things in life seem to go on and on.
I feel overwhelmed with life:
- Not often.
- Every once in a while.
- Fairly often.
- More than others know.

Praising God is a good way to fight being overwhelmed with the bad things in life. Seeing that even the wrath of God in Revelation does come to an end, I can have faith that God will bring even my worst seasons of life to an end. And I can be sure that the "bad" stuff has a purpose and a meaning!

REVELATION 15:3-4

I will re-read the song of Moses that the people sing in **verses 3-4**, and make notes of four different words that mean the most to me, words that describe God and His character:

______________________ ______________________
______________________ ______________________

I will choose one of these words, and look for other places in the Bible where I see that word used. Look up the definition of that word and write it here: ______________________
____.

How will my actions change if I take this characteristic of God to heart?
If God is ______________________, then my ______________________ will be different. I need to work on this.

Ask a friend to keep you accountable. Done; I have someone to help.

SHARE IT

*"Great and marvelous are Your works, Lord God Almighty!
Just and true are Your ways, O King of the saints!"*
~ **Revelation 15:3**

MONDAY WEEK 48

TRUTH: REVELATION 16:1-11

This passage can be terrifying to read; the first four Bowl Judgments sound a lot like the four Trumpet Judgments. Go back to **Revelation 8:6-12**. Match the Bowl Judgments with the trumpet it corresponds with.

First Bowl Judgment	**Trumpet with scorching heat**
Second Bowl Judgment	**Trumpet with water turned blood**
Third Bowl Judgment	**Trumpet with water turned bitter**
Fourth Bowl Judgment	**Trumpet with the sun darkened**

REVELATION 16:9, 11

All of these plagues show the power of God to everyone on earth. But look at the response of the people who don't love God. The plagues should have made them realize their mistakes and repent, but instead they curse God and refuse to change their ways of living.

Has God used things in my life to try to get my attention? ☐ **YES** ☐ **NO**

I'll rate how I respond to God when I see something in my life that needs to change.

Never 1 2 3 4 5 Consistently and quickly

Sometimes God uses other people and their circumstances to bring things to the surface in my own life.

I'll think about a situation that made me stop and think about what God was trying to teach me. What was it? ______________________________

Yesterday, I wrote about a characteristic of God, and how it should affect my life. I paid attention and made sure to live with that reality in mind.

- ☐ Yes, I did that, and I saw a difference in my actions and attitude.
- ☐ I probably should try again today.
- ☐ I really need to focus on God's character.

Do I see the pain in the world as God's way of getting my attention and the attention of others? Here are my thoughts: ______________________________

____

____

SHARE IT

"Pain is God's megaphone to rouse a deaf world."
~ C.S. Lewis

WEEK 48 TUESDAY

TRUTH: REVELATION 16:12-21

REVELATION 16:14

In the past several decades, and throughout history, there have been many important wars: World Wars I and II, Vietnam, Afghanistan, and wars in other countries like Russia and Iraq. Sometimes it seems like the wars in our world will never end. Even to the very end of the world, there are huge wars, but the war that comes with the sixth bowl will be the worst that the world has ever seen. The dragon, the beast, and the false prophet do everything in their power to get all of the kings of the earth to gather for a huge war against God.

Notice the name John uses for God in the face of these armies who are coming against Him: God the ______________________!

When I seem to be up against something too big or too powerful for me to handle, I can remember that God is the Almighty, All Powerful God!
This truth is:

- ☐ Easy for me to remember: I know He is bigger than anything I face!
- ☐ I sometimes take a while to remember all that God says He is.
- ☐ I struggle with this. Where have I seen God work mightily in my life?

It may be helpful to talk this idea out with someone I trust such as a youth leader or a good friend who has a growing relationship with God. I'll ask them to tell me about a specific situation where they have seen God do something incredible.
☐ I did this ☐ I will remember to do this the next time I see ______________________.

HERE'S AN IDEA: Ask your friends this question either in person or on social media: "Question: When have you seen God do something incredible in your life? How have you seen Him be Almighty?"

How do I answer that question? ____
____
____
____

SHARE IT

When I seem to be up against something too big or too powerful for me to handle, I can remember that God is the Almighty God!

WEDNESDAY WEEK 48

TRUTH: REVELATION 17:1-8

This picture of the woman on the scarlet beast can be confusing. But if I think about it in terms of relationships, it makes a little more sense. The woman is a symbol of false teaching and apostasy. Look at **Ezekiel 23:37**. God says worshiping idols, or anything else that takes His place in my life, is as bad as adultery. Can I grasp that idea? God says that when people worship something more than Him, it's as bad as cheating on a wife or a husband!

REVELATION 17:4-6

The woman who represents this kind of misplaced worship is dressed like royalty, and is beautiful to look at, but the truth is that she's filled with death and destruction!

- I have never heard of that before.
- I have heard that idea, but I never realized how serious it was!
- I get it! God takes worship very seriously.
- I need to think about this some more.

REVELATION 17:8

This verse is eerily similar to what we see in **Revelation 1:17-18**, but there are some very significant differences! **Revelation 1:17-18** describes Christ as the One who was ("The First"), the one who died ("I died," and "I have the keys to death and Hades"), and the one who is to come ("I am the living One," and "I am alive forevermore").
In **Revelation 17:8**, we see the beast, the Antichrist, who is trying to imitate Christ to confuse men and lead them in the wrong direction.

Everything that looks good and looks right isn't always something we should follow and marvel at! Sometimes, the most beautiful things are the most dangerous and distracting.

There may be something in my life that has become more important than God. What is it? ______________________________

Do I see anything that needs to change? **YES** **NO**

If yes, what needs to change? ______________________________

SHARE IT

Sometimes, the most beautiful things are the most dangerous and distracting.

WEEK 48 THURSDAY

TRUTH: REVELATION 17:9-18

This passage spans a lot of time and situations - it talks about kings and kingdoms who have been in the past. It tells of how some kings rise and fall, and how the beast ultimately gains control and power over all of the kings that eventually will have power in the future. In the end, the beast even turns on the woman, who seemed to be on his team.

But even through all of these kings and kingdoms, we see the hope that comes from knowing God is King over everything!

REVELATION 17:14

The Lamb, another name for Jesus, the Son of God, is called "L_______ of __________, and K________ of ____________." It says that He will ________________________ the ones who come against Him!

The ones who are with the Lamb are called ____________ and ____________.

REVELATION 17:17

It says that even though man is doing what is wrong, God allows these things to happen until, "the words of God are ______________." This means that God knows what will happen and has it in His plan. Nothing these earthly powers can do will surprise Him, and He will use them for His glory!

Seeing how God is written about in this chapter makes me feel __________________ ____.

My life shows that I believe God is Sovereign and is in control:

Never 1 2 3 4 5 Always

The next time life surprises me with hurt or hardships, I can remember these verses! I will highlight or underline them in my Bible so I can find them easily the next time life throws me a curve.

I might know someone who could use a reminder that God is in control.

I will:
- ☐ Send them a text or call them.
- ☐ Tell them I am praying for them.
- ☐ Write them a note.

SHARE IT

God knows what will happen and has it in His plan.

FRIDAY WEEK 48

TRUTH: ROMANS 9:1-16

ROMANS 9:1-5

Knowing that God's judgment awaits the people I know that are not saved makes me feel:

- Sad.
- Concerned.
- Nothing at all; I actually don't even look at them as not being saved.

ROMANS 9:3

Having my unsaved friends have a relationship with Jesus Christ may mean me going beyond my comfort zone and doing this: ________________________________

____

ROMANS 9:6-13

I am sure I am a child of God because:

- I grew up in a Christian family.
- I was born one.
- I do everything God wants me to do (I might review **Luke 18:18-23**. This young man thought he had done all God wanted him to, also.)
- I put my trust in Jesus Christ alone as my Savior.

I recognize that my trusting in Jesus alone for my salvation is:

- Based on the many good things I did for God.
- Based on God's own grace and mercy.

Look up and define the word ***mercy***. ________________________________

____

Look up and define the word ***compassion***. ____________________________

____

To know that I am a recipient of God's mercy and compassion makes me feel:

____.

When it comes to my salvation in Christ, the one thing I am grateful to God for is:

____.

Write out **Romans 9:6a**: ____

____

SHARE IT

"The Gospel is good news of mercy to the undeserving."
~ John Stott

WEEK 48 SATURDAY

TRUTH: ROMANS 9:17-33

I believe I have abilities, spiritual gifts, and talents that are given to me by God.

☐ **YES** ☐ **NO**

ROMANS 9:17

I have a specific purpose in life. Let me define it this way:
There's a certain thing I want to do to enrich/benefit the lives of others.
It is ______________________________ (e.g., inspire, challenge, serve, give hope, etc.)

There's a certain group of people that I really like to serve/minister to.
They are: ______________________________ (e.g., others in general, underclassmen, other guys, other girls, children, the elderly).

I hope the outcome will be: ____

____

(e.g., it will affect their life and eternity, it will give hope, it will cause them to make their faith their own, etc.).

Now put the blanks all together (This is my purpose statement): ____________________

____

____

(Example: serving others in a way that will affect their life and eternity.
Another example: inspiring underclassmen to live hopeful.)

As far as my purpose in life is concerned or what I think it is,

- ☐ I am absolutely delighted to fulfill it.
- ☐ I am still confused about it and wondering, "Do I have one?"
- ☐ I am so unhappy about it and wish God had other plans for me other than what I have now.

ROMANS 9:20

"Why have you made me like this?" is a question I am asking or have asked God before.

☐ **YES** ☐ **NO**

My prayer in light of all this is:

- ☐ *Lord, I do not understand what You are up to in my life, but I still choose to thank You for it all.*
- ☐ *Lord, in the midst of all my circumstances, I'm going to keep living beyond my selfish side and live my purpose statement.*
- ☐ *Lord, You have a specific plan for me, because You love me specifically and individually.*

SHARE IT

Lord, You have a specific plan for me, because You love me specifically and individually.

SUNDAY WEEK 49

TRUTH: ROMANS 10:1-13

ROMANS 10:1

Paul's heart's desire and prayer to God was for God's chosen people, _______________, to be saved.

My heart's desire and prayer to God for (name of unsaved person) _________________________ is that they may be saved.

Remember that people would have thought Paul would be the LAST person to come to Christ. So pray BIG!

I am committing to pray for this person regularly for this whole:

- [ ] **Week**
- [ ] **Month**
- [ ] **Year**

ROMANS 10:2-4

Doing good things for God with much zeal without the guidance of God's Word is okay.

- [ ] **I agree.**
- [ ] **I don't agree.**

God's righteousness is by faith, but sometimes people try to establish their own way to God by doing: ____.

However, I realize that all that is needed for me to gain God's righteousness is to:
____. **(v. 4)**

ROMANS 10:9-10

Write out these verses in the space provided below:

____

____

____

____

Review the "Romans Road." Work on memorizing it, and check off each verse when done. Once memorized, practice sharing with a friend or family member.

- [ ] **Romans 3:23**
- [ ] **Romans 6:23**
- [ ] **Romans 5:8**
- [ ] **Romans 10:9-10**
- [ ] **Romans 10:13**

SHARE IT

There's nothing like being ready to lovingly, graciously, and accurately share the Gospel!

WEEK 49 MONDAY

TRUTH: ROMANS 10:14-21

ROMANS 10:14-15

It is clear to me that: (check all that apply)

- One has to believe in Jesus first then call on Him for salvation.
- One has to hear God's Word before they can believe.
- Someone has to take the initiative to share God's Word for people to hear it.
- I have a responsibility to tell others about Jesus Christ.

Based on **verse 15** I can say that before God:

- Having beautiful feet is a matter of having a pedicure.
- Having beautiful feet is a matter of preaching the Gospel of Peace.
- Having beautiful feet is not such an issue.

I remember a time when I tried to share the Gospel, and it was not received well. That made me feel ______________________________.

ROMANS 10:16

I know that God is not surprised by this reaction by those who reject Him because He states here that ______________________________.

ROMANS 10:17

If faith in Jesus Christ comes through the hearing of the ____________________, then I realize that I have a responsibility toward those that do not believe in Jesus as their Savior to ______________________________.

In relation to my responsibility toward the lost and the rejection of His Word, I believe **2 Timothy 4:2** is telling me to: ______________________________
______________________________.

In light of today's overall message of telling others about the Gospel of Jesus Christ, I am committing this week to do at least one of the following:

- Share the Gospel with (name of person) ____________________.
- Pray for this missionary today (name) ____________________.
- To give (amount) ______________ toward missions this week.
- To ask my pastor about any upcoming missions trips.
- Share the Gospel with someone at the checkout as GOD prompts me.

SHARE IT

"Never lose heart in the power of the gospel. Do not believe that there exists any man…for whom the gospel is not fitted."
~ Charles Spurgeon

TUESDAY WEEK 49

TRUTH: ROMANS 11:1-12

According to these verses, what I know about Israel is that:
(check any that apply)

- ☐ They are a chosen people.
- ☐ Through Israel we got the Savior Jesus Christ.
- ☐ Through Israel we got the various prophets and the Bible.
- ☐ That even the Jewish people have to believe in Jesus for their salvation.

ROMANS 11:1-2

Based on **verse 1**, since many Jewish people really do not believe in Jesus Christ as their Savior then:

- ☐ God has utterly rejected them too and replaced them with the Church.
- ☐ God has not yet given up on them and still has a plan to bring them to Himself.

Rejection is a horrible word. Let me do a personal inventory. Even though I know Christ as my Savior, do I reject His Word in order to do what I want? Some thoughts:

____

____

Think about yesterday. Would I be defined as **a rejecter of truth** or **a receiver of truth**? (Circle)

ROMANS 11:3-4

I can somehow identify with Elijah's prayer because there have been times when I have felt lonely as a Christian among many non-Christians.

☐ **TRUE** ☐ **FALSE**

Although it may not feel like it, to know that I am not the only Christian and that there are many others out there makes me feel ____________ . Stop and think about this for a minute. There are literally hundreds of teens doing this exact same Quiet Time today!! Whisper a prayer for others who might feel lonely.

ROMANS 11:11

Israel is and always has been God's chosen people. **Psalm 122:6** commands believers to pray for peace in Jerusalem, the capital of God's chosen people, Israel. It really is that important!

But meanwhile, the Gospel was extended to those who are not Jewish, referred to as Gentiles. Praise the LORD, I have the opportunity also to both receive and share the good news of salvation!

SHARE IT

I'm thankful for the gift of salvation God has given to ALL people.

WEEK 49 WEDNESDAY

TRUTH: ROMANS 11:13-24

ROMANS 11:13

Paul knew himself as a missionary to the Gentiles, and I see myself as a missionary to (a person or group of people) ________________________.

My main means of reaching out to the above person/people is through ______________
____.

ROMANS 11:17-24

Match the people to their description.

Some broken off branches	**Saved non-Jewish people**
Wild olive tree	**Israelites that reject Jesus Christ**
Grafted wild olive branch	**Non-Jewish people or Gentile people**

ROMANS 11:20

Write out this verse in the space provided below.

____
____

This has some great practicality for me.
Define the word, UNBELIEF: ____
What is the opposite of unbelief? _______________________
Another word for belief is faith.
According to the end of this verse, what would stop me from believing?______________
____

ROMANS 11:22

This verse speaks of a great character trait of God. What is it? ________________
____

ROMANS 11:23

The fact that God will still bring in believing Israel into His salvation plan is a clear example of God's: (Circle all that apply.)

grace / patience / forgiveness

SHARE IT

"Lovely flowers are the smiles of God's goodness."
~ William Wilberforce

THURSDAY WEEK 49

TRUTH: ROMANS 11:25-36

ROMANS 11:25-28

I just didn't know this about Israel:

- ☐ Their hearts have a partial blindness/hardness over them. (**v. 25**)
- ☐ That GOD still has compassion for them. (**v. 26**)
- ☐ That for this time (the Church age) God has opened salvation to those other than just His chosen Israel. (**v. 28**)

Compare **Deuteronomy 7:7-9** and **Romans 11:29**.
I'll record my response to anyone that may say that God has rejected Israel forever.

____

____

ROMANS 11:30-32

A specific benefit seen in these verses as a result of the temporary disobedience of Israel, is that God has availed to me (as a Gentile) His:

☐ **Grace** ☐ **Mercy** ☐ **Love**

To know that I am a recipient of God's mercy freely given makes me feel

____.

ROMANS 11:33

I believe God's great mercy can never be exhausted.

☐ I believe it. ☐ I think it runs out. ☐ I am not so sure. ☐ I sure do hope so.

Talking about mercy, I am grateful to God that He has shown me mercy particularly in this area of my life: ______________________________.

ROMANS 11:36

If everything is by God, and if I get it through Him to use it for His glory, then I choose to use ______________________ (whatever God has given me) for purposes of ______________________, and through this I believe He will be glorified.

One thing that I am still holding onto that I have not fully dedicated to God for His use and glory is ______________________________.

SHARE IT

"God's mercy and grace give me hope for myself and for our world." ~ Billy Graham

WEEK 49 FRIDAY

TRUTH: ROMANS 12:1-8

ROMANS 12:1

Knowing that I am a child of God through no merit of my own but through an act of God's grace, this verse calls me to present my ______________ as a living sacrifice ________________ and ______________________ to God.

Being a living sacrifice means dedicating my life on a daily basis to God.

☐ **TRUE** ☐ **FALSE**

ROMANS 12:2

One area that I see in my life that has been affected and influenced by the philosophies and mindset of this world (that are contrary to God's Word) is in:

- ☐ The way I think.
- ☐ The way I interact with my parents.
- ☐ The way I interact with my friends.
- ☐ The way I view God.
- ☐ The way I ____.

For me to stop being conformed to the world's way, but instead be transformed (my mind being made new again), I need to change my mind in the way I ____________________ __________________________ so that I can now ____________________________ ________________.

ROMANS 12:3

When evaluating my life, I tend to be:

- ☐ Honest and evaluate myself the way God sees me.
- ☐ Thinking better of myself than I actually am.
- ☐ Unsure of where I really am in my spiritual walk.

In light of the above, this is my prayer: ______________________________________
____
____

ROMANS 12:6

Upon further evaluation of what God is doing in my life and has given me, I believe I:

- ☐ Know what my spiritual gift is.
- ☐ Still do not know what my gift is.
- ☐ I need to talk to ___________________ so they can help me find out what my gift is. Consider a trusted adult!

SHARE IT

"We ought to be living as if Jesus died yesterday, rose this morning, and is coming back this afternoon." ~ *Adrian Rogers*

SATURDAY WEEK 49

TRUTH: ROMANS 12:9-21

ROMANS 12:9

When I tell someone, "I love you," I usually mean it with all my heart.

- That is very true of me all the time.
- That is true of me most of the time.
- That is true of me sometimes.
- That is not always true of me.

One person who I know I have not been genuinely loving towards lately is ______________________, and I believe God is asking me to love them genuinely.

ROMANS 12:10-13

The following would describe me: (check as many as apply)

- I am kind to others.
- I am diligent in all I do.
- I am a person of great hope.
- I am usually a prayerful person.
- I consider others more than I do myself.
- I usually serve God with enthusiasm.
- I am usually patient in difficult times.
- I usually help others.

I am particularly grateful to God for helping me grow in: (choose any area selected above)

____.

The area I am trusting God to help me grow in is: (choose any area not selected above)

____.

ROMANS 12:14-21

I sure need help to grow in the following area(s) too:

- Not to seek revenge toward those who do bad things to me.
- Not to feel jealous over someone else's success.
- Sympathizing with and comforting anyone going through tough times.
- Having humility in relating with all kinds of people.

On a scale of 1 to 5, how have I managed to live at peace with all people in my life?

Not Peacefully 1 2 3 4 5 Very Peacefully

The one person in my life that I have a hard time living at peace with is ____________________________. Instead of not being at peace with them, I will purpose to do good to them by ____.

SHARE IT

"I want the love that cannot help but love; loving, like God, for the very sake of love." ~ A.B. Simpson

WEEK 50 SUNDAY

TRUTH: NAHUM 1:1-15

The Book of Nahum is the sequel to the Book of Jonah. In Jonah, we see God's mercy toward sinful people, giving them a chance to turn away from sin to experience His mercy. In Nahum, we see God's justice when it is evident that people refuse to turn from their sin; so enough is enough. God is communicating to His people, Israel, in the Book of Nahum. While they are now going to experience judgment, He will also comfort them regarding their oppressors.

NAHUM 1:1-3

God's decision-making is perfect. At times He gives mercy to the sinner, but at other times He executes justice.

Does this make me feel **comforted** or **anxious**? (Circle)
Why? ____

NAHUM 1:4-14

When God acts, He is unstoppable because He is all-powerful. There is nothing big enough to stand in His way. God cares for His people and responds when they are attacked.

How does this affect my view toward God? Write your thoughts: ______________

____

NAHUM 1:15

God tells His people to continue living for Him without fear. Bad things were happening, but good things were coming. God always keeps His promises to protect His nation, Israel and His people, the church.

TRUE OR FALSE.

T F God's Word says that He always keeps His promises and has the power to do so.

In what ways do I struggle with believing in God's promises? ______________

____

SHARE IT

Thank God for both His mercy and His justice.

MONDAY WEEK 50

TRUTH: MALACHI 1:1-14

The book of Malachi is both a prophetic book and a plea to the nation of Israel to turn back to God. It is written in a "hypophoric" style, meaning it is one person, in this case God, speaking both sides of a conversation, asking a question, then answering it Himself. God is pointing out to His people that they are phony in their faith. They had gotten to the point that God predicted in **Isaiah 29:13**: *their hearts were far from Him.*

MALACHI 1:1-5

God demonstrates His love for His people Israel, in contrast to His feelings toward the enemies of His people.

As a follower of Jesus, in what ways does God show His love for me? (see **Romans 5:8, 8:28; 2 Corinthians 1:3, 5:17; Philippians 1:6**)

____

MALACHI 1:6-11

God is worthy of both our respect and our best for Him. The people of Israel were giving God whatever was left over after they lived for themselves, instead of giving God their best.

Do I give God my best?

CONSISTENTLY **SOMETIMES** **NOT OFTEN** **NEVER**

What do I ask God to give to me? ____

____

What has God given to me? ____

____

MALACHI 1:12-14

The people of Israel were blessed by God, but they were discontented (***dissatisfied with their circumstances***). They were unthankful and acted as though God was not providing for their needs. They acted as though serving Him was a burden rather than a blessing, and scoffed (*made fun of*) serving God. It would be like saying, "My church stinks!" when really it is my attitude that stinks.

In what ways am I discontented or unthankful for the life, school, family, friends, job, church, and blessings God has given me? ____

____

Do I treat serving God as **a burden** or **a blessing**?

SHARE IT

I want to give God my best, not what's left.

WEEK 50 TUESDAY

TRUTH: **MALACHI 2:1-9**

MALACHI 2:1-4

At this time, the spiritual leaders were twisting God's Word to make rules that allowed them to take advantage of people. They oppressed the poor and made themselves rich from it. God warns them that if they don't turn around, He will curse their life and all the nice things they have.

What kind of warning signs has God put in my life? ______________________

____

What were the results when I either paid attention or ignored them? ______________

____

MALACHI 2:5-7

It was the responsibility of the spiritual leaders to give true instruction. The first spiritual leader of Israel, Levi, obeyed God and did this. He guided many people to live lives that pleased God. His life was one of happiness and peace because He respected God and His Word.

What has God been telling me to do that I have been listening to? ______________

____

What has God been telling me to do that I have NOT been listening to? ____________

____

MALACHI 2:8-9

The current spiritual leaders were not following Levi's example and were leading in ways contrary to God's Word.

God calls on each of us to make disciples as well as encourage each other to obey God's Word.

Do my words lead people to obey God's Word? ☐ **YES** ☐ **NO** ☐ **SOMETIMES**

What specifically needs to change in how I talk and act? ____________________

____

SHARE IT

If you are going to be hated, make sure it's for doing the right thing, the right way, with the right attitude.

WEDNESDAY WEEK 50

TRUTH: MALACHI 2:10-17

MALACHI 2:10-17

At the time this was written, many of the men of Israel were divorcing their wives and marrying women who worshiped false gods. God had commanded in His law to be faithful in marriage and also to never marry outside of His followers because their hearts, households, and loyalties would be divided. They would not be able to fully follow Him, and there would always be severe conflict in their households.

Have I ever betrayed someone or backed out on a commitment?

☐ **YES** ☐ **NO** ☐ **DON'T REMEMBER**

Today our culture celebrates "pluralism" and asks, "Why can't a Muslim and a Jew get married and just get along? Or a Protestant and Catholic, or a Christian and an Atheist?" and so on. Because if they are each true to their faith, they will always be in conflict with each other. To get along, they would have to compromise their beliefs and otherwise be of a particular religion in name only. God wants our full devotion and loyalty.

Do I think it is okay to date or marry someone who is not a faithful believer?

☐ **YES** ☐ **NO** ☐ **NOT SURE** (Hint: see **2 Corinthians 6:14**)

Am I a faithful believer that another faithful believer could date or marry?

☐ **YES** ☐ **NO** ☐ **INCONSISTENT**

To live with a divided loyalty toward God or to live in defiance with known sin in our lives puts us in trouble with God. We may ask God for help and to supply our needs, we may plead, but if we are in open, defiant sin, why should He listen to us? The people talked about in **Malachi** were doing this. Even though these people were defiant toward God and in trouble with God, He was giving them a chance to turn back to Him.

Is there sin in my life that I have not dealt with? ☐ **YES** ☐ **NO** ☐ **NOT SURE**

What is keeping me from turning away from my sin and turning to God?

____

SHARE IT

To fully understand God's grace, we must first understand His demand for complete loyalty.

WEEK 50 THURSDAY

TRUTH: MALACHI 3:1-6

This passage encapsulates prophecy of both the first and second coming of Jesus. In His first coming, He was preceded by His "messenger" who we know to be John the Baptizer. Jesus Himself then came as the messenger of God's Kingdom, and as we know from the Gospels, He was rejected (yet this still fulfilled God's purpose and plan). The second coming of Jesus is referred to here as the "day of His coming." Jesus will claim the earth, which is rightfully His, and will purge sin and wicked people from it. He will fulfill His promises to Israel, and set things right.

MALACHI 3:1

At Jesus' first coming, the people of Israel were seeking a "messiah," but rejected THE Messiah.

Listen to the song, "*King of the World*" by Natalie Grant.

Do I **recognize Jesus for who He truly is: Lord, Master, King, Savior, Sovereign**, or do I **try to repackage Him in a way that fits me**? (Circle)

MALACHI 3:2-3

God will purify those who are of the line of Israel's priests, and as they do their duties, they will be doing them in righteousness.

Do I serve God **with a pure heart** or **out of self-motivation**? (Circle)

MALACHI 3:4-5

"Then" life will be different. The people of God will consistently do what is right, and God will be pleased.

"Then" God will judge and remove those who live in sin.

What do I look forward to in Heaven? ______________________________

____

MALACHI 3:6

God does not change. He keeps His promises. Although He is bringing judgment for their sin at the time **Malachi** was written, and will bring it again in the future, He promised that the people of Israel would have an everlasting place in His eternal Kingdom.

What is my favorite promise from God? ______________________________

____

SHARE IT

God keeps His promises; He never fails.

FRIDAY WEEK 50

TRUTH: MALACHI 3:7-15

For generations, the culture of Israel was not following God with their hearts. They were just going through the motions. As time went on, their attitude toward God soured. They considered it a tedious chore to serve God and held back from sincerely serving Him. Can I relate? ☐ **YES** ☐ **NO**

MALACHI 3:7

Do I follow God's Word, or is my heart divided between myself and God?
☐ I am mostly consistent. ☐ I struggle a lot. ☐ I am just starting.

MALACHI 3:8-9

What in my life truly belongs to God?
☐ Everything ☐ Just big, important things ☐ My spiritual side
(Hint: Everything)

What things in my life do I hold back that belong to God? ______________________

____

MALACHI 3:10-12

Do I believe that I can completely trust God with everything that I am, and everything that I have? ☐ **YES** ☐ **NO** ☐ **SOMETIMES**

In what ways do I trust God to provide for my needs? ______________________

____

How am I a testimony of God's provision in my life? ______________________

____

MALACHI 3:13-15

What are some things that compel me to believe that serving God IS worth it?

____

____

What are some things that compel me to believe that serving God is NOT worth it?

____

____

SHARE IT

"All Christians are but God's stewards. Everything we have is on loan from the Lord, entrusted to us for a while to use in serving Him." ~ John MacArthur

WEEK 50 SATURDAY

TRUTH: MALACHI 3:16-4:6

Today's reading speaks of a day when justice will be served. All those who seem to be getting away with wickedness will get what is coming to them. God is encouraging people to be on the winning side.

MALACHI 3:16

God will put together a record of all those who follow Him, and they will be the ones who will live in eternity with Him in Heaven.

Is my name in that record? ☐ **YES** ☐ **NO** ☐ **NOT SURE**
If your answer is "No" or "Not Sure," please consider the **G O S P E L**:
G O D created us to be with Him.
O U R sins separate us from God.
S I N S cannot be removed by good deeds.
P A Y I N G the price for sin, Jesus died and rose again.
E V E R Y O N E who trusts in Him alone has eternal life.
L I F E with Jesus starts now and lasts forever.

Talk with God now agreeing with Him that you are a sinner, believing that Jesus died to pay the price for your sin, asking Him to allow you to enter into a forever relationship with Him. ☐ Any further questions, contact a church leader.

If your answer is "Yes," will you contact someone whose name is not written in that record and share with them using the **G O S P E L** acrostic above how they can have their name written in the record too? ☐ **YES** ☐ **NO**

MALACHI 4:1

God will bring a day when all those who are evil will be judged.

Do I have a healthy respect for God's judgment? ☐ **YES** ☐ **NO**

MALACHI 4:2-4

On this great day, God's nation Israel will experience victory over those who try to destroy them.

In what ways do I trust God for justice? ______________________________

____

MALACHI 4:5-6

God gave the nation of Israel a sign, which is still to come, that a great prophet Elijah will return, and this will be just before the day of judgment.
Do I believe God will fulfill His promises? ☐ **YES** ☐ **NO**
A promise from God that I will think about today: ______________________________

____

SHARE IT

"God never made a promise that is too good to be true."
~ D.L. Moody

SUNDAY WEEK 51

TRUTH: REVELATION 19:1-10

How can I read this passage and not get caught up in the celebration?! This whole scene is remarkable and full of loud praise and lots of voices singing praises to God for His faithfulness! The prophecies from so long ago were finally being fulfilled! I see God's judgment falling on the sins of those who did not believe in Him, and I see Him answering the questions of His saints back in **Revelation 6:10**. He has finally avenged the blood of the people who had chosen death instead of recanting their trust in God.

Through these 10 verses, I see examples of God's faithfulness. It may have been different than people expected, and it may have taken longer than they expected, but God comes through with His promises!

God's faithfulness is something I believe in:

Never 1 2 3 4 5 Always

When I pray, and I don't see Him answering the way I thought He would, how do I respond? ______________________________

There are times when I haven't been able to see His faithfulness, yet these verses:

- ☐ Encourage me to keep believing.
- ☐ Make me angry, because I'm not sure I can believe it.
- ☐ Confuse me, because I don't know what I'm missing.
- ☐ Challenge me to make my faith grow through the hard times.

REVELATION 19:10

The angel who is talking to John is insistent that John not worship him because he was only a servant with John. He told John to worship Whom? ________

Think about the things that pull my attention away from worshiping Jesus such as a sport, another person, being accepted, or being seen as attractive, etc. Write down the top two things that distract me from worshiping Jesus as I should.

1) ______________________ **2)** ______________________

I will ask a youth leader or mentor to help me learn how to worship Jesus in every area of my life. ☐ **AGREE** ☐ **DISAGREE**

SHARE IT

God comes through with His promises!

WEEK 51 MONDAY

TRUTH: REVELATION 19:11-21

REVELATION 19:11-13

This passage starts with a magnificent picture of who Christ is and His majesty and power that will be seen at the very end of time. He comes with an entire army of soldiers who are ready to fight with Him. The scene is bright and huge and awe-inspiring.

REVELATION 19:11

Jesus is the rider on the white horse. John says here that He is called **F** ____________________ **and T**__________. That's not just His name, but His CHARACTER!

How has Jesus been faithful and true to me? ________________________________

____

Have I been faithful and true to Him lately? ☐ **YES** ☐ **NO**

REVELATION 19:13

What name is given to Jesus here? The **W**__________ **of G**______

John who wrote Revelation also wrote the Gospel of John. Read **John 1:1-2**. Note this very specific connection: Jesus was the Living Word of God at the beginning, and He will be the Living Word at the end.

REVELATION 19:21

Everyone who stands against Jesus is killed by the ______________ coming out of His mouth. What an awesome picture of the power of the Word of God! Not only the Bible, but the Person!

How does **Hebrews 4:12** describe the Word of God? ____________________________

____

How often do I spend time with this incredibly powerful book and Person? ___________

____

I'll write out a Bible verse that means a lot to me.

____

____

____

Why is this verse so meaningful to me? ________________________________

____

☐ I will share this verse and why it's meaningful to me with someone today.

SHARE IT

"The Bible is no mere book, but a Living Creature, with a power that conquers all that oppose it." ~ Napoleon Bonaparte

TUESDAY WEEK 51

TRUTH: REVELATION 20:1-15

This could be a really overwhelming passage. It talks about a thousand years, the dead rising again, a great white throne, a huge judgment, books, people who will be judged by what is written in them, Death and Hades, and Satan. There is so much that happens! But one great truth comes through it all: Death and Satan will be defeated and finally dethroned by God! The promises that God made through Jesus, about death being defeated and those who believed in His name being saved, are being fulfilled!

There are a lot of really intense pictures in this passage. I'll circle which picture caught my attention the most:

Revelation 20:2 – Satan being bound for a thousand years

Revelation 20:7-10 – The great battle after Satan is allowed out of his captivity

Revelation 20:11-13 – The Great White Throne Judgment

Revelation 20:14-15 – Death and Hades being thrown into the Lake of Fire

Why did this make such an impression on me? What did it make me think of?

____

____

REVELATION 20:15

This is a very direct and striking verse. It says that anyone whose name is not in the Book of Life will end up with Satan and Death in the Lake of Fire.

Does this make me nervous? ☐ **YES** ☐ **NO**
If this makes me nervous, I'll talk with a trusted adult such as my youth leader or pastor today!

Is there anyone I know who I'm not sure has their name in the Book of Life? ☐ **YES** ☐ **NO**

THIS IS SO IMPORTANT: it's bigger than life or death! I will write the names of a few friends who God is leading me to talk to about Him and His salvation through Jesus and the cross. I commit to praying for them and asking God to give me an opportunity to share His love with them.

____

SHARE IT

"The saddest road to hell is the one that runs under the pulpit, past the Bible, and through the middle of warnings and invitations." ~ J.C. Ryle

WEEK 51 WEDNESDAY

TRUTH: REVELATION 21:1-8

It's almost like John knew that the last 20 chapters had been really heavy, so he decided to write something hopeful in this chapter. But it wasn't John's idea, this is what comes next in God's story! We see the beautiful picture of Heaven and earth being made new. After so many judgments and so much destruction, there wouldn't be much left. God will make a brand new earth and a brand new Heaven. He says that He is making everything new. This doesn't just apply to the physical world, but the principle can be applied to me! Everything that I was before knowing Christ is made ________________ when I come to know Him! (**2 Corinthians 5:17**).

When I hear this kind of hope, what's my gut reaction?

- ☐ I'm not sure I can believe it, it's too good to be true!
- ☐ I shake my head; no way it's going to happen. I've done too much.
- ☐ I want to believe it! It sounds so amazing!
- ☐ I do believe it! It's a beautiful and real truth! I can't wait!

Are there things in my life I wish I could make new right now? ☐ **YES** ☐ **NO**
Spend some time right now writing down a prayer surrendering them to Jesus asking Him to make them new.

____

____

____

____

REVELATION 21:3-4

In this section I see the promises of how things will be. What is my favorite part?

____

REVELATION 21:5-6

Strong promises coming directly from the throne of God!

I'll write these verses out on a 3 x 5 card.

I'll take those promises and place them somewhere I'll be able to remind myself of them. God is timeless, and He is Sovereign. Nothing happens outside of His view. I'll try to live in light of that truth, and see how small problems become when I can remember Who God is!

SHARE IT

"The most thrilling thing about Heaven is that Jesus Christ will be there. I will see Him face to face." ~ Billy Graham

THURSDAY WEEK 51

TRUTH: REVELATION 21:9-27

REVELATION 21:12, 14

This passage is a rush of pictures and descriptions. Can I imagine how John must have felt, being taken to see such a beautiful sight? It almost feels as if he can't find enough words that would describe what he's seeing well enough. But there are some very important facts that can't be overlooked. First, the city that John sees makes a pretty big deal out of the twelve tribes of Israel, with each tribe's name being on one of the 12 gates. This makes it clear that the Old Testament is very important. It's not just setting the stage for the New Testament, but it has incredible significance for all eternity.

Here's a challenge: When's the last time I read the Old Testament?

- ☐ I've never really thought about it.
- ☐ I know I've read some of it, but I never realized it was so important.
- ☐ I know all of the popular stories, but maybe I'm missing something.

I'll make it a goal to read through one of the books of the Old Testament in the next week and come back and check off that I did it.

☐ **YES! I READ IT! DATE** ______________________________

The next big thing to notice is that each disciple's name was written on one of the 12 foundations of the great city. Imagine John's surprise when he saw his own name! How would I be feeling if I were in John's shoes? ______________________________

____

REVELATION 21:22-27

Read this again. Does it strike me as incredible? Everyone in this city will walk with God. There will be no need for a sun, because the Lamb will be the light; there will be no barriers or walls between God and men any longer. The city's description was gorgeous, but the most beautiful thing will be the communion with God Himself!

I'll write out a prayer right now and talk to God like I would if I were in that city. I have communion with Him right now even if I can't see it or always feel it. I'll ask God to help me know Him more today.

____

____

____

____

______________________________*. Amen.*

SHARE IT

The most beautiful thing about Heaven will be spending time with God Himself!

WEEK 51 FRIDAY

TRUTH: REVELATION 22:1-9

REVELATION 22:1-2

This passage might sound a little familiar. Go back to the very beginning of the Bible, and read **Genesis 2:8-10**. We see the picture of creation, and the Garden of Eden, and how things were supposed to be. List the two items that are found in each passage, between **Revelation 22:1-2** and **Genesis 2:9-10**.

Revelation 22:1 and **Genesis 2:10**:
The ______________________________

Revelation 22:2 and **Genesis 2:9**:
The ______________________________

How cool is it that the Bible starts this way, and ends this way?

REVELATION 22:6

God has made many promises to believers throughout Scripture, and here, He reassures me that His Words and His promises are
______________________________ and ______________________________.

The fact that this is repeated over and over again makes it even more powerful. Some people might want to rationalize or explain God's Word away, but He makes it very clear that what He says matters! And He lets John know that what he is seeing and hearing is true, and that it will actually happen.

Do I believe it? ☐ **YES** ☐ **NO** ☐ **I HAVE A HARD TIME BELIEVING IT SOMETIMES.**

Do I live as if every word in the Bible from Genesis through Revelation is true?
☐ **YES** ☐ **NO**

I'll write out something I have a hard time believing in the Bible, and ask a trusted adult/friend to pray with me that I'll be able to believe what God has promised!

____

____

____

REVELATION 22:8-9

These verses sound just like **Revelation 19:9-10**. John is again reminded that the only Person that he is allowed to worship is God.

If I prayerfully search my heart is there any person or thing that I am worshiping besides God right now? ☐ **YES** ☐ **NO**

I will spend time confessing this and surrendering this to God. ☐

SHARE IT

God's Words are Faithful and True.

SATURDAY WEEK 51

TRUTH: REVELATION 22:10-21

REVELATION 22:12

"I am coming quickly!" God is very direct with His warning and announcement. He could come at any time, and it's going to happen soon! Sometimes I get caught up in the minutes and hours and years of everyday life, but I have to remember that God doesn't run on a schedule like I do. A day is like a thousand years, and a thousand years is like a day to Him. What might seem like a long time to me is a blink of an eye to Him!

REVELATION 22:17

This is a beautiful invitation: everyone is invited to ____________. One word, but it means so much! It promises acceptance and entrance. It promises that those who answer the call to "Come" will be allowed to come into the Kingdom, if they'll only listen to the Spirit.

Do I understand the picture of those who are spiritually thirsty? Water isn't something I drink just because I like it. I drink it because I need it to LIVE! Is this comparison accidental? No way! Jesus knows that the only way for me to truly live is to come to Him!

How often do I go to Jesus for everyday things (stress, worries, concerns, desires)?

Never 1 2 3 4 5 Always

Can people tell that Jesus is in my life? ☐ **YES** ☐ **NO**

In what area of my life is it hardest to keep Jesus first place?

- ☐ My words - I know I would speak differently if He were around.
- ☐ My actions - I don't always think about Him before I do something.
- ☐ My thoughts - If my thoughts were visible to others, I'd be embarrassed.
- ☐ My activities - Time with Jesus and in the Word get put on the back burner.

Think about if I knew Jesus was coming back today, what would I do differently?

____

Would there be any conversations I would want to have and with whom?

____

Who do I know who needs to hear about the love of Jesus before He returns?

____

SHARE IT

Jesus knows that the only way for me to truly live is to come to Him!

WEEK 52 SUNDAY

TRUTH: ROMANS 13:1-14

The authorities that God has placed in my life:
At home ______________________________
At church ______________________________
At school ______________________________
In my country ______________________________

From the above list, sometimes I feel like ______________________________ is in this position of authority by mistake. The reason I feel this way is because ______________________________.

I am in agreement with **verse 1** that ALL authority is appointed by God.

- ☐ I totally agree.
- ☐ I somewhat agree.
- ☐ I find it hard to believe this.

When it comes to authority:

- ☐ I find no problem whatsoever in obeying authority.
- ☐ It usually is a challenge for me to obey authority.
- ☐ I feel the authority should earn my respect and obedience.

Compare **Romans 13:2, 5** and **1 Peter 2:13-14**.
Obedience to authority is a matter of:

- ☐ Personal preference.
- ☐ My friend's opinion.
- ☐ What political party the leader belongs to.
- ☐ Obedience to God's Word.

The times I find it hard to obey authority is when ______________________________.

However, Lord, I pray that regardless of what the authority does, that You help me to ______________________________.

If there is anything that may make me run into trouble with authority, it may be:

- ☐ That I am not fulfilling the responsibilities they give to me like homework, chores, speed limits, etc. (**v. 7**)
- ☐ That I am choosing not to love others as I ought to. (**vv. 8-10**)
- ☐ That I am just sloppy in my spiritual life and in life generally. (**v. 11**)
- ☐ That I am involved in some sinful/dark habits. (**v. 12**)

SHARE IT

Obedience to authority is a matter of obedience to God's Word.

MONDAY WEEK 52

TRUTH: ROMANS 14:1-12

ROMANS 14:1-3

The following statement(s) would be true of me:
- ☐ Anyone who does not agree with my views is obviously wrong.
- ☐ I believe anyone doing things contrary to my ways and preferences is wrong.
- ☐ On things that are not against the Bible, I believe in an individual's free choice.

With those who I think are not as spiritually mature as I am, I tend to:
- ☐ Be somewhat impatient with their immaturity.
- ☐ Be somewhat understanding and seek to help them.
- ☐ Avoid them since we are not at the same level.
- ☐ Let them know, or think in my mind, how they need to grow up.

In all honesty sometimes (name) ______________________________ tends to rub me the wrong way with their immaturity.

I believe **verse 1** is calling me to ______________________________ this person even though they are less mature in their spiritual life.

For me to graciously receive a less mature person may mean that I may have to ask God to get rid of the following in me: (circle any that apply)

Arguments/disputes with them **Despising their behavior**

Judging everything they do **Showing contempt to them**

I think that some things that I may be doing that are not sinful but may be a problem to a less mature person include: ____.

TRUE OR FALSE.

T F According to this passage, the immature believer just has to grow up and deal with whatever I may be doing that may affect them.

T F Since I am the more mature believer, then it is my responsibility to let go of some of the things for the sake of the weak/immature believer.

ROMANS 14:12

Knowing that I shall give an account of everything I am doing in my life, including how I treat the weaker believer, means that I may need to: ____________________________

____.

SHARE IT

"Truth-oriented Christians love studying Scripture and theology. But sometimes they're quick to judge and slow to forgive. They're strong on truth, weak on grace."
~ Randy Alcorn

WEEK 52 TUESDAY

TRUTH: ROMANS 14:13-23

ROMANS 14:13

If I cherish something and I am asked to give it up for the sake of another believer:
- I would definitely not give it up because I think it's unfair to me.
- It would be hard to do so, but I would give it up anyway.
- I would find ways of helping the other person accept it.

Someone may stumble (*slip into a morally negative situation*) if they:
- Listen to the music I listen to.
- Watch the movies I watch.
- View my social media page.
- Other: ______________________.
- Go to the places I go.
- Interact with my friends.
- See my life at home.
- Go through my phone.

For me to RESOLVE not to be a stumbling block to people in the above area(s) means that I may have to: ____

____

What would make my letting go such a hard thing to do for the sake of another?

____

What would make it easy for me to let go for the sake of another?

____

ROMANS 14:17-18

My self-denial for the sake of another is seen before God as:
- Pointless
- Good
- A waste
- It doesn't concern God at all.

RESOLUTION TIME:
Trusting that God is leading me to be sensitive to other believers, I am today making a resolution to specifically let go of ____

____.

SHARE IT

"A Pharisee is hard on others and easy on himself, but a spiritual man is easy on others and hard on himself."
~ A.W. Tozer

WEDNESDAY WEEK 52

TRUTH: ROMANS 15:1-16

Looking back through this Quiet Time, I realize God has brought growth in this area of my life:

____

____

ROMANS 15:1-7

I am also aware that ______________________ may be struggling with this same area. The following is my plan on how God can use me to help them grow too:

____

____.

Whenever I help someone in need, I usually find myself doing this so that
- God is glorified. (**v. 6**)
- I am known as a nice and helpful person.
- The person in need is encouraged and benefits from the help.

My attitude toward someone who does not recognize me or thank me when I help them out is usually:
- "How ungrateful can this person be? Not even a thank you?!"
- "Well, I am glad they are better, and I was able to help anyway."
- "Never am I helping this person again."
- "I hope they thank God for what He has done through me."

I notice that my attitude above is **in line** **not in line** with **verse 7** and so I believe this is another area in my life that:
- I need to praise God for.
- I need to ask God to help me change in.

ROMANS 15:13

As I look toward "The God of hope" to help me and my friends to be Christ-like, the one thing I am praying about is:
- Being filled with joy and peace in believing that one day we will be like Christ.
- To have great hope by the power of the Holy Spirit even as He works in us.

Today I shall **send a note** **message** **text** **verse 13** to the friend I mentioned above: ______________________.

SHARE IT

Hope is not a whim or a wish. It's a Rock on which I stand. That Rock is Christ.

WEEK 52 THURSDAY

TRUTH: ROMANS 15:17-33

The response from my friend I sent the verse to yesterday was:

- Encouraging.
- Exciting.
- There was no response.
- Not what I expected.
- I have not yet sent it, but I shall do so ______________________________.

ROMANS 15:17-19

Looking at how I have been able to share the Gospel both in the past and most recently, I am thankful for:

- A person who has gotten saved ________________________.
- A person who has encouraged me through this _______________.
- A person who listened to me share even if they are not yet saved _____________.
- What effect my sharing has had on _______________________.

ROMANS 15:20

One place God is placing on my heart to make it "My aim to preach the Gospel" is:

- With my unsaved family members.
- With friends I hang out with.
- With my unsaved neighbors.
- With those I just bump into, for example, the checkout person, etc.
- ____

ROMANS 15:22, 30-32

One place I know that the Gospel is prohibited or restricted from being preached freely is ________________________.

With the above place in mind, I am committing myself:

- **today** - **this whole week** - **this month** to earnestly pray for the missionaries there, that:

- They may be delivered from their persecutors.
- That they may find people to partner with them in their ministry.
- That God may fill them with joy even in the midst of persecution.
- That they would find moments of refreshment from the Lord and other believers.

One local missionary serving here in my church/town/city/state/country that I know of is ___________________________________.

One way I will stand with this missionary is by:

- **Sending them financial support.** - **Praying.** - **Visiting.**

SHARE IT

"Every Christian a missionary; every non-Christian a mission-field." ~ Winkie Pratney

FRIDAY WEEK 52

TRUTH: ROMANS 16:1-16

ROMANS 16:1-2

People that God has placed in my life that have been helpful to me and many others are:
1. ______________________________
2. ______________________________
3. ______________________________

ROMANS 16:3-4

People that God has placed in my life that have been selfless in their service to the church are:
1. ______________________________
2. ______________________________
3. ______________________________

ROMANS 16:7-9

People that God has placed in my life that have been alongside me in hard times are:
1. ______________________________
2. ______________________________
3. ______________________________

Read **Proverbs 18:24**. This reminds me of the role I have to play in being a friend to others. Just as the above have been to me, then I purpose to:

Be helpful to ____________________ by ______________________________
____.

Offer selfless service to ____________________ by ______________________________
____.

Be an encouragement to ____________________ by ______________________________
____.

My prayer for the people above who have been a blessing to me is:

____
____
____
____
____

SHARE IT

"There is no exercise better for the heart than reaching down and lifting people up." ~ John Holmes

WEEK 52 SATURDAY

TRUTH: ROMANS 16:17-27

ROMANS 16:17

To those causing divisions in the church, I am encouraged to join in with them.

☐ **TRUE** ☐ **FALSE**

To those teaching false doctrine, I am called to

☐ **Debate with them.** ☐ **Avoid them.** ☐ **Just listen to them, but not buy in.**

One sure way I can ensure that I do not fall for false teaching is by studying the Bible thoroughly and regularly. And I can also:

- ☐ Listen to strong Bible teachers.
- ☐ Check out for myself to see if what I hear others speak about the Bible is true.
- ☐ Just believe anyone, at any time, without checking into it.
- ☐ Ask questions respectfully on lessons I hear from my Youth Pastor. (He would LOVE that I'm engaged in the teaching and wanting to learn!)

When it comes to a daily study of the Bible, then I rate myself as:

Struggling 1 2 3 4 5 Consistent

ROMANS 16:19

The reputation I have among many that know me is that I: ______________________________
____.

This is something I definitely need to:

- ☐ Praise God for.
- ☐ Be concerned about.
- ☐ Seek help from ______________________________.

My obedience and my character at:

Home is ☐ **Good.** ☐ **Not good at all.** ☐ **Is improving.**

Church is ☐ **Good.** ☐ **Not good at all.** ☐ **Is improving.**

School is ☐ **Good.** ☐ **Not good at all.** ☐ **Is improving.**

REVIEW TIME:

As I have gone through the book of Romans in my quiet time, the one thing that has stood out, encouraged, or changed me is: ______________________________
____.

SHARE IT

"Until you have given up yourself to Him, you will not have a real self." ~ C.S. Lewis

Quiet Time Schedule Options

The following chart displays the Bible books and chapters for this year's quiet times. All quiet times cover the same passages each day so the whole family can stay connected to God's Word. Two schedules have been included or you can create your own for your group or family.

WEEKS 1 THROUGH 26

WEEK #	BOOKS - CHAPTERS	2018-19 ACADEMIC SCHEDULE	2019 CALENDAR SCHEDULE
WEEK 1	Philippians 1-2	Aug 26 - Sep 1	Dec 30 - Jan 5
WEEK 2	Philippians 2-4	Sep 2 - Sep 8	Jan 6 - Jan 12
WEEK 3	Job 1-13	Sep 9 - Sep 15	Jan 13 - Jan 19
WEEK 4	Job 14-42	Sep 16 - Sep 22	Jan 20 - Jan 26
WEEK 5	Psalms 104-105	Sep 23 - Sep 29	Jan 27 - Feb 2
WEEK 6	John 1	Sep 30 - Oct 6	Feb 3 - Feb 9
WEEK 7	John 2-3, Psalm 119	Oct 7 - Oct 13	Feb 10 - Feb 16
WEEK 8	Psalm 119	Oct 14 - Oct 20	Feb 17 - Feb 23
WEEK 9	John 4-5	Oct 21 - Oct 27	Feb 24 - Mar 2
WEEK 10	John 5, Psalm 119	Oct 28 - Nov 3	Mar 3 - Mar 9
WEEK 11	Psalm 119, John 1-6	Nov 4 - Nov 10	Mar 10 - Mar 16
WEEK 12	John 6-8	Nov 11 - Nov 17	Mar 17 - Mar 23
WEEK 13	John 8, Psalm 107	Nov 18 - Nov 24	Mar 24 - Mar 30
WEEK 14	Psalm 107, Ezekiel 1-3, 36	Nov 25 - Dec 1	Mar 31 - Apr 6
WEEK 15	Ezekiel 37-44	Dec 2 - Dec 8	Apr 7 - Apr 13
WEEK 16	Ezekiel 47, 1 Kings 1-6	Dec 9 - Dec 15	Apr 14 - Apr 20
WEEK 17	1 Kings 11-17	Dec 16 - Dec 22	Apr 21 - Apr 27
WEEK 18	1 Kings 18-21	Dec 23 - Dec 29	Apr 28 - May 4
WEEK 19	1 Kings 22, John 9-10	Dec 30 - Jan 5	May 5 - May 11
WEEK 20	John 10-11	Jan 6 - Jan 12	May 12 - May 18
WEEK 21	John 12, Psalms 114-115	Jan 13 - Jan 19	May 19 - May 25
WEEK 22	Psalms 116-118, Exodus 1-2	Jan 20 - Jan 26	May 26 - Jun 1
WEEK 23	Exodus 2-5	Jan 27 - Feb 2	Jun 2 - Jun 8
WEEK 24	Exodus 6-9	Feb 3 - Feb 9	Jun 9 - Jun 15
WEEK 25	Exodus 9-11, Ephesians 1	Feb 10 - Feb 16	Jun 16 - Jun 22
WEEK 26	Ephesians 2-3	Feb 17 - Feb 23	Jun 23 - Jun 29

Quiet Time Schedule Options

WEEKS 27 THROUGH 52

WEEK #	BOOKS - CHAPTERS	2018-19 ACADEMIC SCHEDULE	2019 CALENDAR SCHEDULE
WEEK 27	Ephesians 4-5	Feb 24 - Mar 2	Jun 30 - Jul 6
WEEK 28	Ephesians 5-6, John 13	Mar 3 - Mar 9	Jul 7 - Jul 13
WEEK 29	John 13-15	Mar 10 - Mar 16	Jul 14 - Jul 20
WEEK 30	John 16-18	Mar 17 - Mar 23	Jul 21 - Jul 27
WEEK 31	John 18-20	Mar 24 - Mar 30	Jul 28 - Aug 3
WEEK 32	John 20-21, Exodus 12	Mar 31 - Apr 6	Aug 4 - Aug 10
WEEK 33	Exodus 13-16	Apr 7 - Apr 13	Aug 11 - Aug 17
WEEK 34	Exodus 16-17, Psalms 106, 108	Apr 14 - Apr 20	Aug 18 - Aug 24
WEEK 35	Exodus 19-32	Apr 21 - Apr 27	Aug 25 - Aug 31
WEEK 36	Exodus 32-40	Apr 28 - May 4	Sep 1 - Sep 7
WEEK 37	Romans 1-3	May 5 - May 11	Sep 8 - Sep 14
WEEK 38	Romans 3-6	May 12 - May 18	Sep 15 - Sep 21
WEEK 39	Romans 7-8, 2 Kings 1-2	May 19 - May 25	Sep 22 - Sep 28
WEEK 40	2 Kings 2-6	May 26 - Jun 1	Sep 29 - Oct 5
WEEK 41	2 Kings 6-17	Jun 2 - Jun 8	Oct 6 - Oct 12
WEEK 42	2 Kings 17-23, 2 Timothy 1	Jun 9 - Jun 15	Oct 13 - Oct 19
WEEK 43	2 Timothy 1-3	Jun 16 - Jun 22	Oct 20 - Oct 26
WEEK 44	2 Timothy 3-4, Revelation 6-7	Jun 23 - Jun 29	Oct 27 - Nov 2
WEEK 45	Revelation 8-13, 1 Peter 1	Jun 30 - Jul 6	Nov 3 - Nov 9
WEEK 46	1 Peter 1-3	Jul 7 - Jul 13	Nov 10 - Nov 16
WEEK 47	1 Peter 4-5, Revelation 14	Jul 14 - Jul 20	Nov 17 - Nov 23
WEEK 48	Revelation 15-17, Romans 9	Jul 21 - Jul 27	Nov 24 - Nov 30
WEEK 49	Romans 10-12	Jul 28 - Aug 3	Dec 1 - Dec 7
WEEK 50	Nahum 1, Malachi 1-4	Aug 4 - Aug 10	Dec 8 - Dec 14
WEEK 51	Revelation 19-22	Aug 11 - Aug 17	Dec 15 - Dec 21
WEEK 52	Romans 13-16	Aug 18 - Aug 24	Dec 22 - Dec 28

Request a viewbook at **admissions@wol.org**

Apply online at **wordoflife.edu** or call **1.800.331.9673**

Request More Information

Name: ____________

Address: ____________

City: ________ State: ________ Zipcode: ________

Email: ________ Phone: ________

Date of Birth: __ / __ / __ Current Grade: FR SO JR SR

Word of **Life**
Bible Institute

NO POSTAGE
NECESSARY
IF MAILED
IN THE
UNITED STATES

BUSINESS REPLY MAIL
FIRST-CLASS MAIL PERMIT NO. 1 SCHROON LAKE NY
POSTAGE WILL BE PAID BY ADDRESSEE

WORD OF LIFE FELLOWSHIP
PO BOX 600
SCHROON LAKE NY 12870-9986